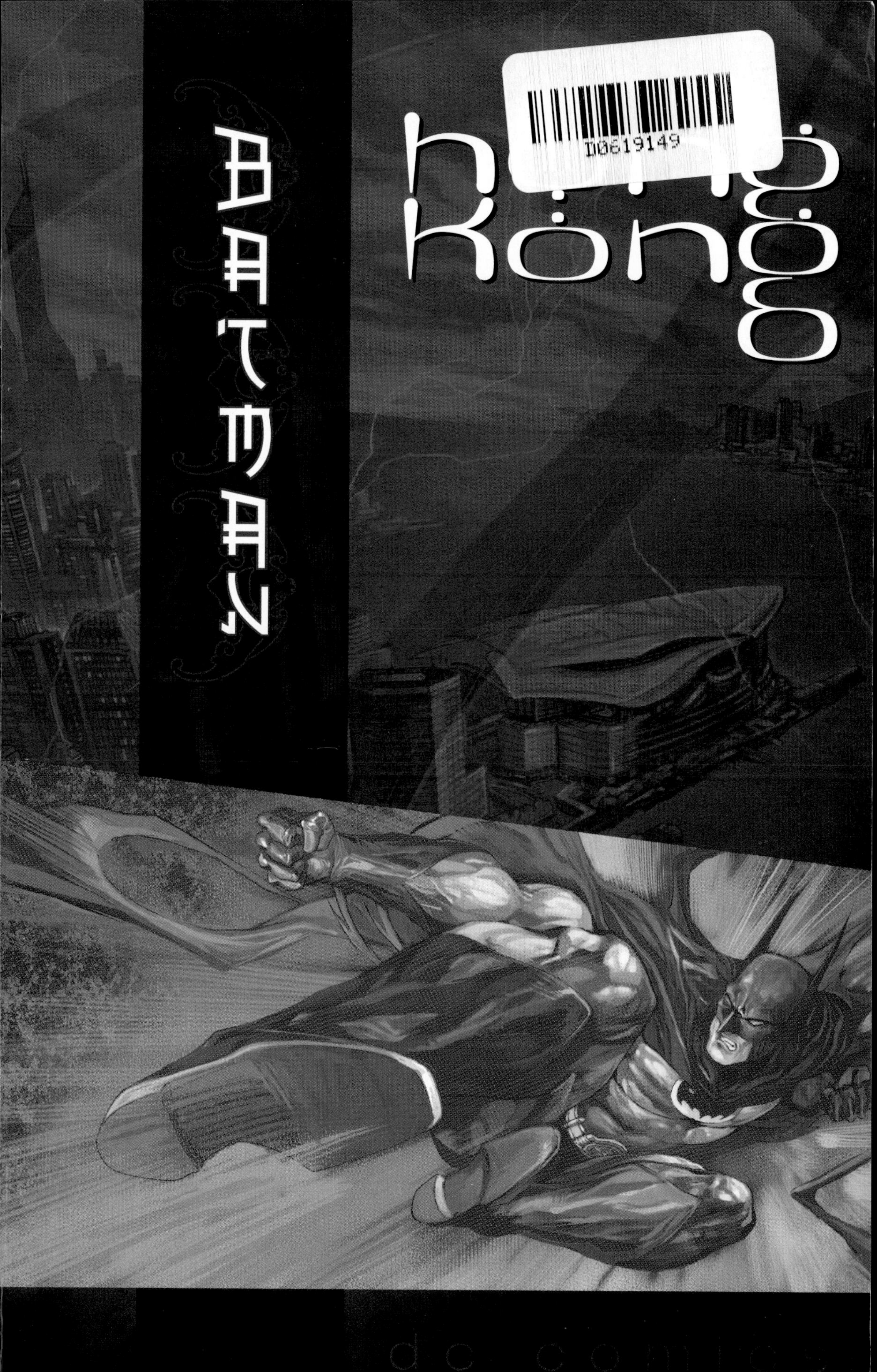
BATMAN
Hong Kong
dc comics

WRITER doug moench

ARTIST tony wong

LETTERING BY KURT HATHAWAY

SPECIAL THANKS TO MR. KHOO FUK LUNG

BATMAN CREATED BY BOB KANE

Dan DiDio, *VP-Editorial* • Andy Helfer, *Group Editor* • Harvey Richards, *Assistant Editor*
Amie Brockway-Metcalf, *Art Director* • Paul Levitz, *President & Publisher*
Georg Brewer, *VP-Design & Retail Product Development* • Richard Bruning, *VP-Creative Director*
Patrick Caldon, *Senior VP-Finance & Operations* • Chris Caramalis, *VP-Finance*
Terri Cunningham, *VP-Managing Editor* • Alison Gill, *VP-Manufacturing*
Lillian Laserson, *Senior VP & General Counsel* • David McKillips, *VP-Advertising*
John Nee, *VP-Business Development* • Cheryl Rubin, *VP-Licensing & Merchandising*
Bob Wayne, *VP-Sales & Marketing*

Batman: Hong Kong. Published by DC Comics, 1700 Broadway, New York, NY 10019.

Printed in Canada.
DC Comics - A Warner Bros. Entertainment Company.

COVER ART: TONY WONG
LOGO DESIGN: TERRY MARKS

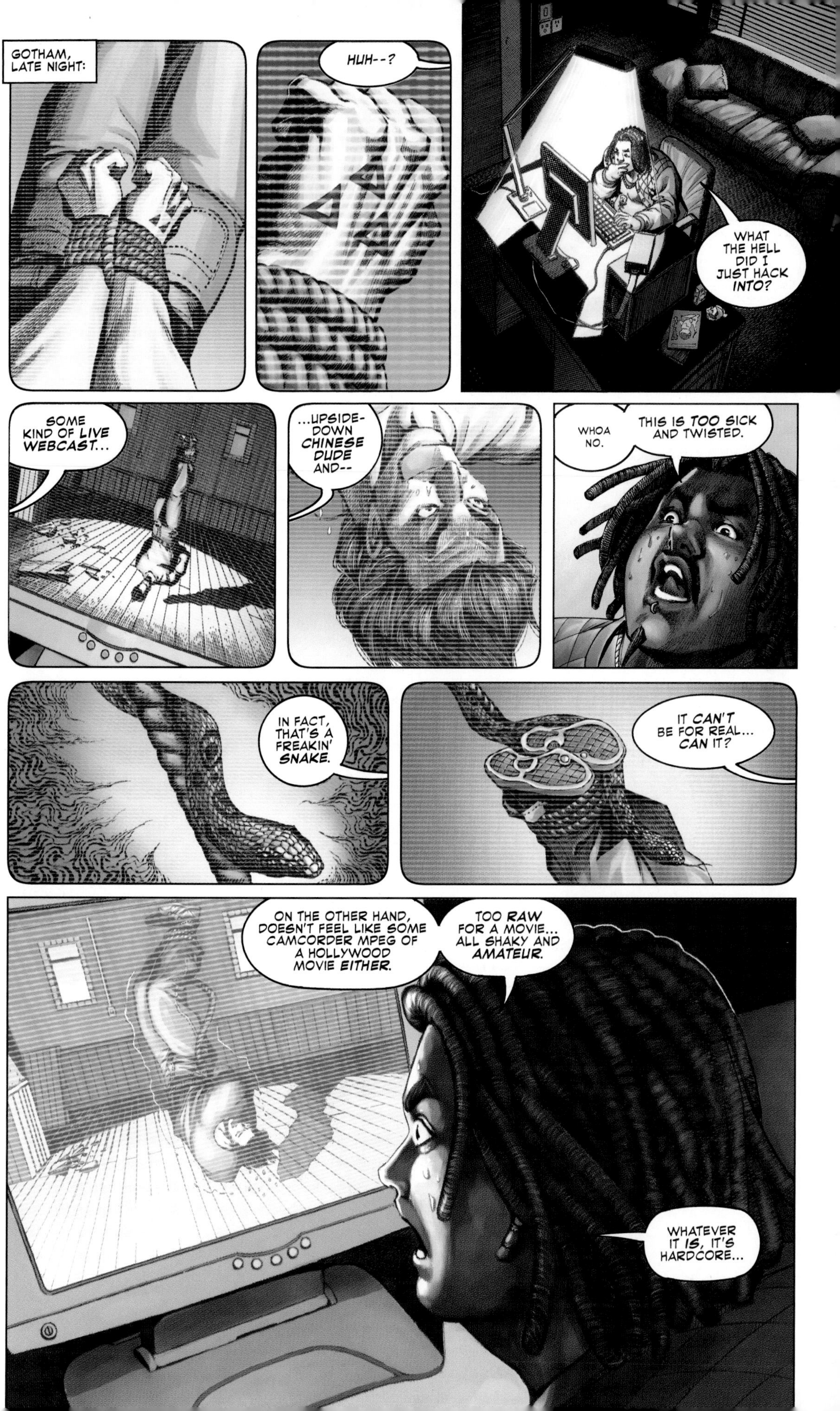
GOTHAM, LATE NIGHT:
HUH--?
WHAT THE HELL DID I JUST HACK INTO?
SOME KIND OF LIVE WEBCAST...
...UPSIDE-DOWN CHINESE DUDE AND--
WHOA NO.
THIS IS TOO SICK AND TWISTED.
IN FACT, THAT'S A FREAKIN' SNAKE.
IT CAN'T BE FOR REAL... CAN IT?
ON THE OTHER HAND, DOESN'T FEEL LIKE SOME CAMCORDER MPEG OF A HOLLYWOOD MOVIE EITHER.
TOO RAW FOR A MOVIE... ALL SHAKY AND AMATEUR.
WHATEVER IT IS, IT'S HARDCORE...

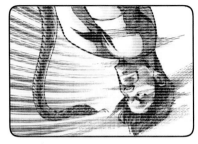

...IT'S REAL.

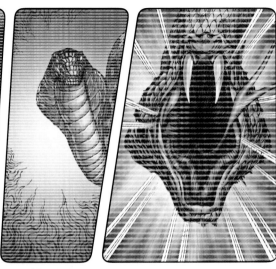

YAAHH!!

IT BIT HIM!

FREAKIN' FANGED HIS FACE!

AGAIN-- AND AGAIN!

--AND NOW...THE SNAKE'S LEAVIN'.

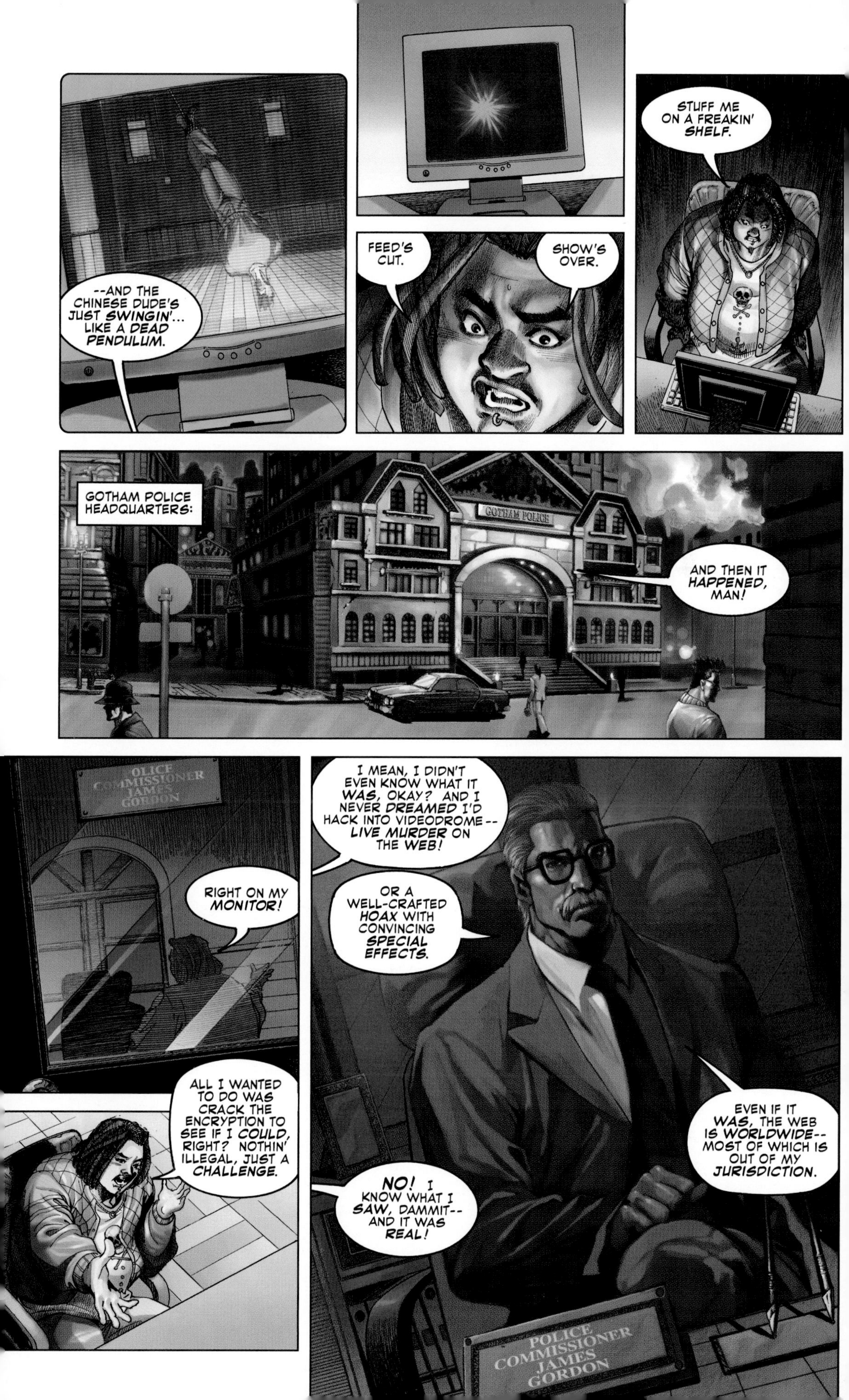
--AND THE CHINESE DUDE'S JUST SWINGIN'... LIKE A DEAD PENDULUM.
FEED'S CUT.
SHOW'S OVER.
STUFF ME ON A FREAKIN' SHELF.
GOTHAM POLICE HEADQUARTERS:
GOTHAM POLICE
AND THEN IT HAPPENED, MAN!
POLICE COMMISSIONER JAMES GORDON
RIGHT ON MY MONITOR!
I MEAN, I DIDN'T EVEN KNOW WHAT IT WAS, OKAY? AND I NEVER DREAMED I'D HACK INTO VIDEODROME--LIVE MURDER ON THE WEB!
OR A WELL-CRAFTED HOAX WITH CONVINCING SPECIAL EFFECTS.
ALL I WANTED TO DO WAS CRACK THE ENCRYPTION TO SEE IF I COULD, RIGHT? NOTHIN' ILLEGAL, JUST A CHALLENGE.
EVEN IF IT WAS, THE WEB IS WORLDWIDE--MOST OF WHICH IS OUT OF MY JURISDICTION.
NO! I KNOW WHAT I SAW, DAMMIT--AND IT WAS REAL!
POLICE COMMISSIONER JAMES GORDON

YOU'RE *RIGHT,* COMMISSIONER, IT *COULD* HAVE HAPPENED ANYWHERE--FLOATING I.S.P., UNTRACEABLE SOURCE--BUT YOU'RE ALSO *WRONG.*

WHAT I SAW HAPPENED *RIGHT HERE* ON *YOUR TURF*--IN GOTHAM.

HOW CAN YOU BE SO *SURE?*

BECAUSE WHEN THE WEBCAM FOLLOWED THE DAMN *KILLER-SNAKE,* THE VIEW INCLUDED A *WINDOW*--AND OUT THAT WINDOW WAS *COIT TOWER.*

ALL RIGHT, LEAVE YOUR NAME, NUMBER, AND A *STATEMENT* WITH THE OFFICER OUTSIDE-- BUT THERE'S STILL NOT MUCH WE CAN *DO.*

EVEN IF SOMEONE *WAS* KILLED, WE NEED THE *BODY.*

YOU MEAN THAT'S *IT?*

FOR NOW, YES.

NO CORPSE, NO MURDER.

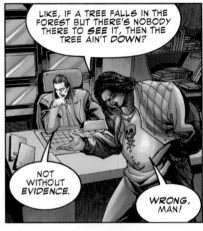

LIKE, IF A TREE FALLS IN THE FOREST BUT THERE'S NOBODY THERE TO *SEE* IT, THEN THE TREE AIN'T *DOWN?*

NOT WITHOUT *EVIDENCE.*

WRONG, MAN!

"IF THE TREE *FELL,* IT'S *DOWN*--AND IN *THIS* CASE, SOMEBODY *DID* SEE IT! *ME*--RIGHT ON MY FREAKIN' *SCREEN!*

"THAT WEBCAST MURDER *HAPPENED,* MAN..."

YOU *TOO,* HUH?

"...WHETHER *YOU* FIND THE BODY OR *NOT!*"

DON'TCHA JUST *HATE* IT WHEN THE WORLD TURNS UPSIDE DOWN?

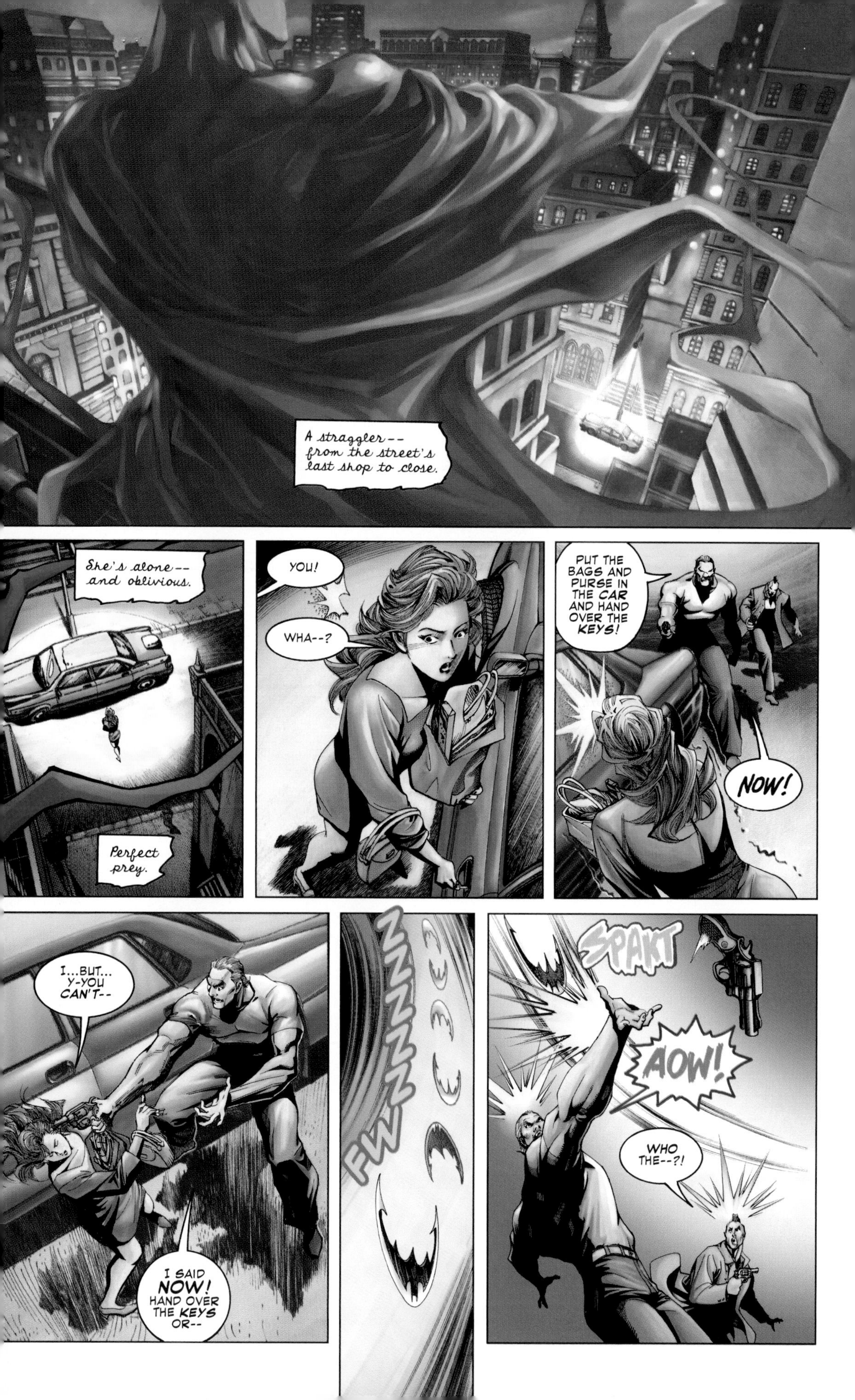
A straggler-- from the street's last shop to close.
She's alone-- and oblivious.
Perfect prey.
YOU!
WHA--?
PUT THE BAGS AND PURSE IN THE CAR AND HAND OVER THE KEYS!
NOW!
I...BUT... Y-YOU CAN'T--
I SAID NOW! HAND OVER THE KEYS OR--
FWNNNNN
SPAKT
AOW!
WHO THE--?!

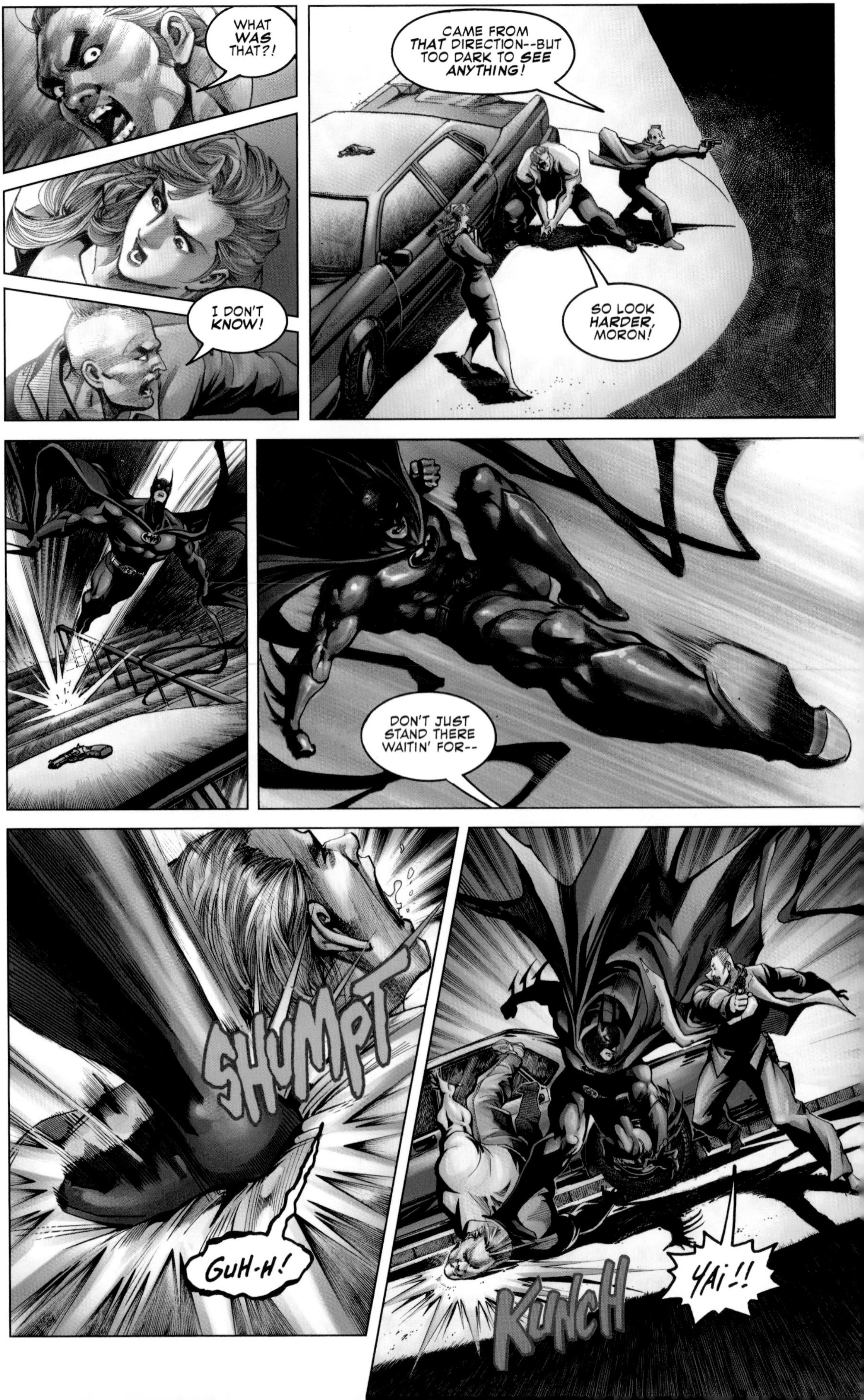
WHAT WAS THAT?!
I DON'T KNOW!
CAME FROM THAT DIRECTION--BUT TOO DARK TO SEE ANYTHING!
SO LOOK HARDER, MORON!
DON'T JUST STAND THERE WAITIN' FOR--
SHUMPT
GUH-H!
KUNCH
YAI!!

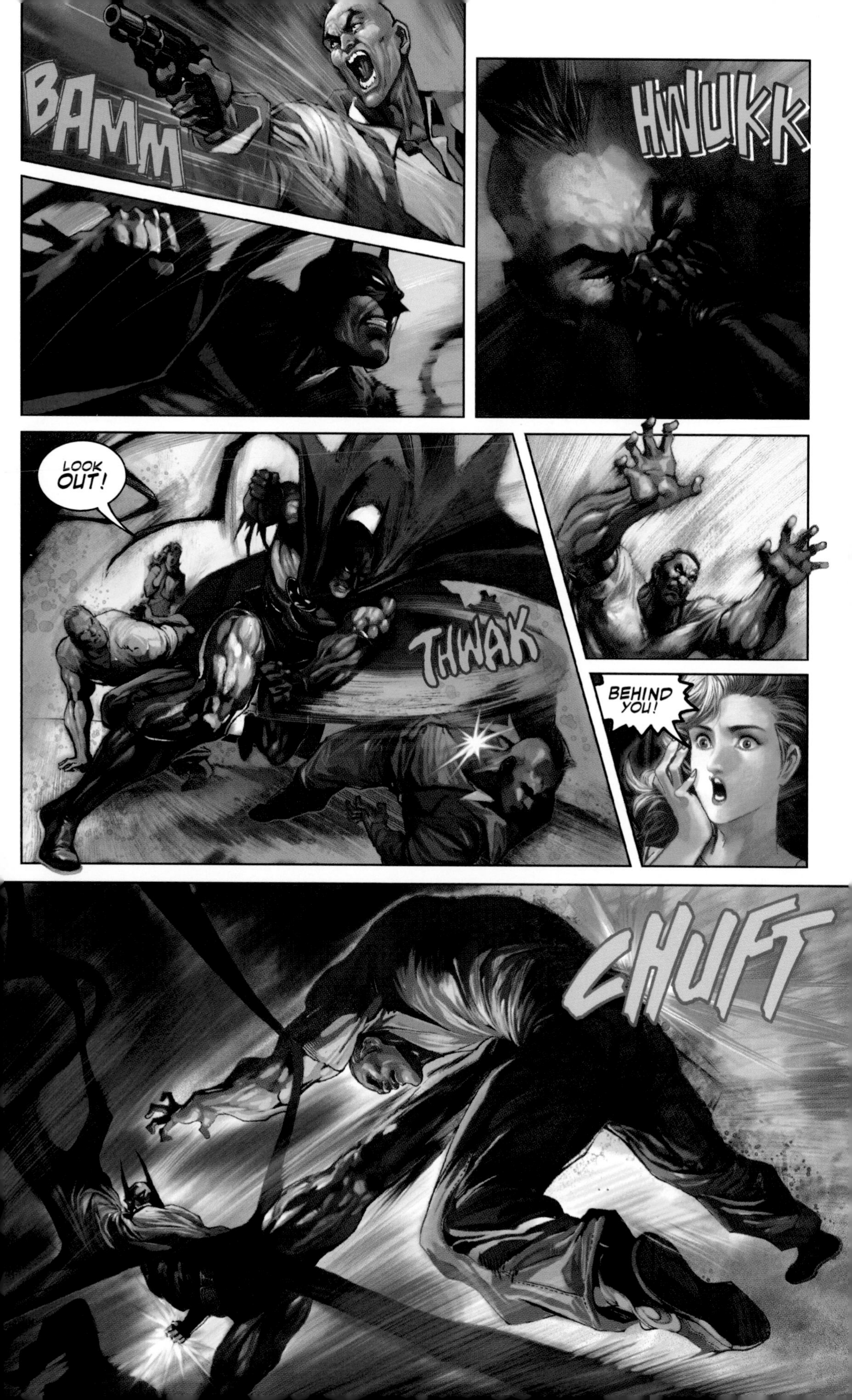
BAMM
HWUKK
LOOK OUT!
THWAK
BEHIND YOU!
CHUFT

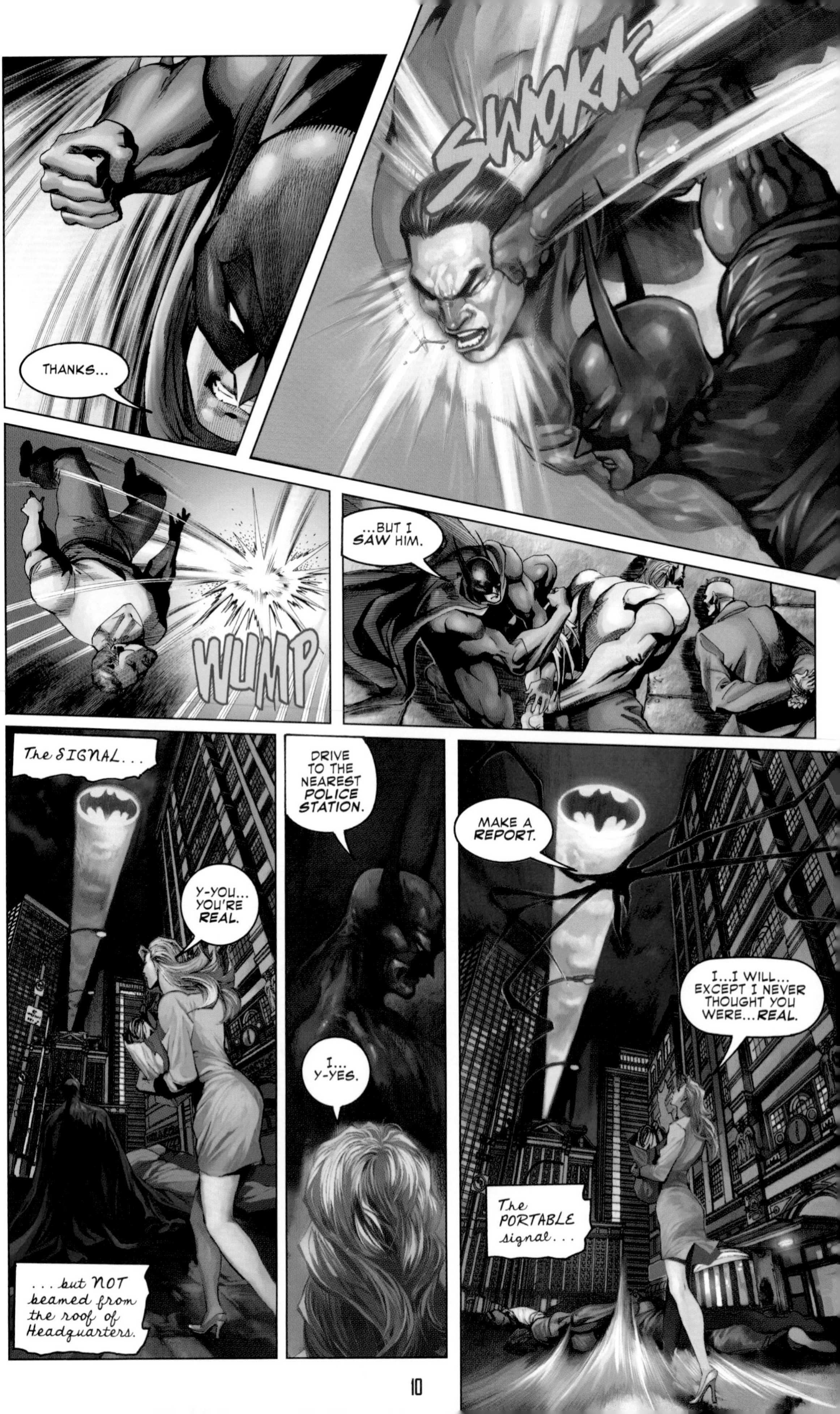
THANKS...
SWOKK
WUMP
...BUT I SAW HIM.
The SIGNAL...
Y-YOU... YOU'RE REAL.
...but NOT beamed from the roof of Headquarters.
DRIVE TO THE NEAREST POLICE STATION.
I... Y-YES.
MAKE A REPORT.
I...I WILL... EXCEPT I NEVER THOUGHT YOU WERE...REAL.
The PORTABLE signal...

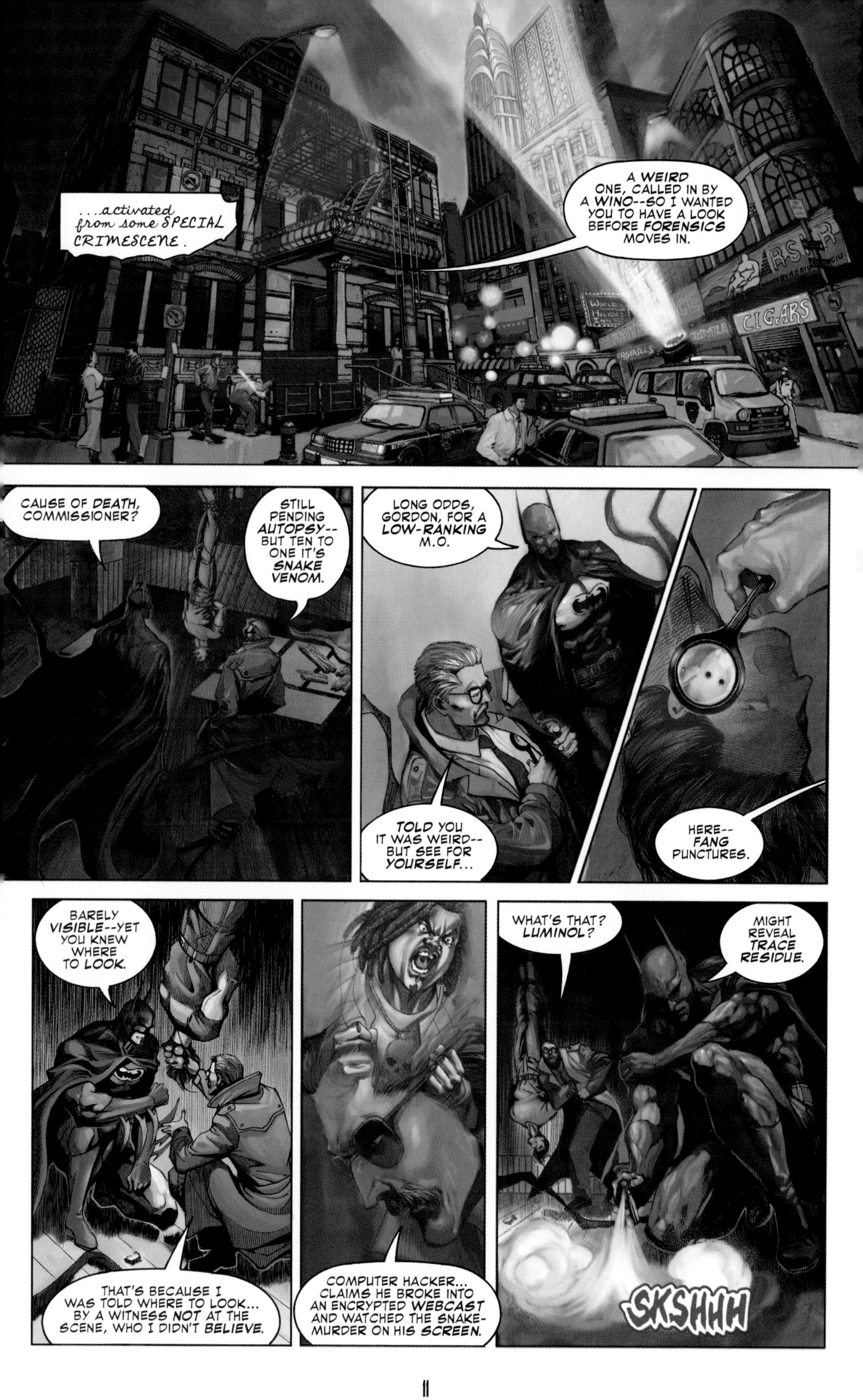
...activated from some SPECIAL CRIMESCENE.
A WEIRD ONE, CALLED IN BY A WINO--SO I WANTED YOU TO HAVE A LOOK BEFORE FORENSICS MOVES IN.
CIGARS
CAUSE OF DEATH, COMMISSIONER?
STILL PENDING AUTOPSY--BUT TEN TO ONE IT'S SNAKE VENOM.
LONG ODDS, GORDON, FOR A LOW-RANKING M.O.
TOLD YOU IT WAS WEIRD--BUT SEE FOR YOURSELF...
HERE--FANG PUNCTURES.
BARELY VISIBLE--YET YOU KNEW WHERE TO LOOK.
THAT'S BECAUSE I WAS TOLD WHERE TO LOOK... BY A WITNESS NOT AT THE SCENE, WHO I DIDN'T BELIEVE.
COMPUTER HACKER... CLAIMS HE BROKE INTO AN ENCRYPTED WEBCAST AND WATCHED THE SNAKE-MURDER ON HIS SCREEN.
WHAT'S THAT? LUMINOL?
MIGHT REVEAL TRACE RESIDUE.
SKSHHH

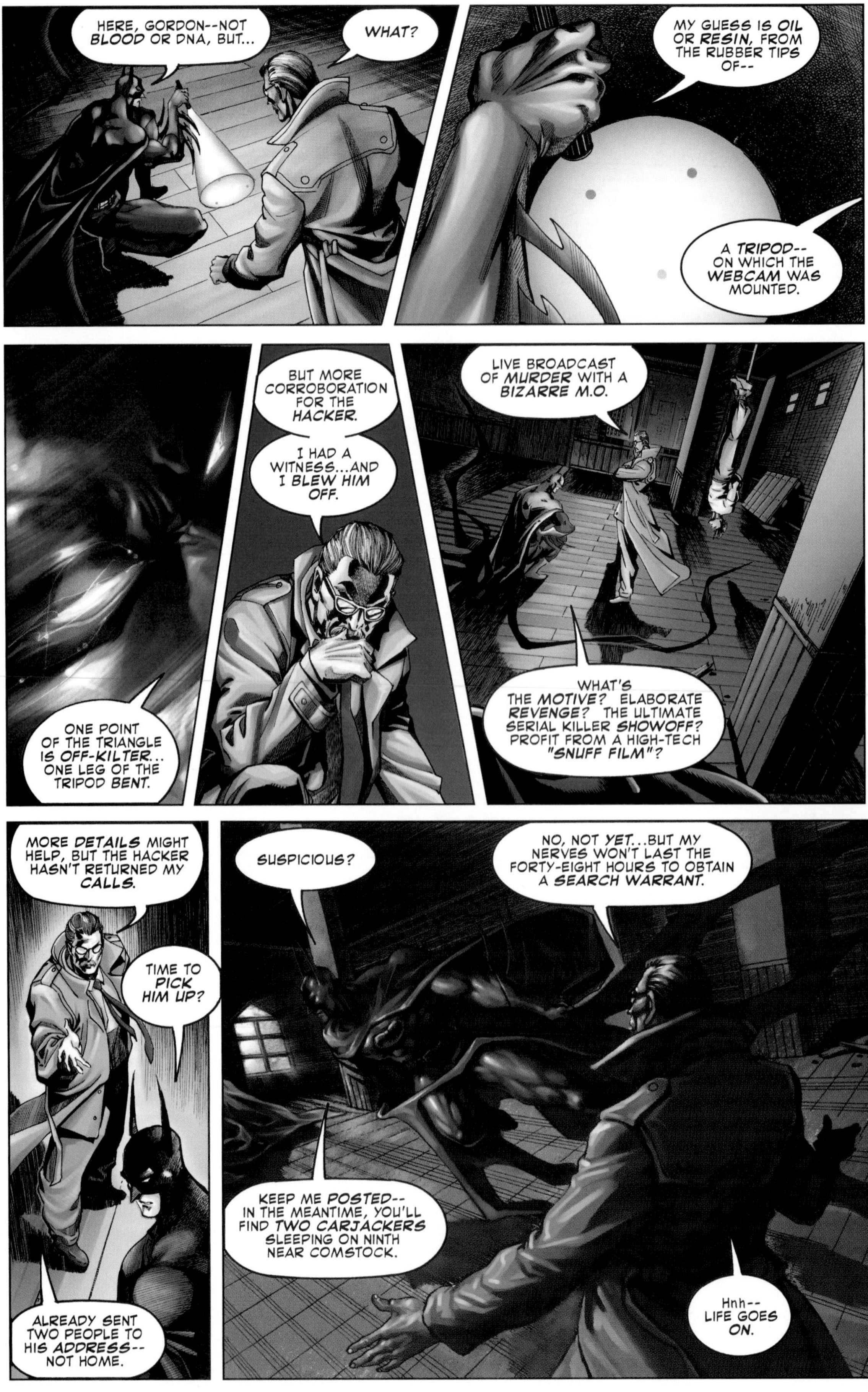

HERE, GORDON--NOT BLOOD OR DNA, BUT...
WHAT?
MY GUESS IS OIL OR RESIN, FROM THE RUBBER TIPS OF--
A TRIPOD-- ON WHICH THE WEBCAM WAS MOUNTED.
ONE POINT OF THE TRIANGLE IS OFF-KILTER... ONE LEG OF THE TRIPOD BENT.
BUT MORE CORROBORATION FOR THE HACKER.
I HAD A WITNESS...AND I BLEW HIM OFF.
LIVE BROADCAST OF MURDER WITH A BIZARRE M.O.
WHAT'S THE MOTIVE? ELABORATE REVENGE? THE ULTIMATE SERIAL KILLER SHOWOFF? PROFIT FROM A HIGH-TECH "SNUFF FILM"?
MORE DETAILS MIGHT HELP, BUT THE HACKER HASN'T RETURNED MY CALLS.
TIME TO PICK HIM UP?
ALREADY SENT TWO PEOPLE TO HIS ADDRESS-- NOT HOME.
SUSPICIOUS?
NO, NOT YET...BUT MY NERVES WON'T LAST THE FORTY-EIGHT HOURS TO OBTAIN A SEARCH WARRANT.
KEEP ME POSTED-- IN THE MEANTIME, YOU'LL FIND TWO CARJACKERS SLEEPING ON NINTH NEAR COMSTOCK.
Hnh-- LIFE GOES ON.

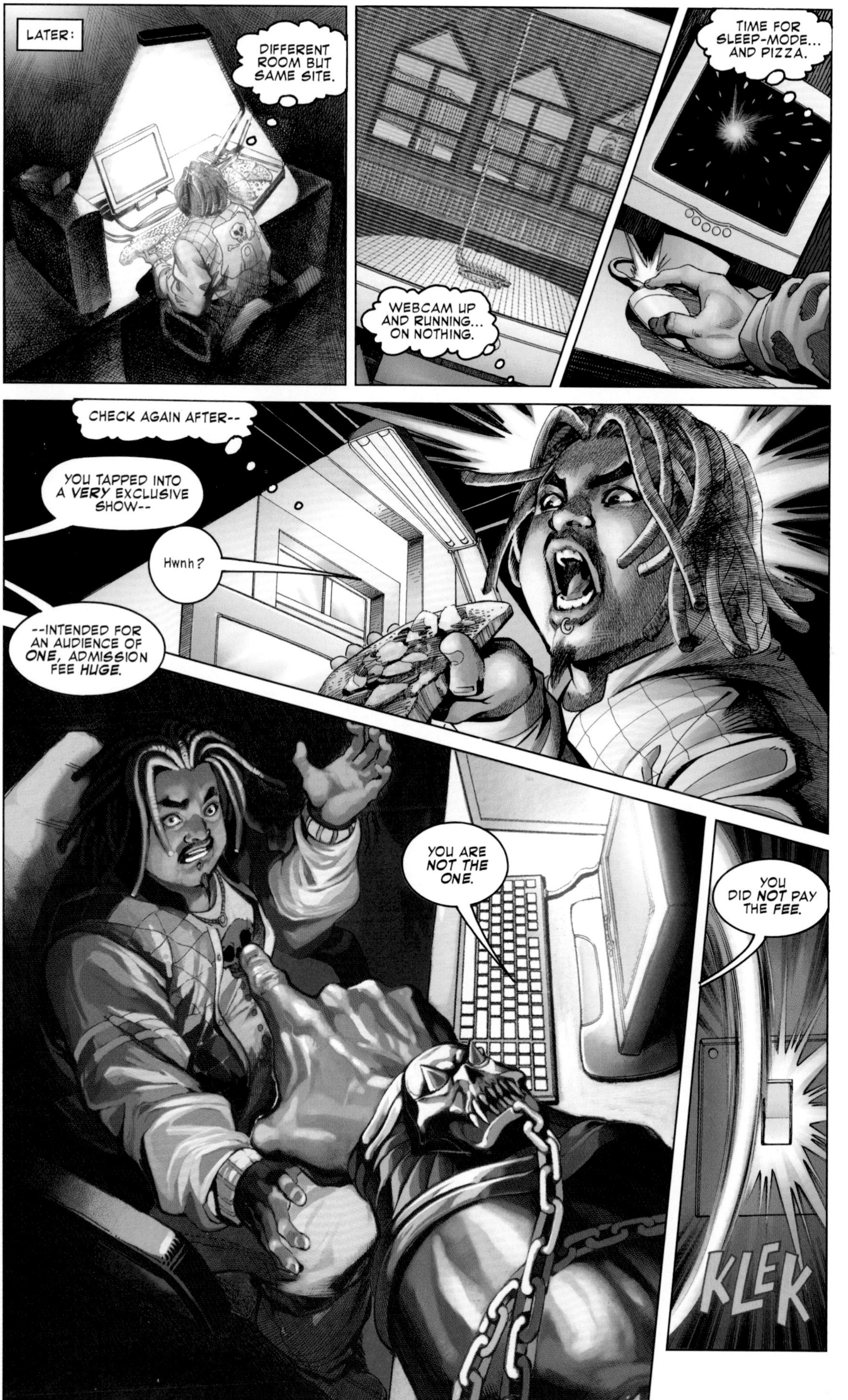
LATER:
DIFFERENT ROOM BUT SAME SITE.
WEBCAM UP AND RUNNING... ON NOTHING.
TIME FOR SLEEP-MODE... AND PIZZA.
CHECK AGAIN AFTER--
YOU TAPPED INTO A VERY EXCLUSIVE SHOW--
Hwnh?
--INTENDED FOR AN AUDIENCE OF ONE, ADMISSION FEE HUGE.
YOU ARE NOT THE ONE.
YOU DID NOT PAY THE FEE.
KLEK

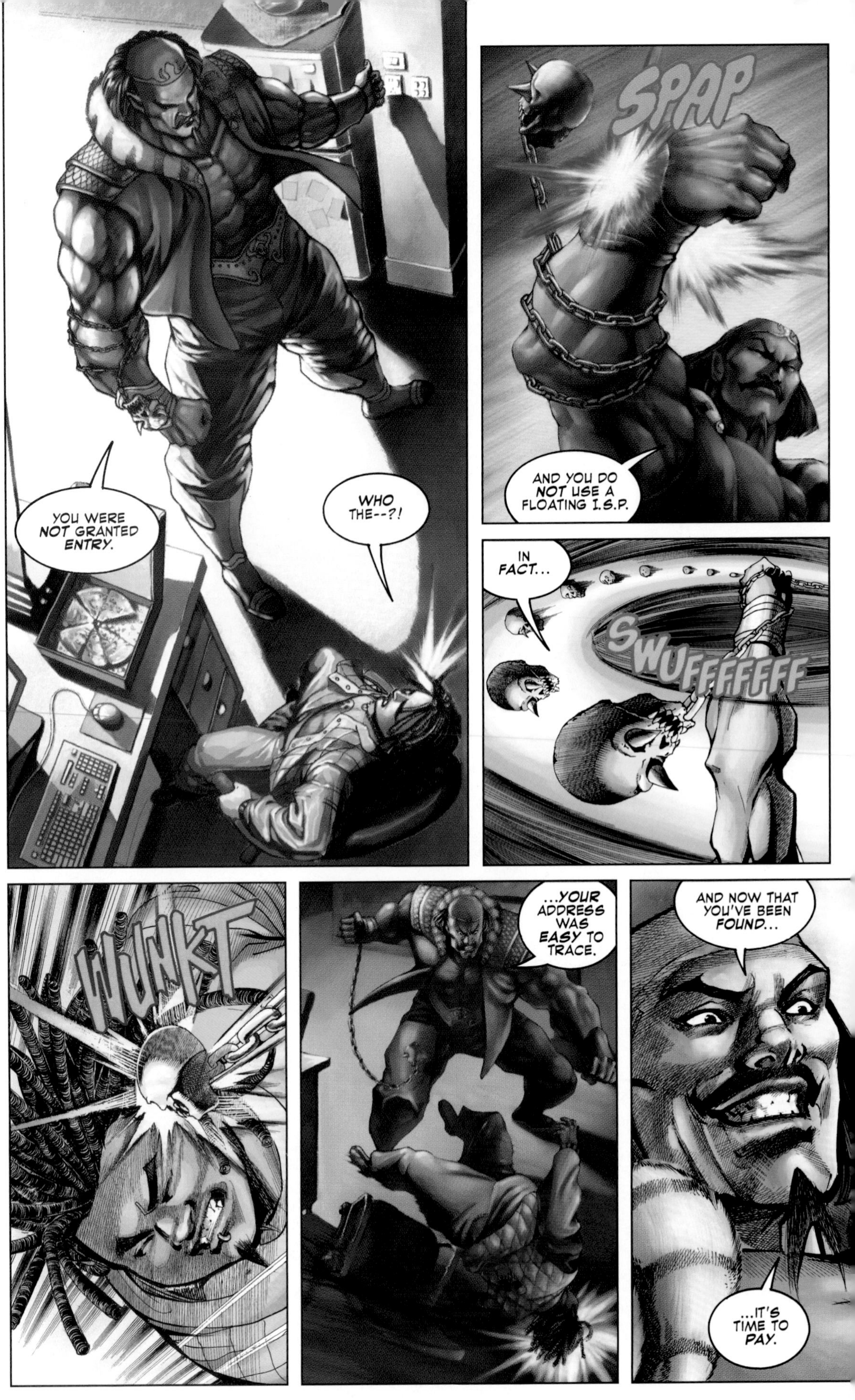
YOU WERE NOT GRANTED ENTRY.
WHO THE--?!
SPAP
AND YOU DO NOT USE A FLOATING I.S.P.
IN FACT...
SWUFFFFFFF
WUNKT
...YOUR ADDRESS WAS EASY TO TRACE.
AND NOW THAT YOU'VE BEEN FOUND...
...IT'S TIME TO PAY.

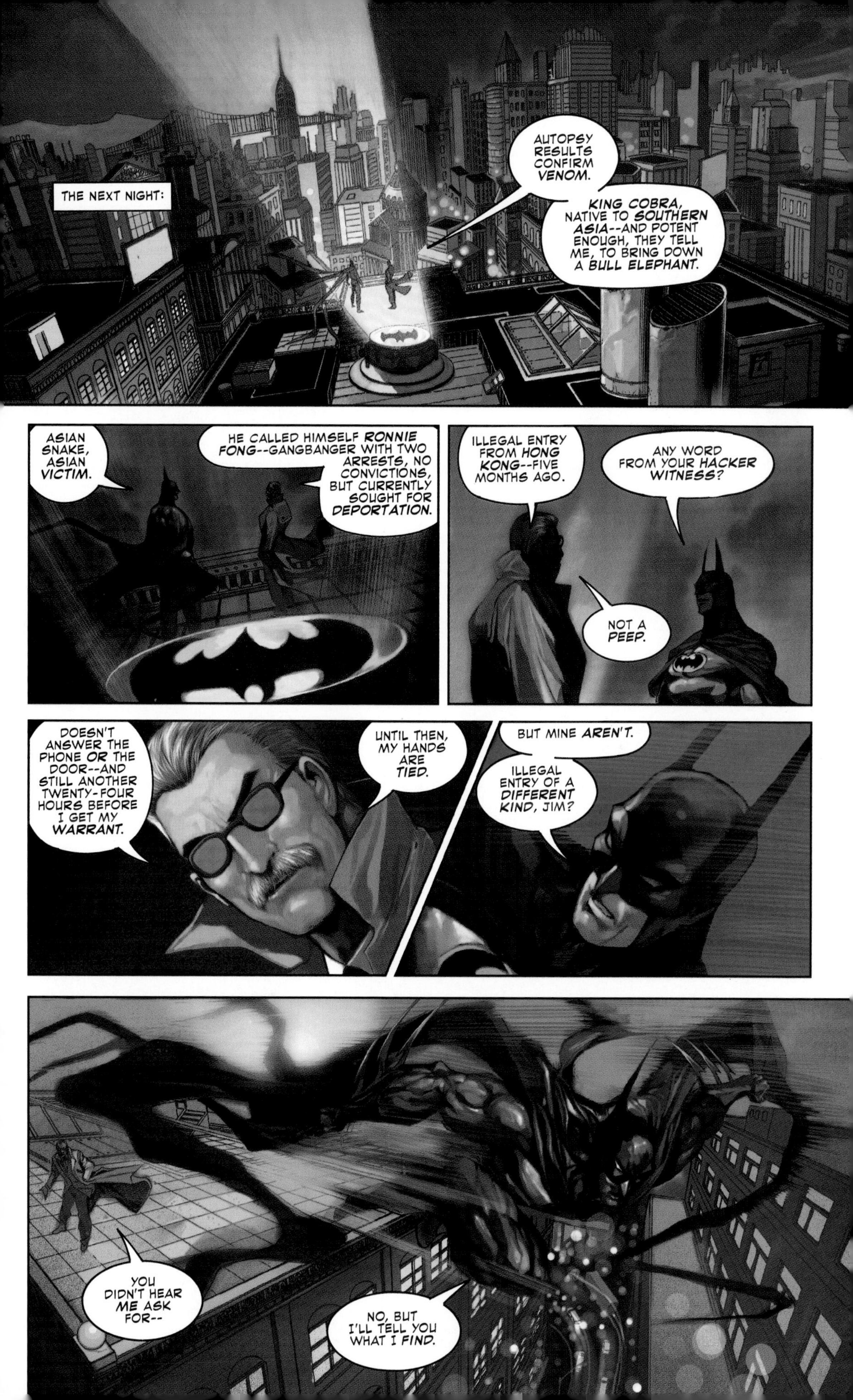
THE NEXT NIGHT:
AUTOPSY RESULTS CONFIRM VENOM.
KING COBRA, NATIVE TO SOUTHERN ASIA--AND POTENT ENOUGH, THEY TELL ME, TO BRING DOWN A BULL ELEPHANT.
ASIAN SNAKE, ASIAN VICTIM.
HE CALLED HIMSELF RONNIE FONG--GANGBANGER WITH TWO ARRESTS, NO CONVICTIONS, BUT CURRENTLY SOUGHT FOR DEPORTATION.
ILLEGAL ENTRY FROM HONG KONG--FIVE MONTHS AGO.
ANY WORD FROM YOUR HACKER WITNESS?
NOT A PEEP.
DOESN'T ANSWER THE PHONE OR THE DOOR--AND STILL ANOTHER TWENTY-FOUR HOURS BEFORE I GET MY WARRANT.
UNTIL THEN, MY HANDS ARE TIED.
BUT MINE AREN'T.
ILLEGAL ENTRY OF A DIFFERENT KIND, JIM?
YOU DIDN'T HEAR ME ASK FOR--
NO, BUT I'LL TELL YOU WHAT I FIND.

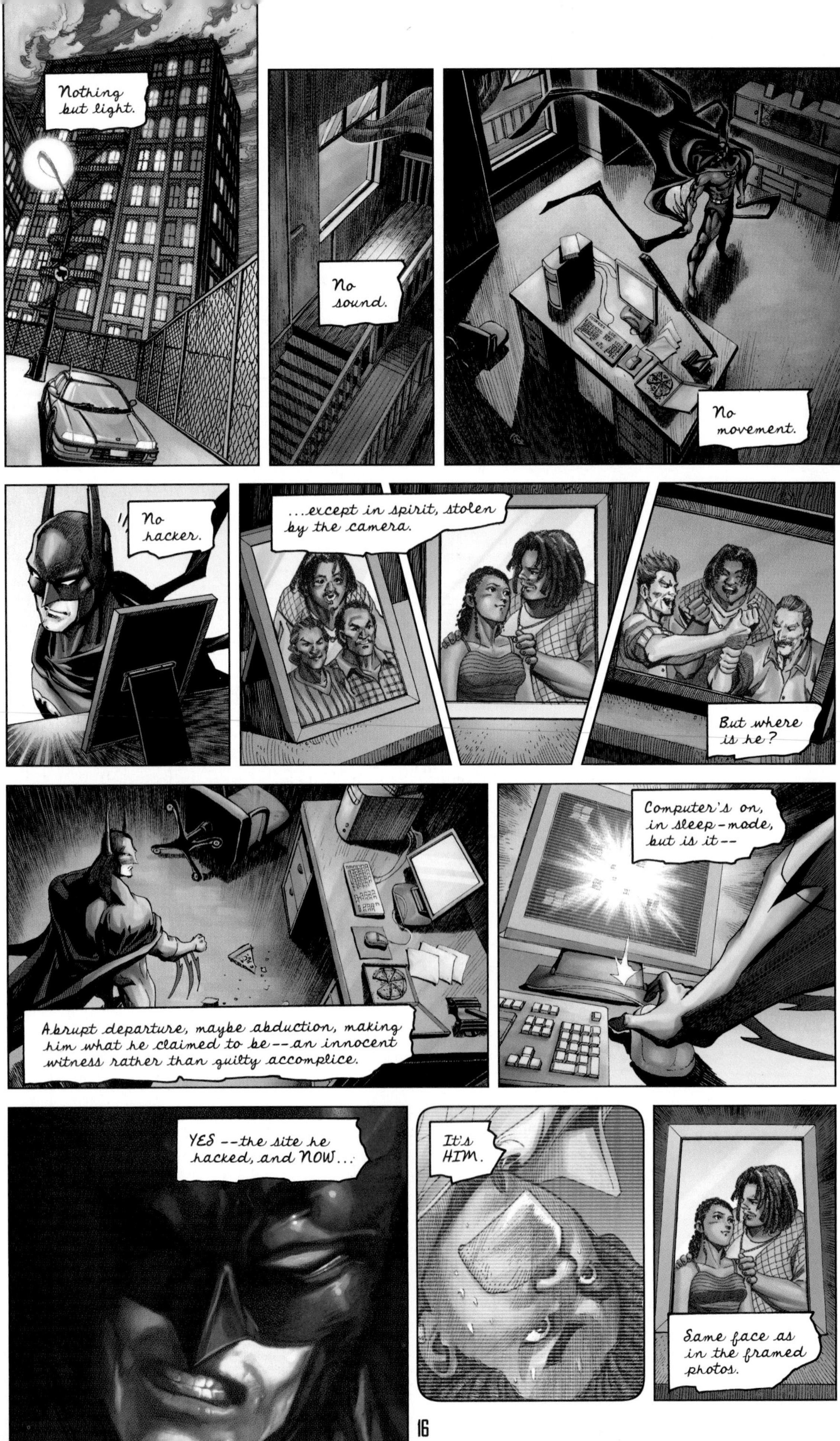
Nothing but light.
No sound.
No movement.
No hacker.
...except in spirit, stolen by the camera.
But where is he?
Abrupt departure, maybe abduction, making him what he claimed to be--an innocent witness rather than guilty accomplice.
Computer's on, in sleep-mode, but is it--
YES--the site he hacked, and NOW...
It's HIM.
Same face as in the framed photos.

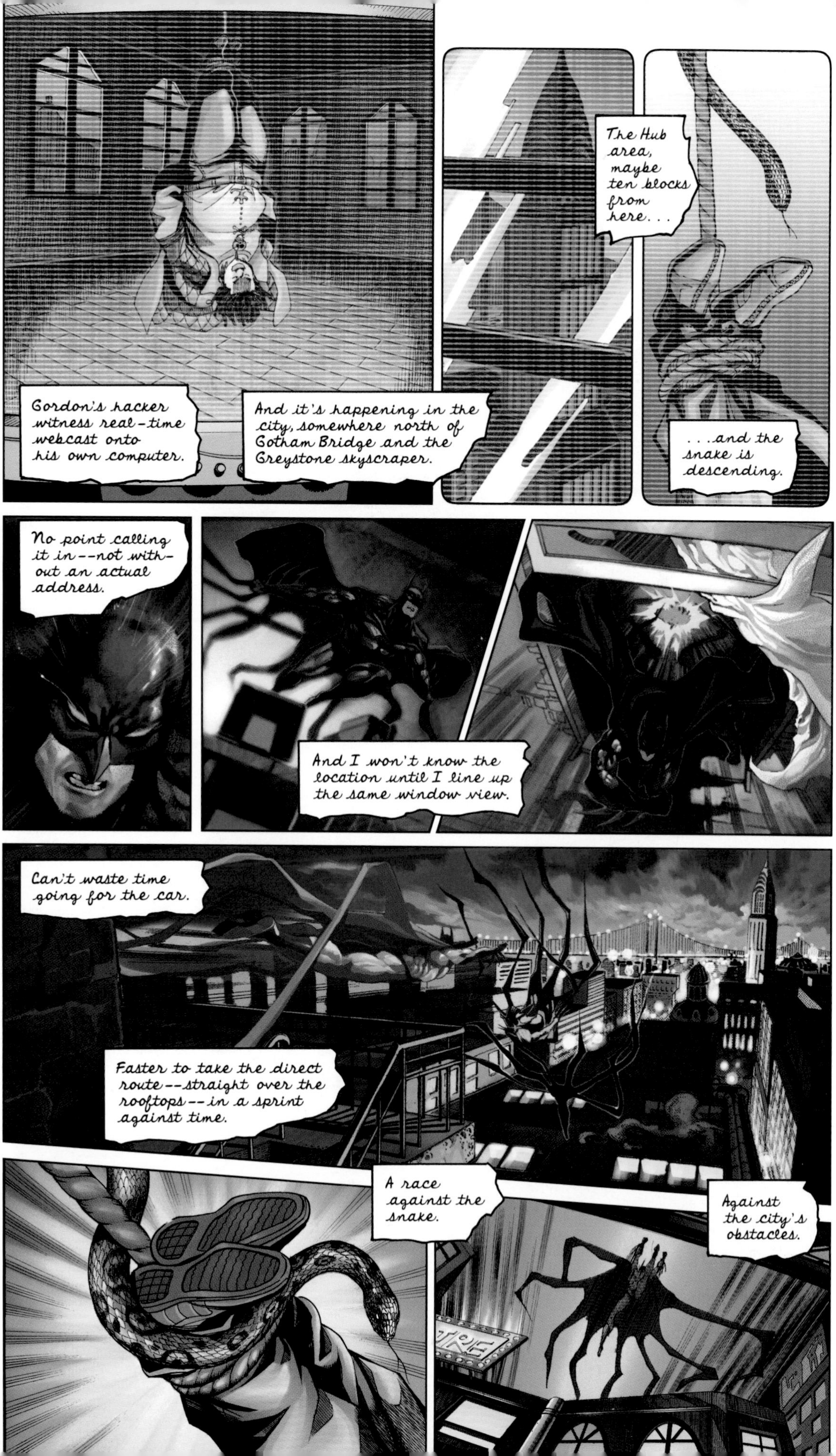
Gordon's hacker witness real-time webcast onto his own computer.
And it's happening in the city, somewhere north of Gotham Bridge and the Greystone skyscraper.
The Hub area, maybe ten blocks from here...
...and the snake is descending.
No point calling it in--not without an actual address.
And I won't know the location until I line up the same window view.
Can't waste time going for the car.
Faster to take the direct route--straight over the rooftops--in a sprint against time.
A race against the snake.
Against the city's obstacles.

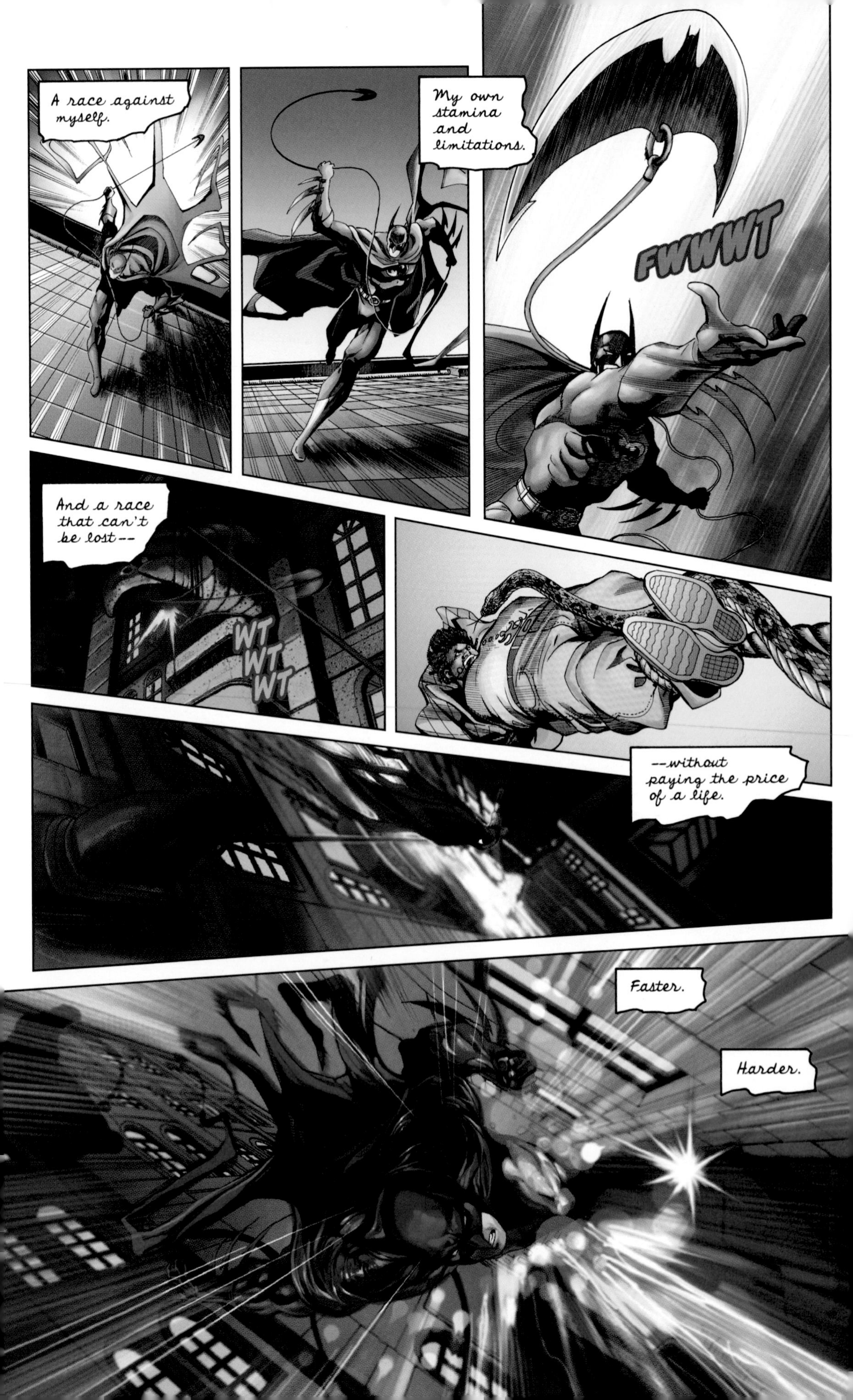
A race against myself.
My own stamina and limitations.
FWWWT
And a race that can't be lost--
WT WT WT
--without paying the price of a life.
Faster.
Harder.

Can't let up for a single step.

Flat-out and nonstop all the way.

CITY
SALE
ENT

Spend everything -- down to the last drop of adrenaline and beyond.

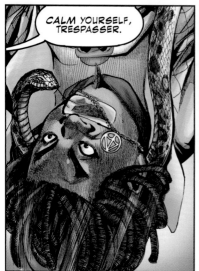

CALM YOURSELF, TRESPASSER.

THE COBRA WILL *NOT* STRANGLE YOU.

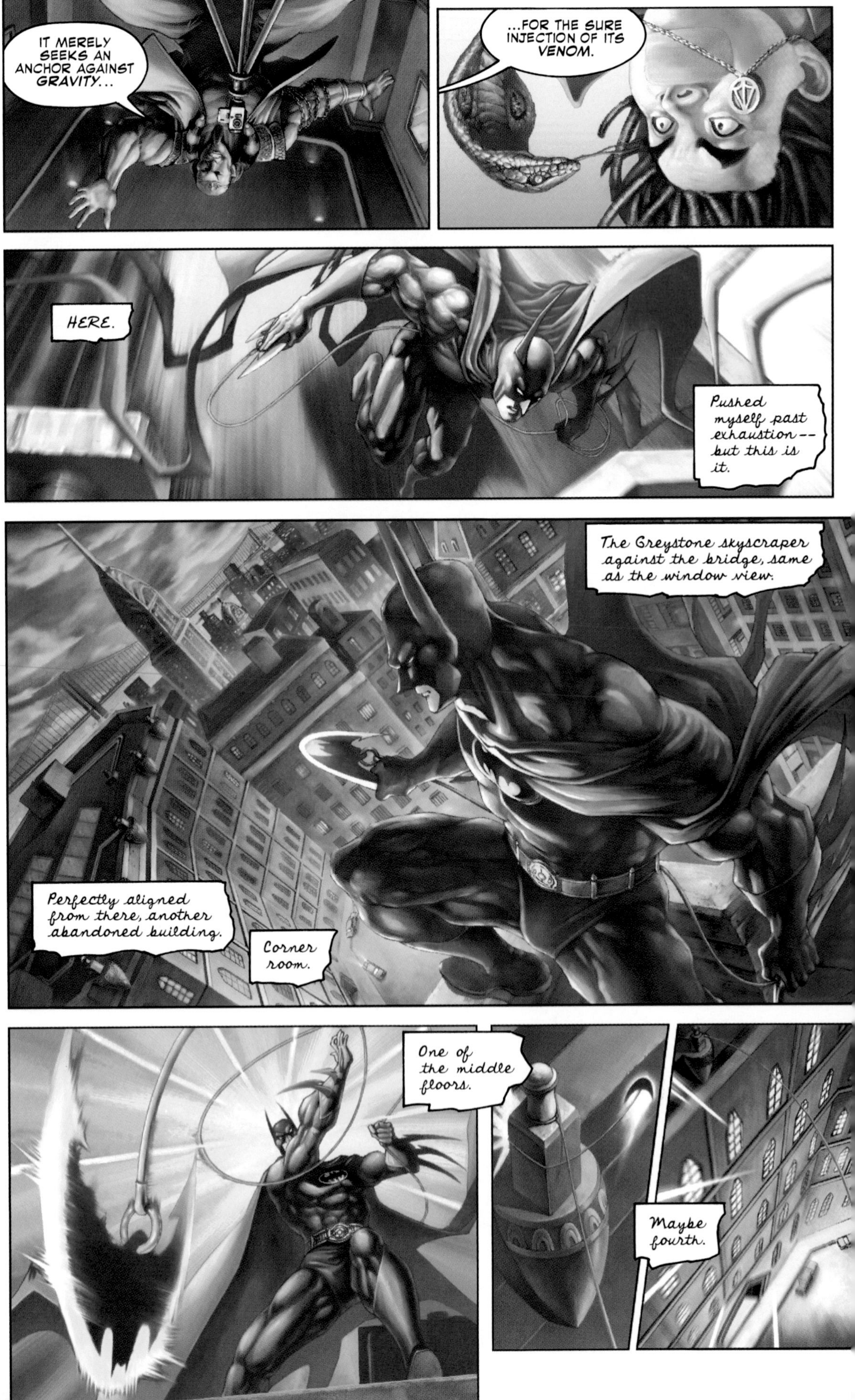
IT MERELY SEEKS AN ANCHOR AGAINST GRAVITY...
...FOR THE SURE INJECTION OF ITS VENOM.
HERE.
Pushed myself past exhaustion-- but this is it.
The Greystone skyscraper against the bridge, same as the window view.
Perfectly aligned from there, another abandoned building.
Corner room.
One of the middle floors.
Maybe fourth.

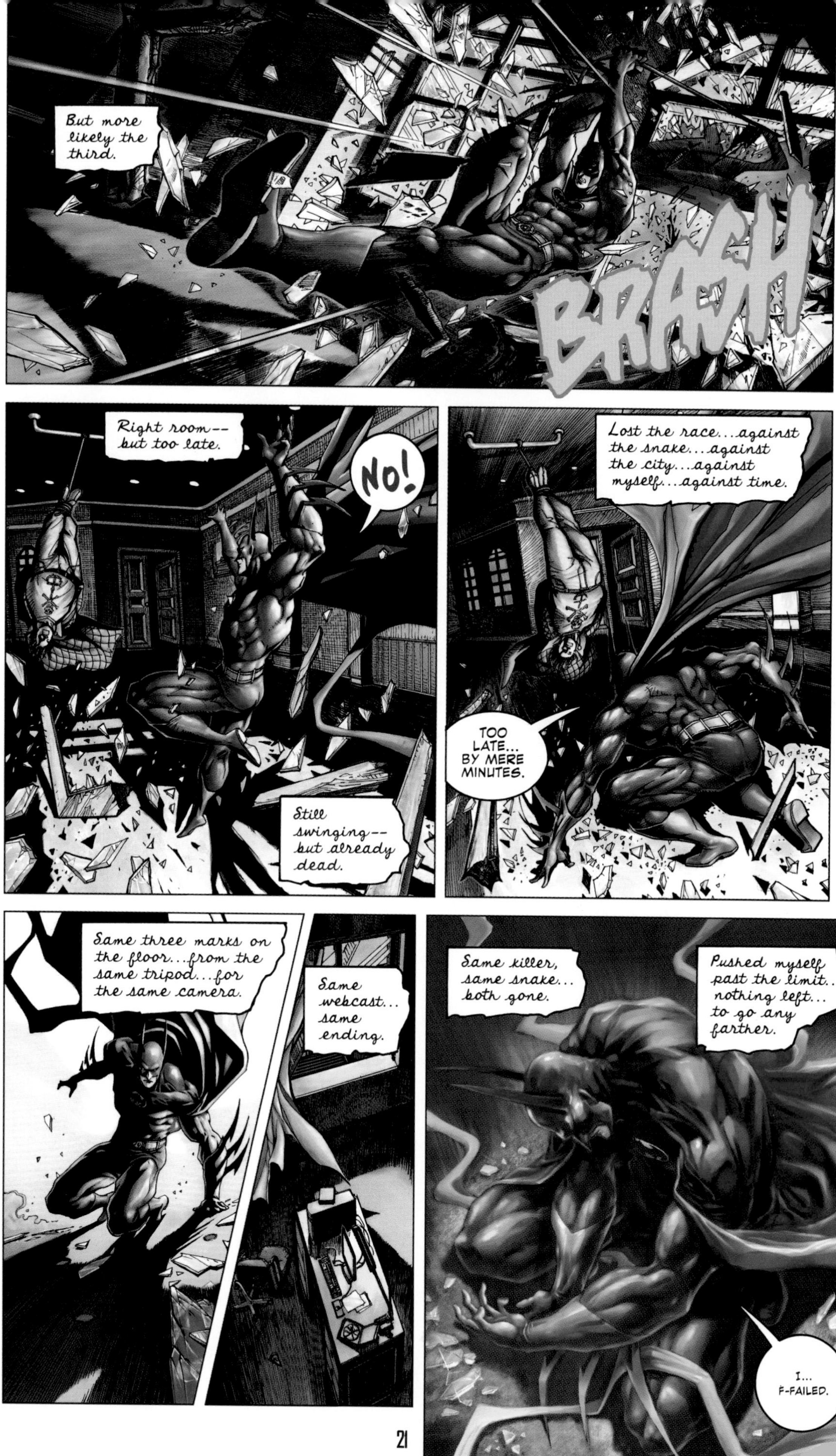
But more likely the third.
BRASH
Right room-- but too late.
NO!
Still swinging-- but already dead.
Lost the race...against the snake...against the city...against myself...against time.
TOO LATE... BY MERE MINUTES.
Same three marks on the floor...from the same tripod...for the same camera.
Same webcast... same ending.
Same killer, same snake... both gone.
Pushed myself past the limit... nothing left... to go any farther.
I... F-FAILED.

KOWLOON PENINSULA, HONG KONG, TWO WEEKS LATER:

JOHNNY? IT'S ME AND *ANGELA*! YOU *HERE*, JOHNNY?

YO, IT'S ME--BENNY! WHERE THE HELL ARE Y--

AAAIIIIEEE

EASY, ANGELA!

WHOEVER IT WAS...THEY'RE *LONG GONE*.

BUT...H-HE'S *DEAD*, BENNY! J-JOHNNY'S *DEAD*!

WH-WHO... WHO WOULD WANT TO *KILL* HIM, BENNY?

NOT *THIEVES*, ANGELA...

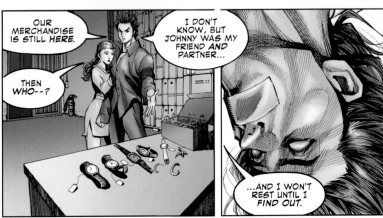

OUR MERCHANDISE IS STILL *HERE*.

THEN WHO--?

I DON'T KNOW, BUT JOHNNY WAS MY FRIEND AND PARTNER...

...AND I WON'T REST UNTIL I FIND OUT.

22

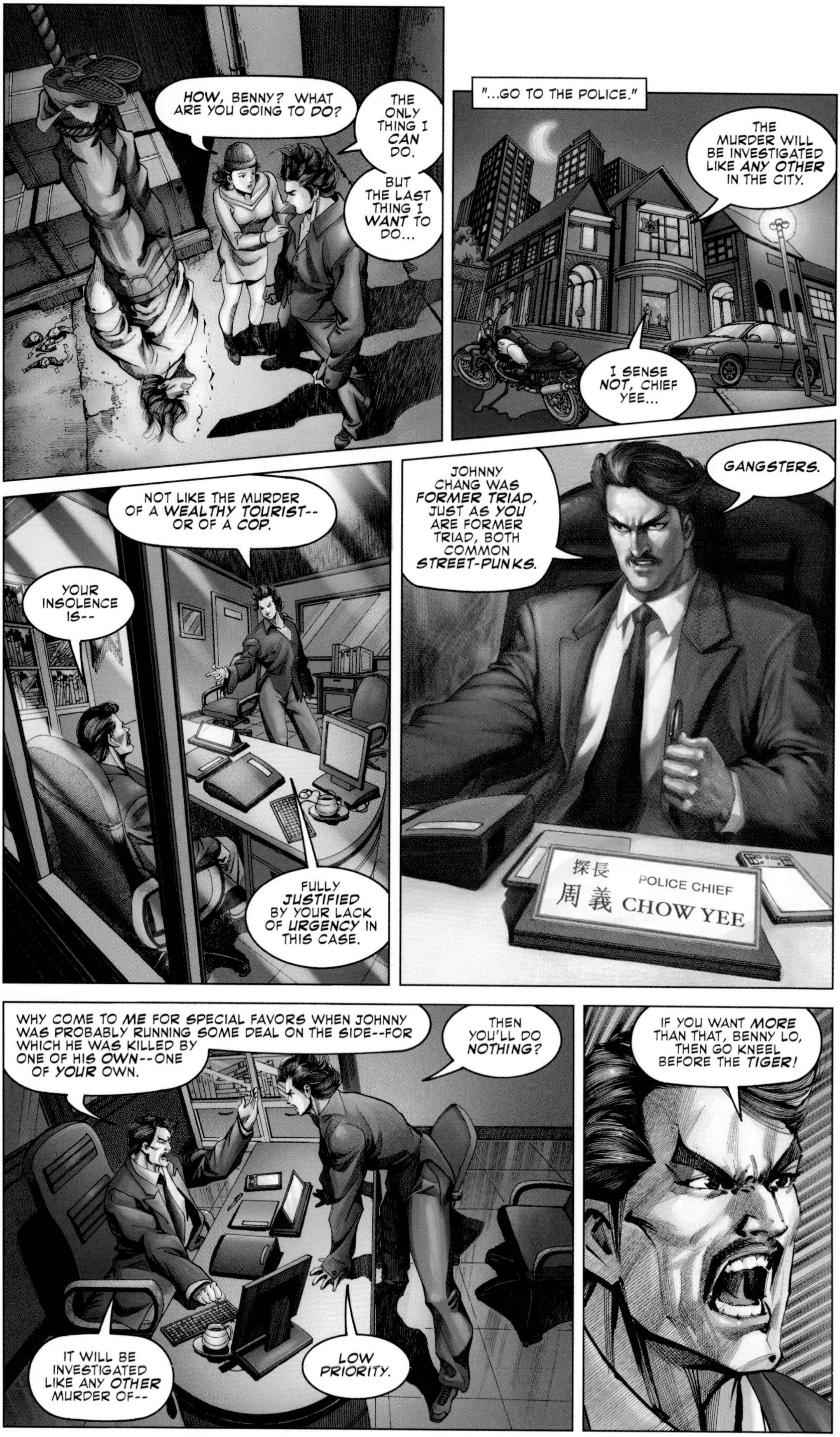

HOW, BENNY? WHAT ARE YOU GOING TO DO?
THE ONLY THING I CAN DO.
BUT THE LAST THING I WANT TO DO...
"...GO TO THE POLICE."
THE MURDER WILL BE INVESTIGATED LIKE ANY OTHER IN THE CITY.
I SENSE NOT, CHIEF YEE...
NOT LIKE THE MURDER OF A WEALTHY TOURIST--OR OF A COP.
YOUR INSOLENCE IS--
FULLY JUSTIFIED BY YOUR LACK OF URGENCY IN THIS CASE.
JOHNNY CHANG WAS FORMER TRIAD, JUST AS YOU ARE FORMER TRIAD, BOTH COMMON STREET-PUNKS.
GANGSTERS.
探長
周義
POLICE CHIEF
CHOW YEE
WHY COME TO ME FOR SPECIAL FAVORS WHEN JOHNNY WAS PROBABLY RUNNING SOME DEAL ON THE SIDE--FOR WHICH HE WAS KILLED BY ONE OF HIS OWN--ONE OF YOUR OWN.
THEN YOU'LL DO NOTHING?
IT WILL BE INVESTIGATED LIKE ANY OTHER MURDER OF--
LOW PRIORITY.
IF YOU WANT MORE THAN THAT, BENNY LO, THEN GO KNEEL BEFORE THE TIGER!

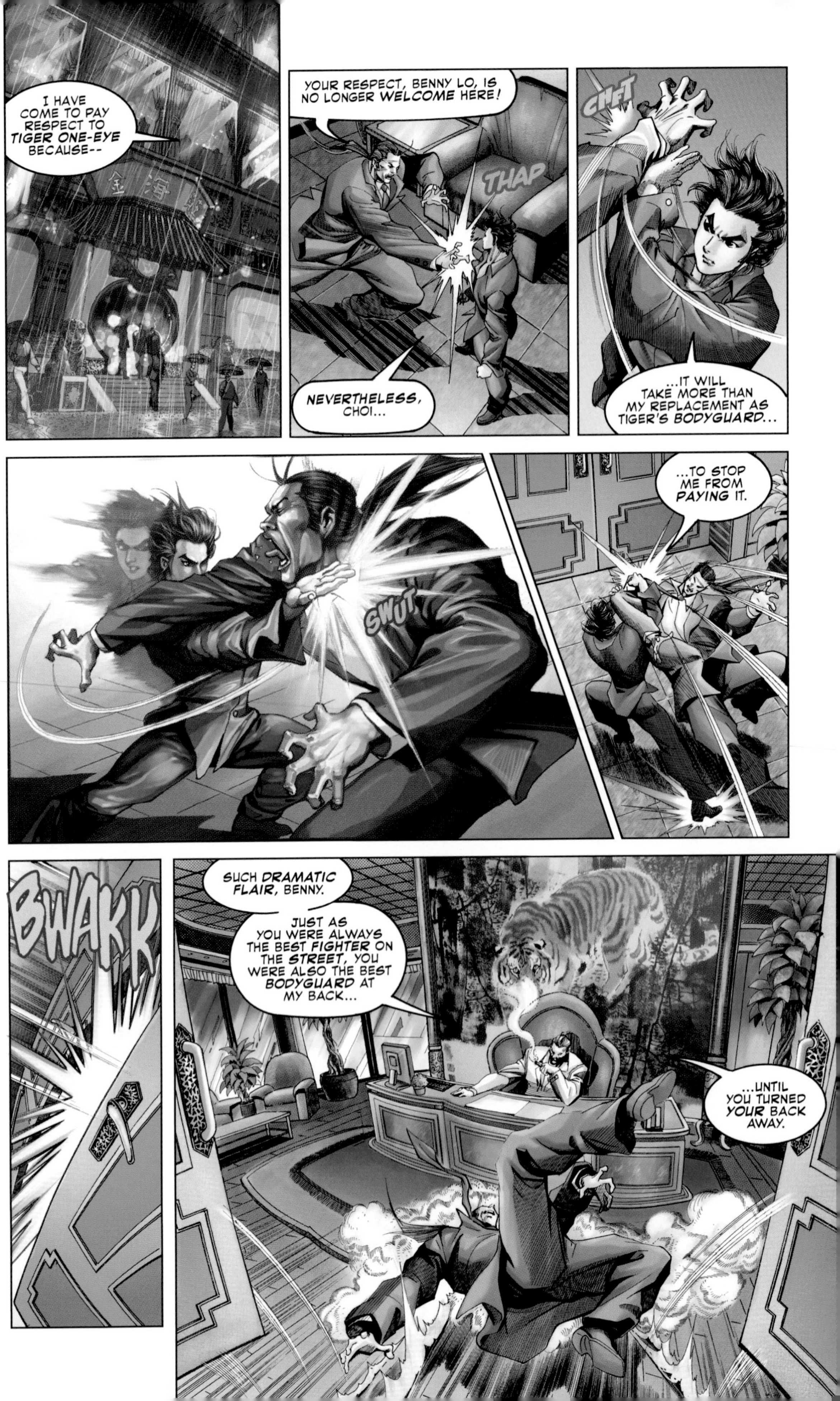
I HAVE COME TO PAY RESPECT TO TIGER ONE-EYE BECAUSE--
YOUR RESPECT, BENNY LO, IS NO LONGER WELCOME HERE!
THAP
NEVERTHELESS, CHOI...
CHFT
...IT WILL TAKE MORE THAN MY REPLACEMENT AS TIGER'S BODYGUARD...
SWUT
...TO STOP ME FROM PAYING IT.
BWAKK
SUCH DRAMATIC FLAIR, BENNY.
JUST AS YOU WERE ALWAYS THE BEST FIGHTER ON THE STREET, YOU WERE ALSO THE BEST BODYGUARD AT MY BACK...
...UNTIL YOU TURNED YOUR BACK AWAY.

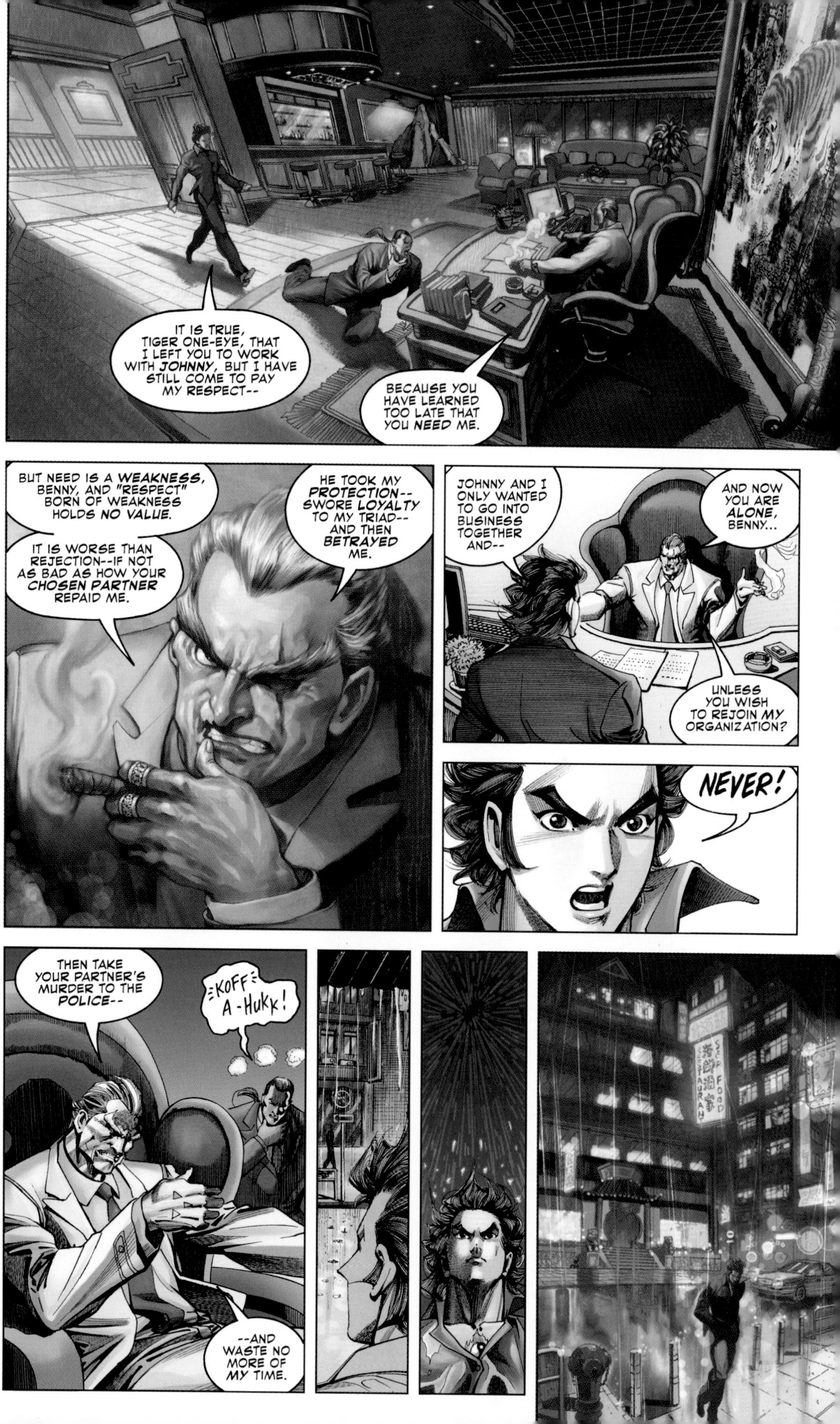
IT IS TRUE, TIGER ONE-EYE, THAT I LEFT YOU TO WORK WITH JOHNNY, BUT I HAVE STILL COME TO PAY MY RESPECT--
BECAUSE YOU HAVE LEARNED TOO LATE THAT YOU NEED ME.
BUT NEED IS A WEAKNESS, BENNY, AND "RESPECT" BORN OF WEAKNESS HOLDS NO VALUE.
IT IS WORSE THAN REJECTION--IF NOT AS BAD AS HOW YOUR CHOSEN PARTNER REPAID ME.
HE TOOK MY PROTECTION--SWORE LOYALTY TO MY TRIAD--AND THEN BETRAYED ME.
JOHNNY AND I ONLY WANTED TO GO INTO BUSINESS TOGETHER AND--
AND NOW YOU ARE ALONE, BENNY...
UNLESS YOU WISH TO REJOIN MY ORGANIZATION?
NEVER!
THEN TAKE YOUR PARTNER'S MURDER TO THE POLICE--
KOFF A-HUKK!
--AND WASTE NO MORE OF MY TIME.
SEA FOOD
RESTAURANT

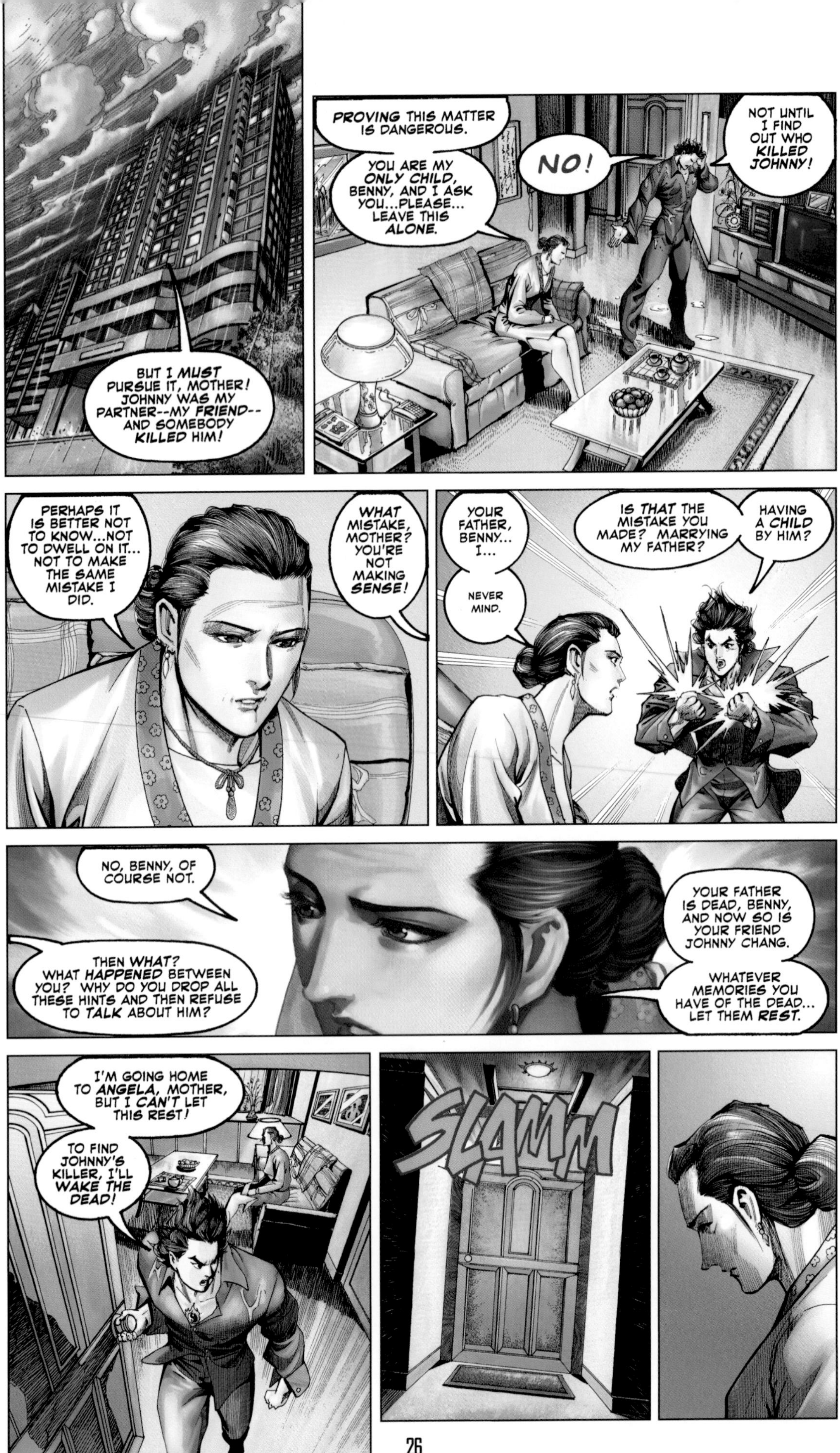
BUT I MUST PURSUE IT, MOTHER! JOHNNY WAS MY PARTNER--MY FRIEND--AND SOMEBODY KILLED HIM!
PROVING THIS MATTER IS DANGEROUS.
YOU ARE MY ONLY CHILD, BENNY, AND I ASK YOU...PLEASE... LEAVE THIS ALONE.
NO!
NOT UNTIL I FIND OUT WHO KILLED JOHNNY!
PERHAPS IT IS BETTER NOT TO KNOW...NOT TO DWELL ON IT... NOT TO MAKE THE SAME MISTAKE I DID.
WHAT MISTAKE, MOTHER? YOU'RE NOT MAKING SENSE!
YOUR FATHER, BENNY... I...
NEVER MIND.
IS THAT THE MISTAKE YOU MADE? MARRYING MY FATHER?
HAVING A CHILD BY HIM?
NO, BENNY, OF COURSE NOT.
THEN WHAT? WHAT HAPPENED BETWEEN YOU? WHY DO YOU DROP ALL THESE HINTS AND THEN REFUSE TO TALK ABOUT HIM?
YOUR FATHER IS DEAD, BENNY, AND NOW SO IS YOUR FRIEND JOHNNY CHANG.
WHATEVER MEMORIES YOU HAVE OF THE DEAD... LET THEM REST.
I'M GOING HOME TO ANGELA, MOTHER, BUT I CAN'T LET THIS REST!
TO FIND JOHNNY'S KILLER, I'LL WAKE THE DEAD!
SLAMM

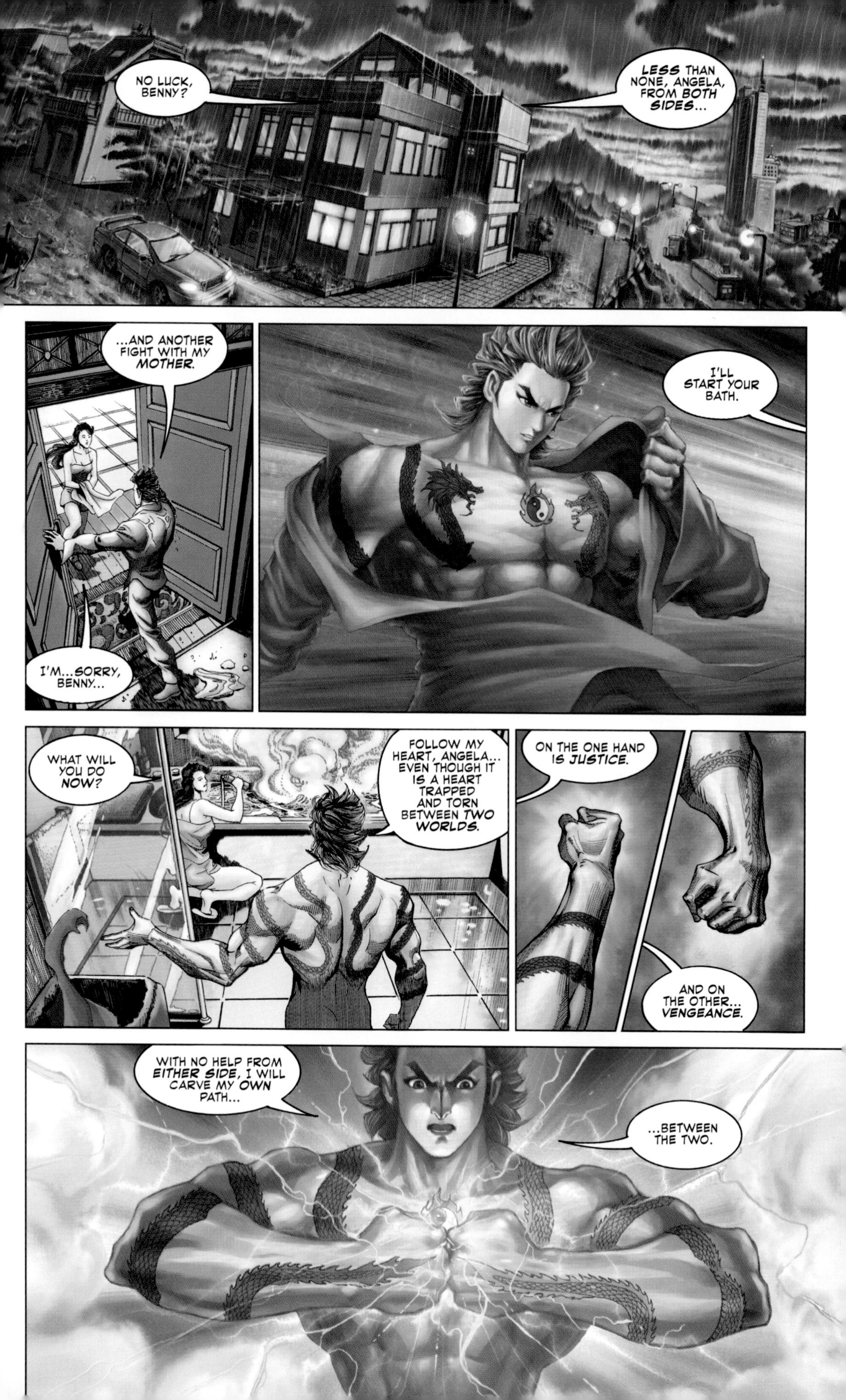
NO LUCK, BENNY?
LESS THAN NONE, ANGELA, FROM BOTH SIDES...
...AND ANOTHER FIGHT WITH MY MOTHER.
I'M...SORRY, BENNY...
I'LL START YOUR BATH.
WHAT WILL YOU DO NOW?
FOLLOW MY HEART, ANGELA... EVEN THOUGH IT IS A HEART TRAPPED AND TORN BETWEEN TWO WORLDS.
ON THE ONE HAND IS JUSTICE.
AND ON THE OTHER... VENGEANCE.
WITH NO HELP FROM EITHER SIDE, I WILL CARVE MY OWN PATH...
...BETWEEN THE TWO.

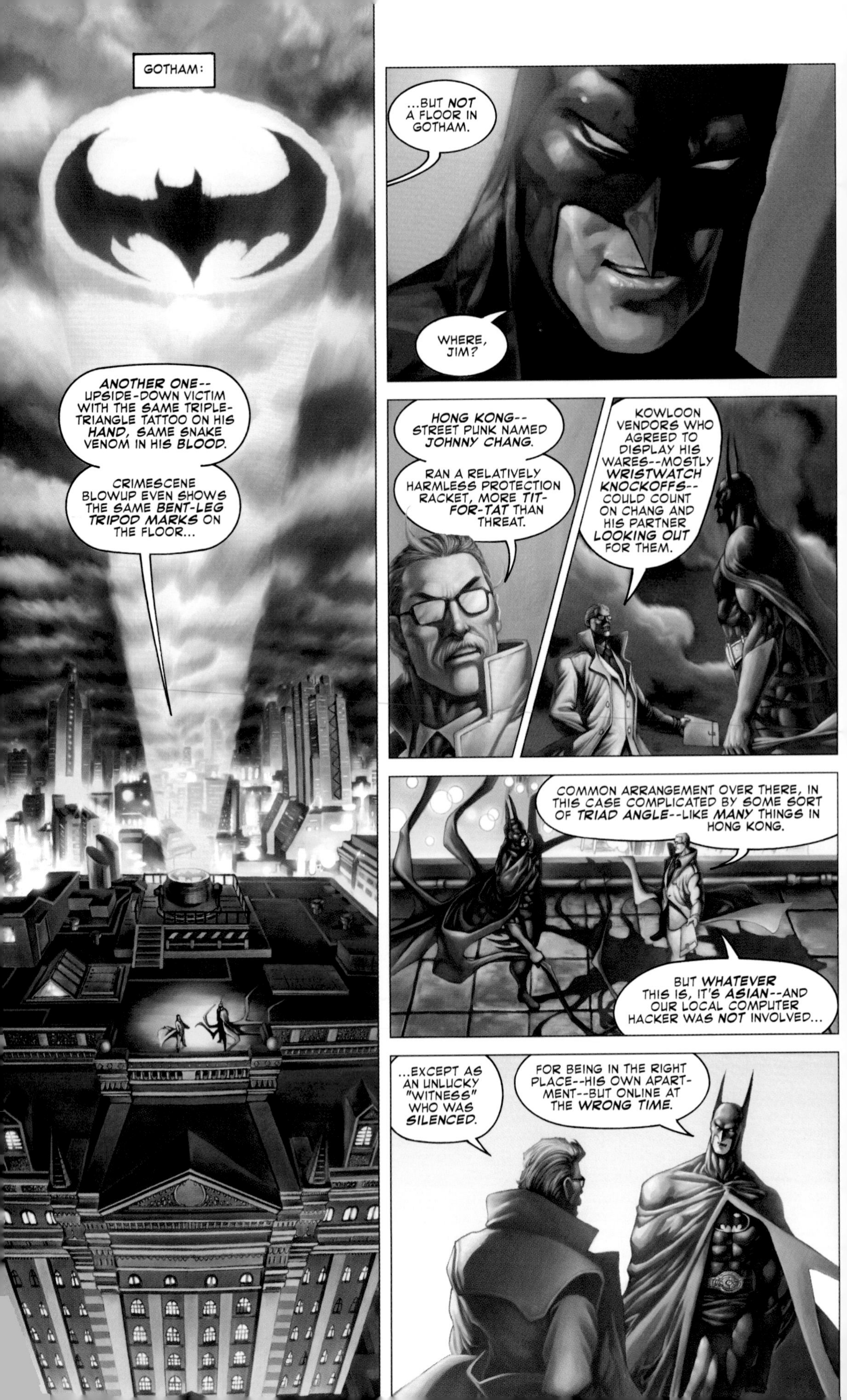
GOTHAM:
ANOTHER ONE--UPSIDE-DOWN VICTIM WITH THE SAME TRIPLE-TRIANGLE TATTOO ON HIS HAND, SAME SNAKE VENOM IN HIS BLOOD.
CRIMESCENE BLOWUP EVEN SHOWS THE SAME BENT-LEG TRIPOD MARKS ON THE FLOOR...
...BUT NOT A FLOOR IN GOTHAM.
WHERE, JIM?
HONG KONG--STREET PUNK NAMED JOHNNY CHANG.
RAN A RELATIVELY HARMLESS PROTECTION RACKET, MORE TIT-FOR-TAT THAN THREAT.
KOWLOON VENDORS WHO AGREED TO DISPLAY HIS WARES--MOSTLY WRISTWATCH KNOCKOFFS--COULD COUNT ON CHANG AND HIS PARTNER LOOKING OUT FOR THEM.
COMMON ARRANGEMENT OVER THERE, IN THIS CASE COMPLICATED BY SOME SORT OF TRIAD ANGLE--LIKE MANY THINGS IN HONG KONG.
BUT WHATEVER THIS IS, IT'S ASIAN--AND OUR LOCAL COMPUTER HACKER WAS NOT INVOLVED...
...EXCEPT AS AN UNLUCKY "WITNESS" WHO WAS SILENCED.
FOR BEING IN THE RIGHT PLACE--HIS OWN APARTMENT--BUT ONLINE AT THE WRONG TIME.

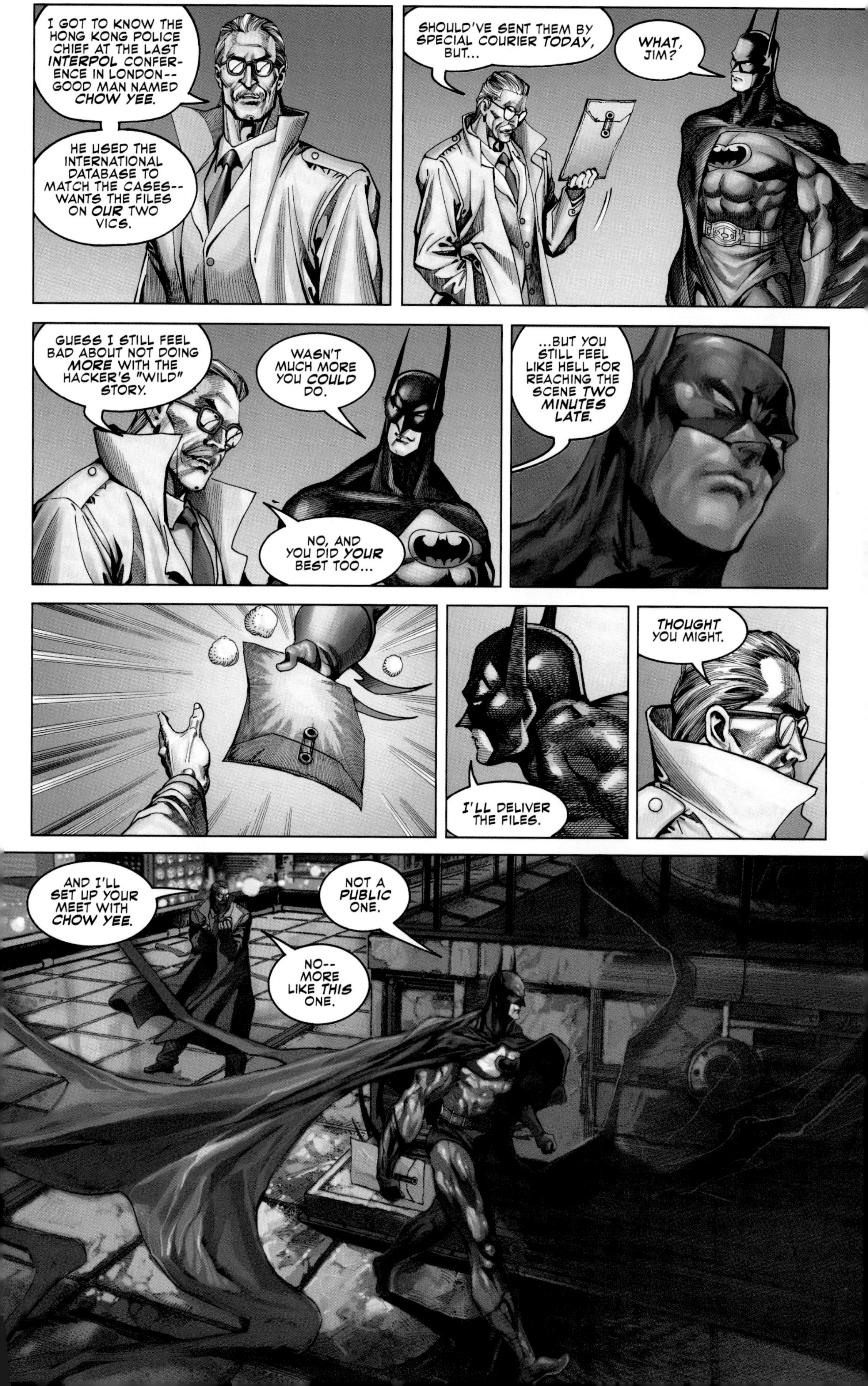
I GOT TO KNOW THE HONG KONG POLICE CHIEF AT THE LAST INTERPOL CONFERENCE IN LONDON-- GOOD MAN NAMED CHOW YEE.
HE USED THE INTERNATIONAL DATABASE TO MATCH THE CASES-- WANTS THE FILES ON OUR TWO VICS.
SHOULD'VE SENT THEM BY SPECIAL COURIER TODAY, BUT...
WHAT, JIM?
GUESS I STILL FEEL BAD ABOUT NOT DOING MORE WITH THE HACKER'S "WILD" STORY.
WASN'T MUCH MORE YOU COULD DO.
NO, AND YOU DID YOUR BEST TOO...
...BUT YOU STILL FEEL LIKE HELL FOR REACHING THE SCENE TWO MINUTES LATE.
I'LL DELIVER THE FILES.
THOUGHT YOU MIGHT.
AND I'LL SET UP YOUR MEET WITH CHOW YEE.
NOT A PUBLIC ONE.
NO-- MORE LIKE THIS ONE.

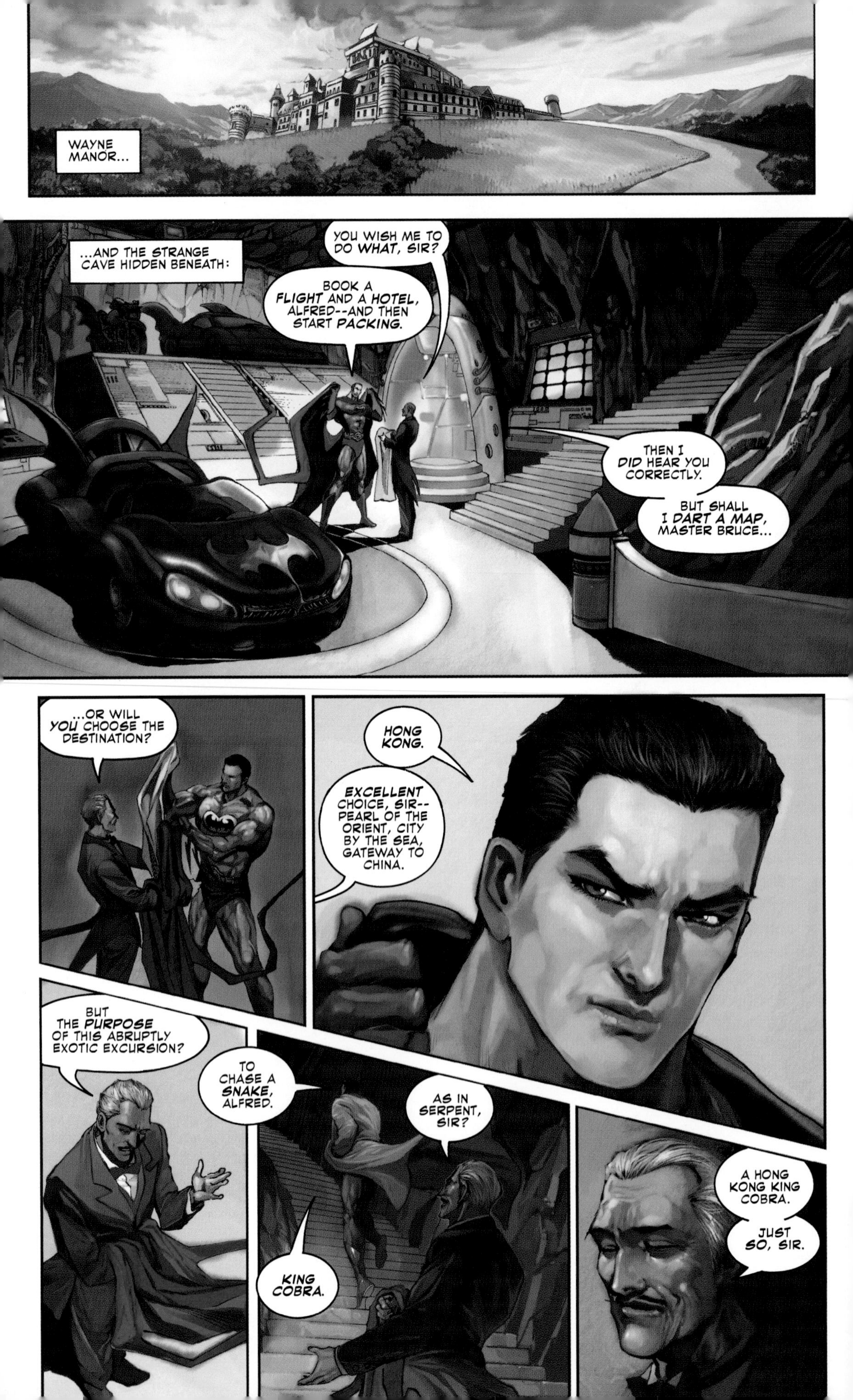
WAYNE MANOR...
...AND THE STRANGE CAVE HIDDEN BENEATH:
YOU WISH ME TO DO WHAT, SIR?
BOOK A FLIGHT AND A HOTEL, ALFRED--AND THEN START PACKING.
THEN I DID HEAR YOU CORRECTLY.
BUT SHALL I DART A MAP, MASTER BRUCE...
...OR WILL YOU CHOOSE THE DESTINATION?
HONG KONG.
EXCELLENT CHOICE, SIR--PEARL OF THE ORIENT, CITY BY THE SEA, GATEWAY TO CHINA.
BUT THE PURPOSE OF THIS ABRUPTLY EXOTIC EXCURSION?
TO CHASE A SNAKE, ALFRED.
AS IN SERPENT, SIR?
KING COBRA.
A HONG KONG KING COBRA.
JUST SO, SIR.

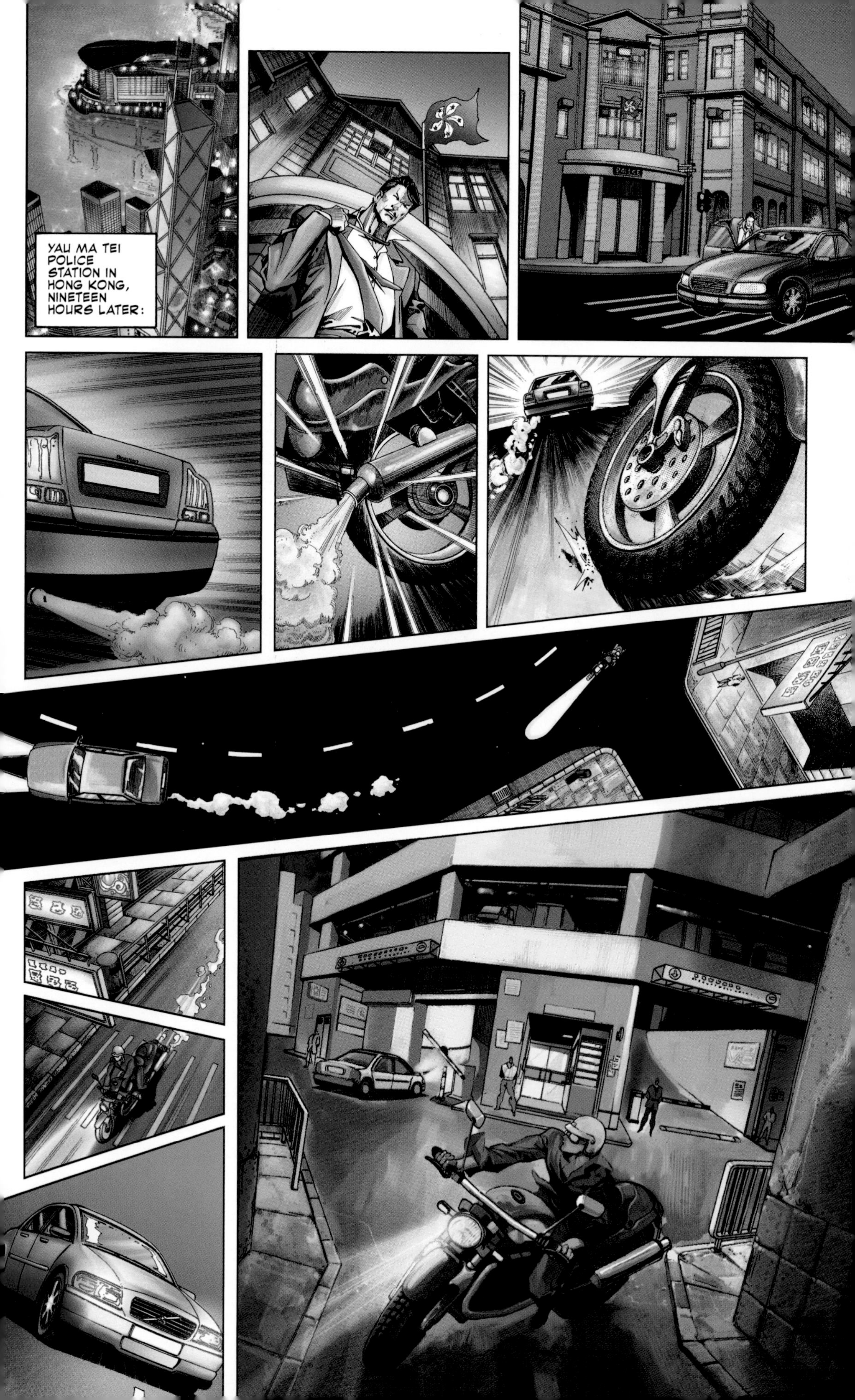
YAU MA TEI POLICE STATION IN HONG KONG, NINETEEN HOURS LATER:

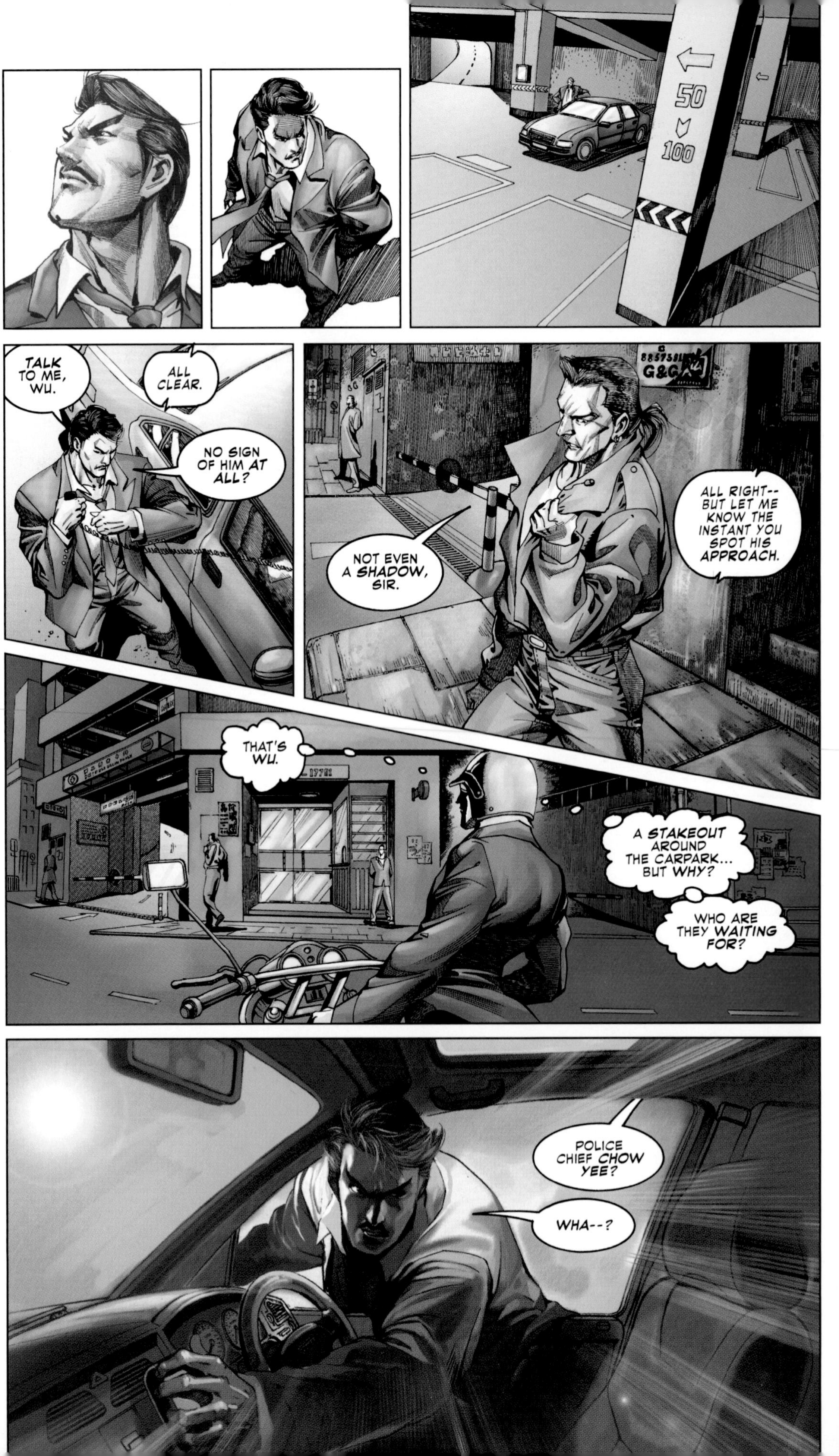
50
100
TALK TO ME, WU.
ALL CLEAR.
NO SIGN OF HIM AT ALL?
NOT EVEN A SHADOW, SIR.
ALL RIGHT-- BUT LET ME KNOW THE INSTANT YOU SPOT HIS APPROACH.
G&G
THAT'S WU.
A STAKEOUT AROUND THE CARPARK... BUT WHY?
WHO ARE THEY WAITING FOR?
POLICE CHIEF CHOW YEE?
WHA--?

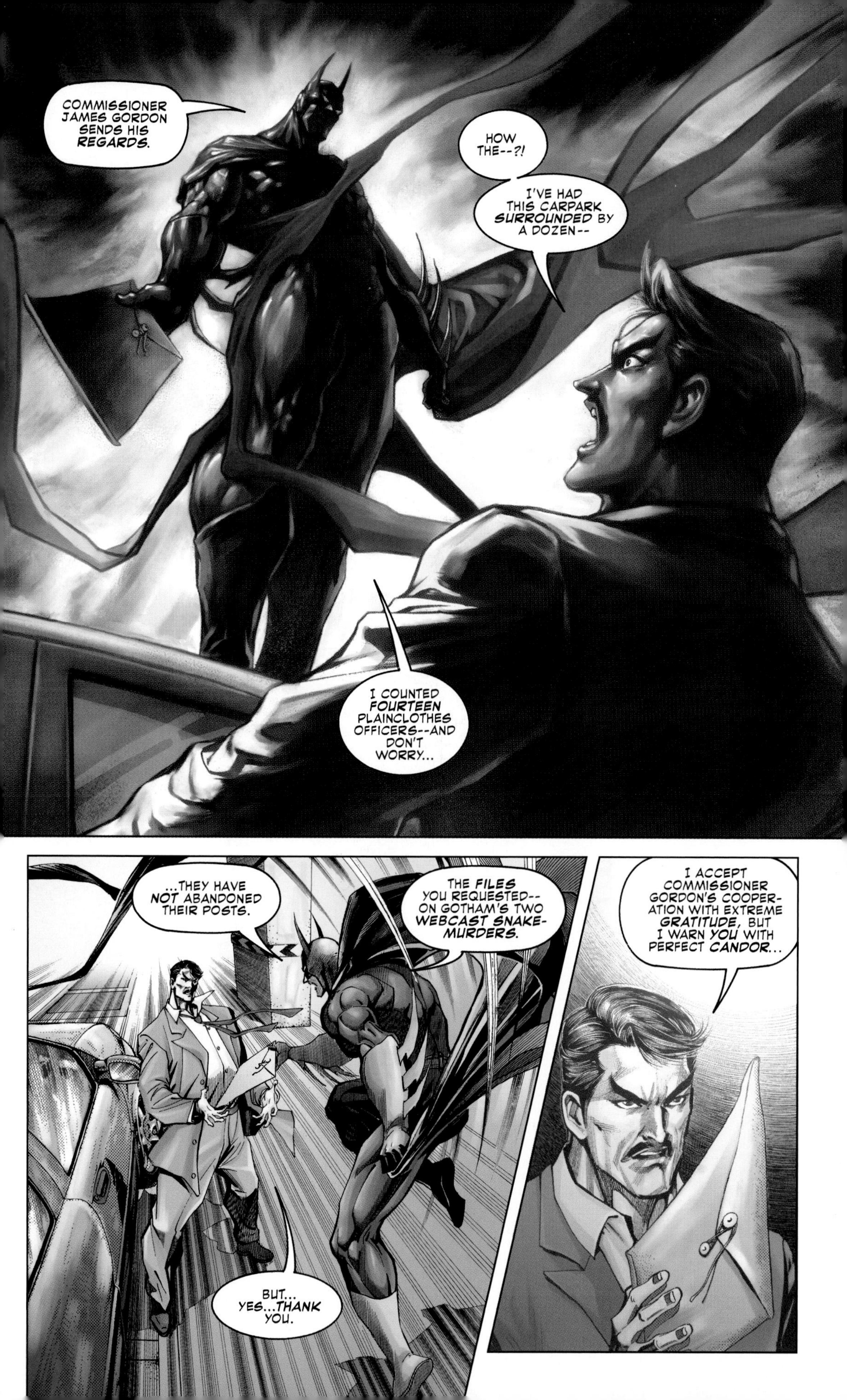
COMMISSIONER JAMES GORDON SENDS HIS REGARDS.
HOW THE--?!
I'VE HAD THIS CARPARK SURROUNDED BY A DOZEN--
I COUNTED FOURTEEN PLAINCLOTHES OFFICERS--AND DON'T WORRY...
...THEY HAVE NOT ABANDONED THEIR POSTS.
THE FILES YOU REQUESTED-- ON GOTHAM'S TWO WEBCAST SNAKE-MURDERS.
BUT... YES...THANK YOU.
I ACCEPT COMMISSIONER GORDON'S COOPERATION WITH EXTREME GRATITUDE, BUT I WARN YOU WITH PERFECT CANDOR...

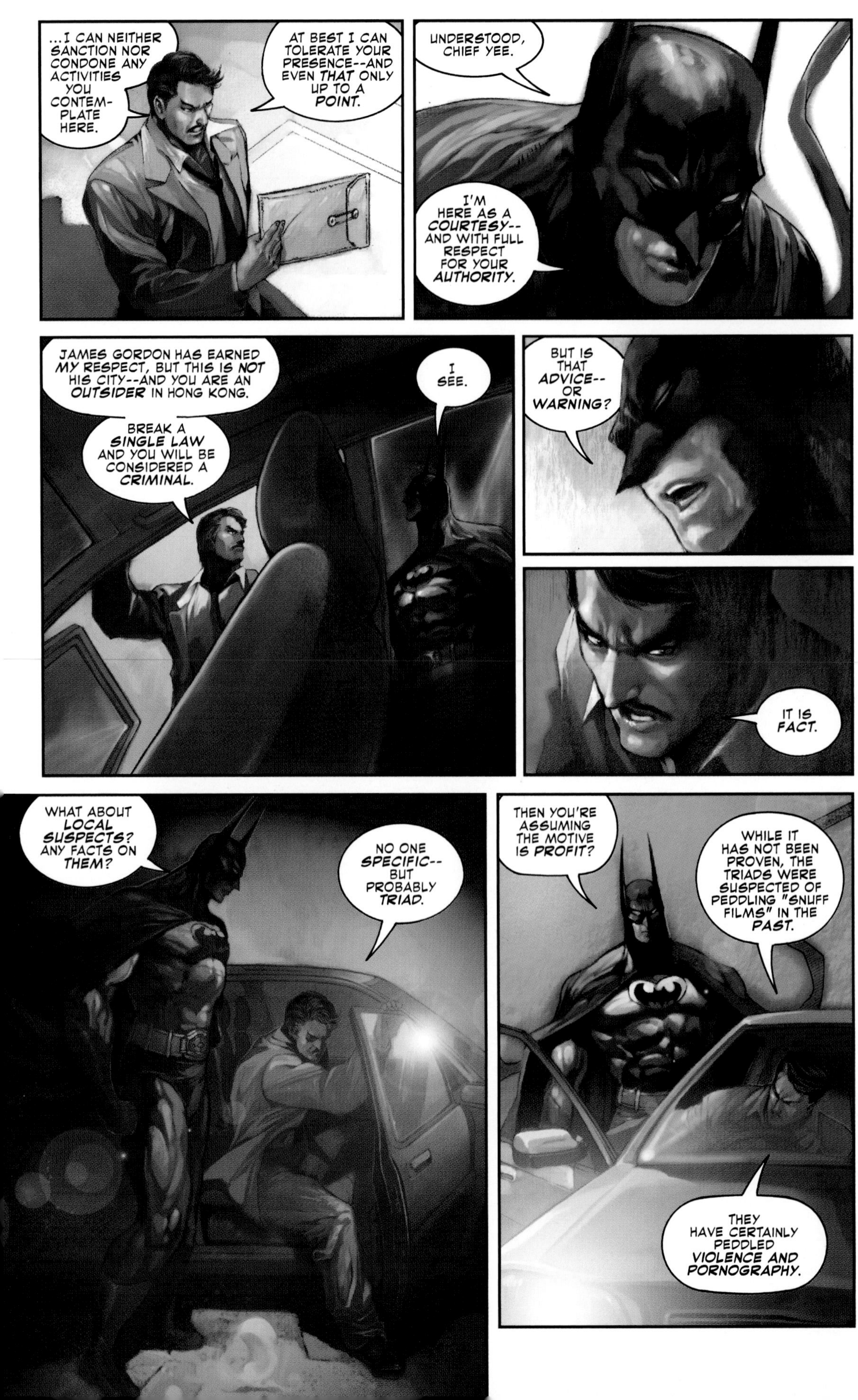
...I CAN NEITHER SANCTION NOR CONDONE ANY ACTIVITIES YOU CONTEMPLATE HERE.
AT BEST I CAN TOLERATE YOUR PRESENCE--AND EVEN THAT ONLY UP TO A POINT.
UNDERSTOOD, CHIEF YEE.
I'M HERE AS A COURTESY--AND WITH FULL RESPECT FOR YOUR AUTHORITY.
JAMES GORDON HAS EARNED MY RESPECT, BUT THIS IS NOT HIS CITY--AND YOU ARE AN OUTSIDER IN HONG KONG.
BREAK A SINGLE LAW AND YOU WILL BE CONSIDERED A CRIMINAL.
I SEE.
BUT IS THAT ADVICE--OR WARNING?
IT IS FACT.
WHAT ABOUT LOCAL SUSPECTS? ANY FACTS ON THEM?
NO ONE SPECIFIC--BUT PROBABLY TRIAD.
THEN YOU'RE ASSUMING THE MOTIVE IS PROFIT?
WHILE IT HAS NOT BEEN PROVEN, THE TRIADS WERE SUSPECTED OF PEDDLING "SNUFF FILMS" IN THE PAST.
THEY HAVE CERTAINLY PEDDLED VIOLENCE AND PORNOGRAPHY.

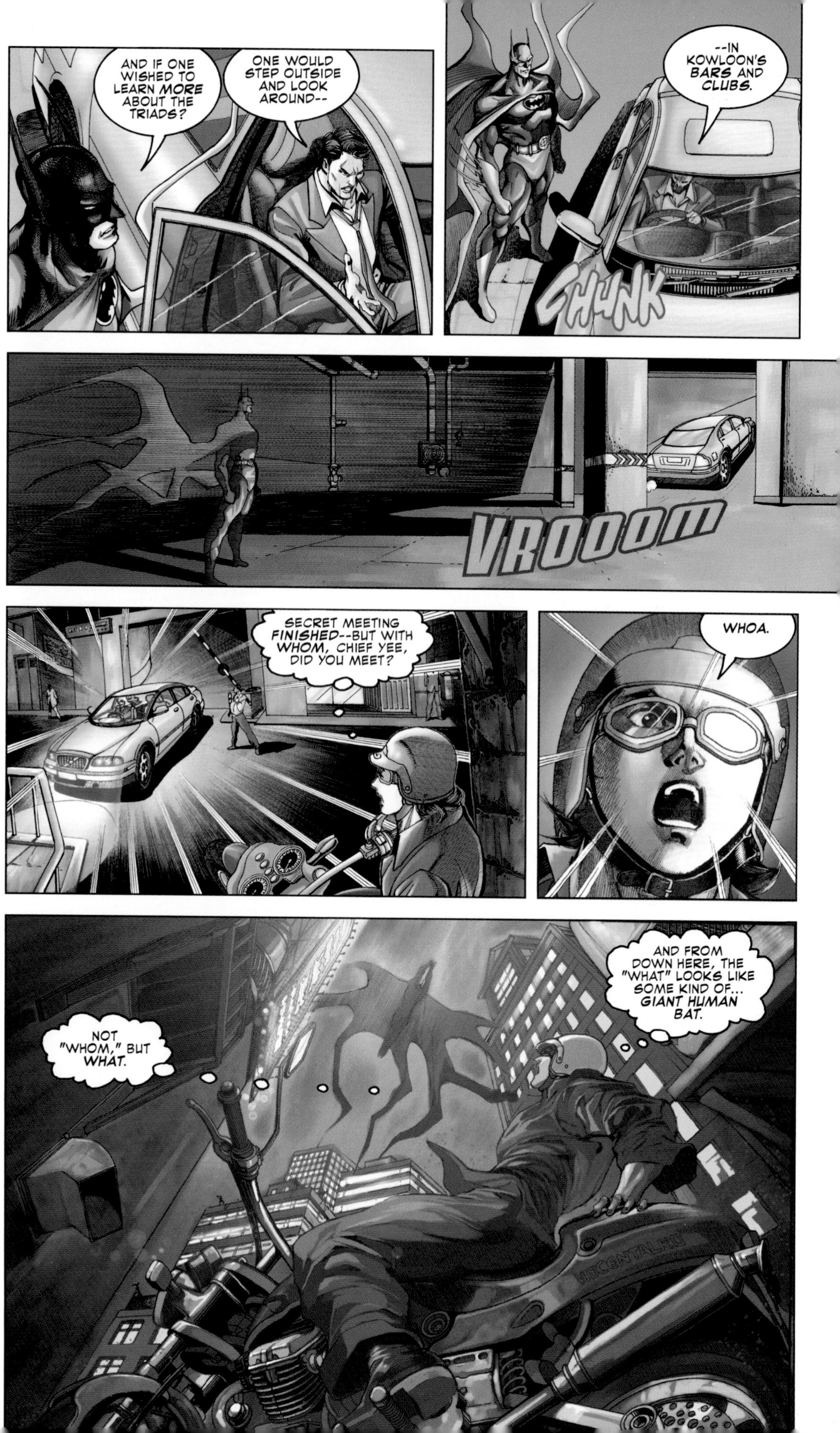
AND IF ONE WISHED TO LEARN MORE ABOUT THE TRIADS?
ONE WOULD STEP OUTSIDE AND LOOK AROUND--
--IN KOWLOON'S BARS AND CLUBS.
CHUNK
VROOOM
SECRET MEETING FINISHED--BUT WITH WHOM, CHIEF YEE, DID YOU MEET?
WHOA.
NOT "WHOM," BUT WHAT.
AND FROM DOWN HERE, THE "WHAT" LOOKS LIKE SOME KIND OF... GIANT HUMAN BAT.

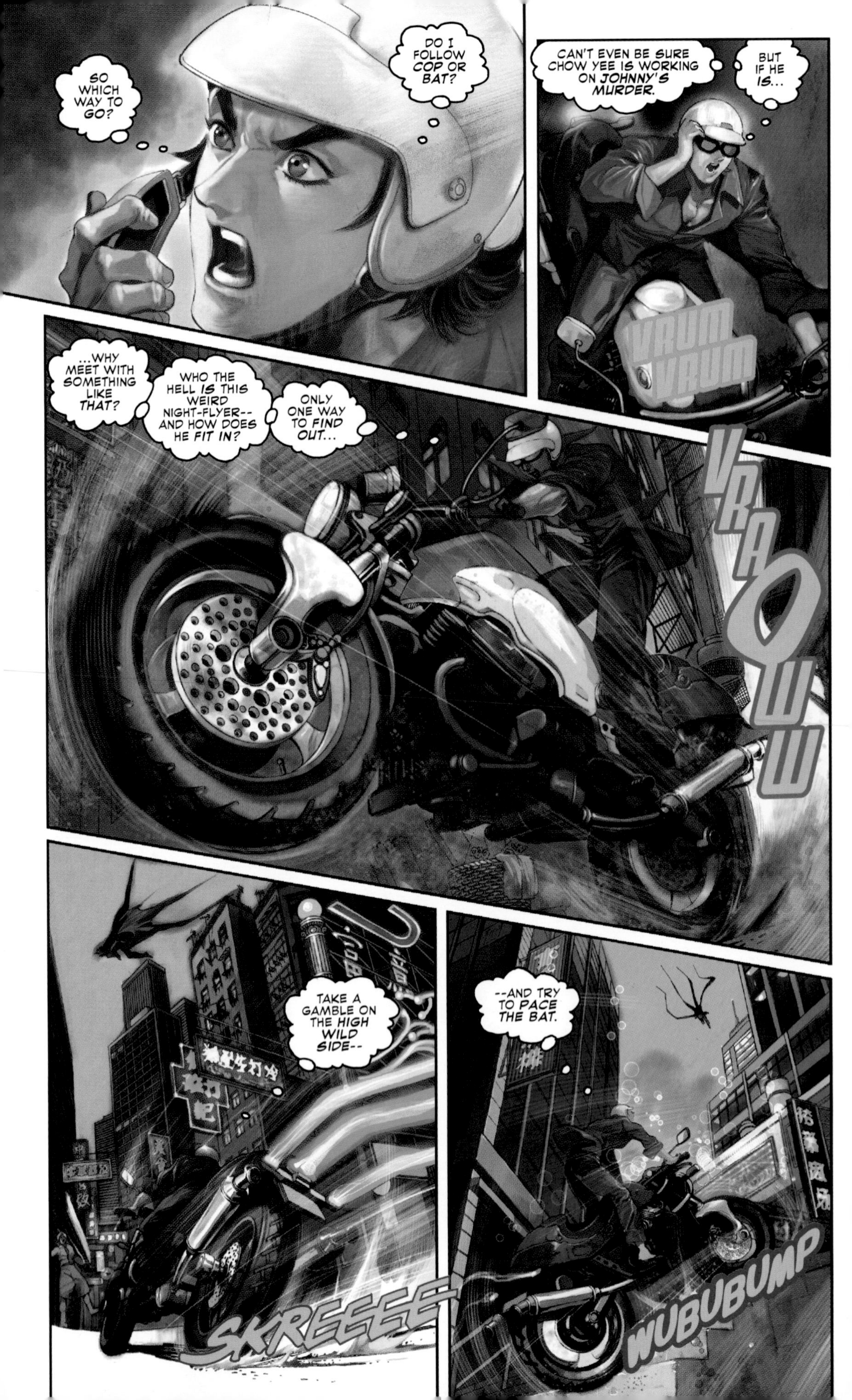
SO WHICH WAY TO GO?
DO I FOLLOW COP OR BAT?
CAN'T EVEN BE SURE CHOW YEE IS WORKING ON JOHNNY'S MURDER.
BUT IF HE IS...
VRUM VRUM
...WHY MEET WITH SOMETHING LIKE THAT?
WHO THE HELL IS THIS WEIRD NIGHT-FLYER-- AND HOW DOES HE FIT IN?
ONLY ONE WAY TO FIND OUT...
VRAOWW
TAKE A GAMBLE ON THE HIGH WILD SIDE--
SKREEEEE
--AND TRY TO PACE THE BAT.
WUBUBUMP

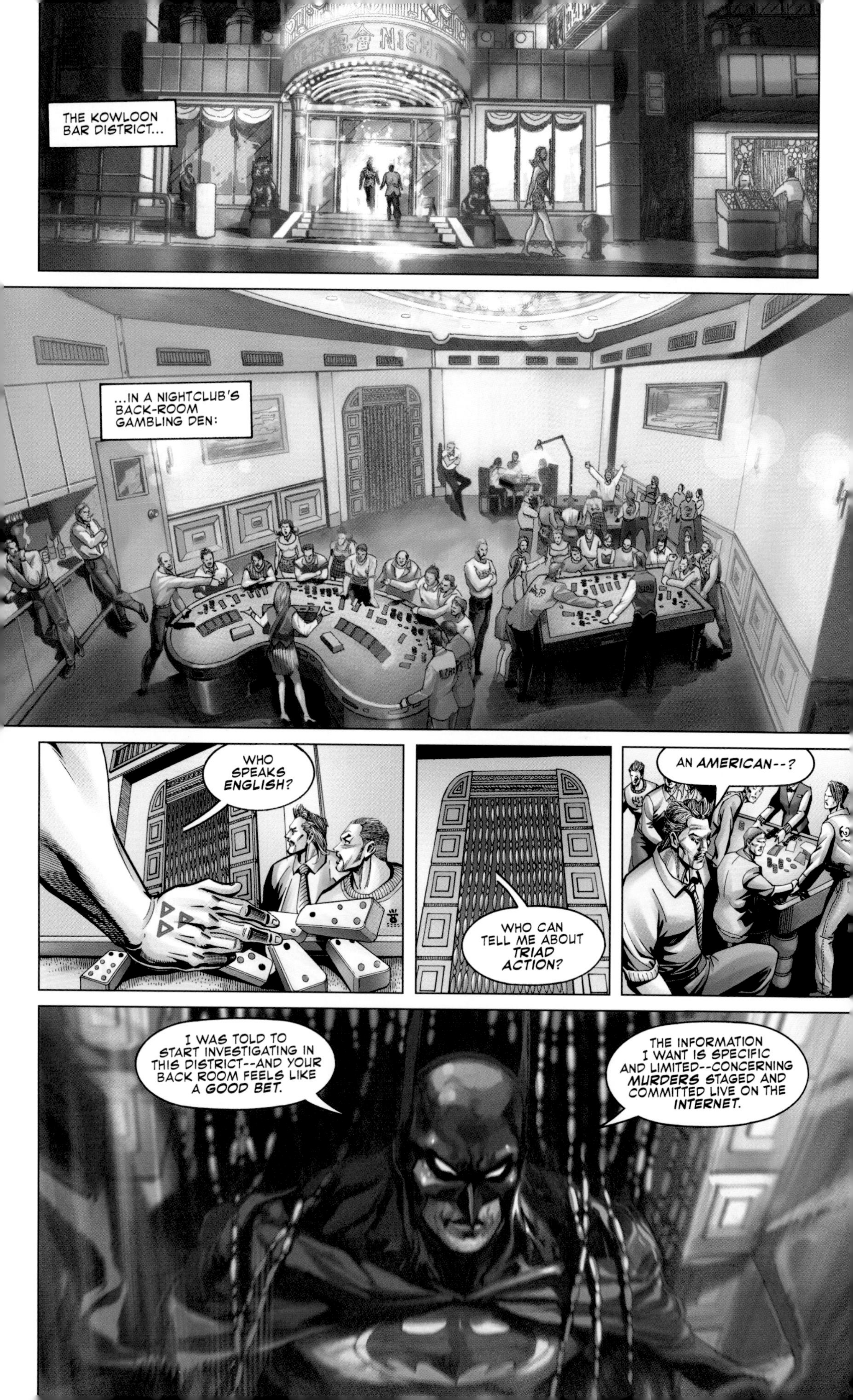
THE KOWLOON BAR DISTRICT...
...IN A NIGHTCLUB'S BACK-ROOM GAMBLING DEN:
WHO SPEAKS ENGLISH?
WHO CAN TELL ME ABOUT TRIAD ACTION?
AN AMERICAN--?
I WAS TOLD TO START INVESTIGATING IN THIS DISTRICT--AND YOUR BACK ROOM FEELS LIKE A GOOD BET.
THE INFORMATION I WANT IS SPECIFIC AND LIMITED--CONCERNING MURDERS STAGED AND COMMITTED LIVE ON THE INTERNET.

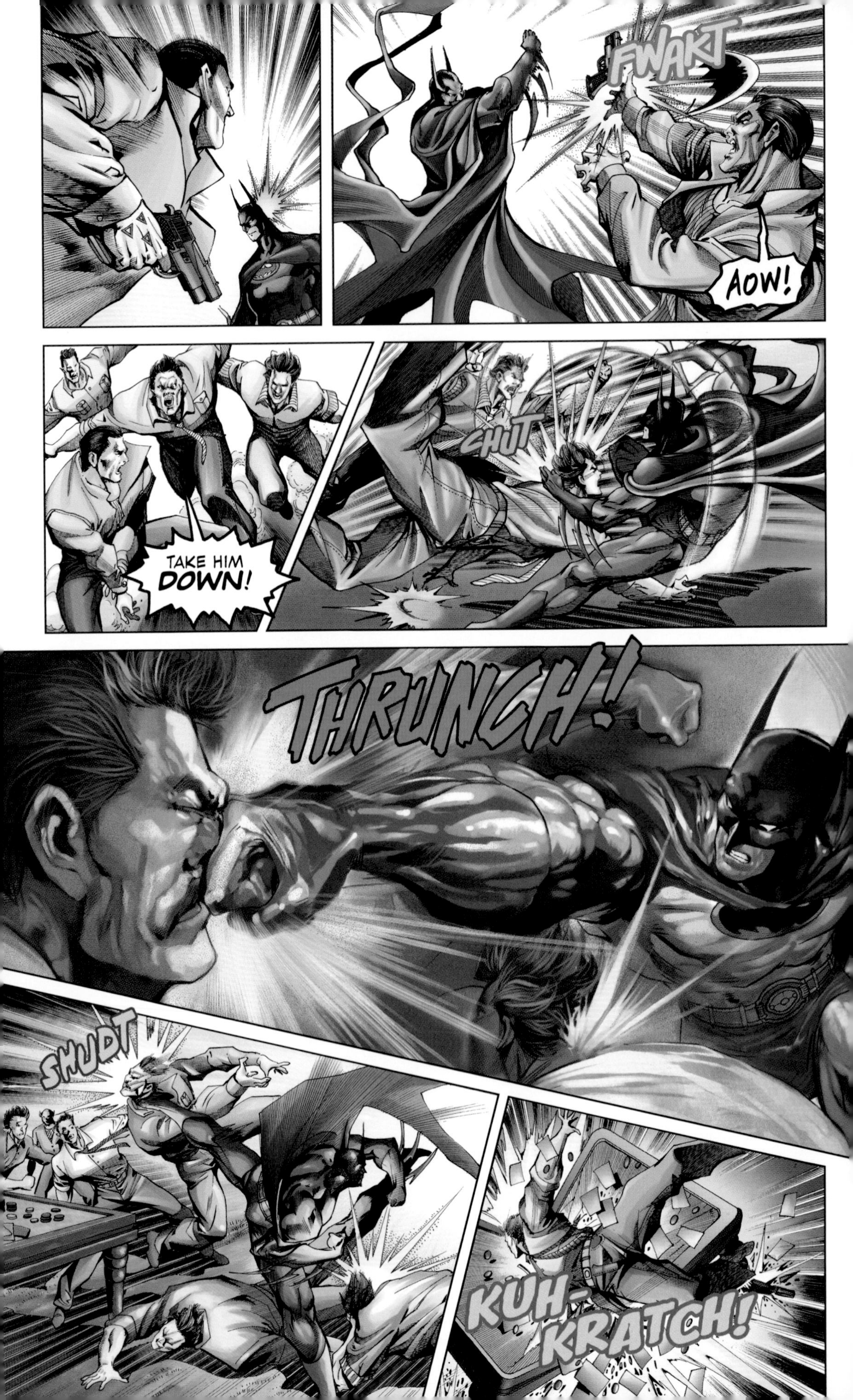
FWAKT
AOW!
TAKE HIM DOWN!
CHUT
THRUNCH!
SHUDT
KUH-KRATCH!

KUKK

CHUFT

SWFFF

FWUFFT

SWUKK

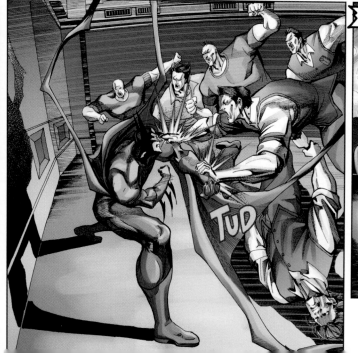

TUD

YEAH!!

GO, BABY, GO!

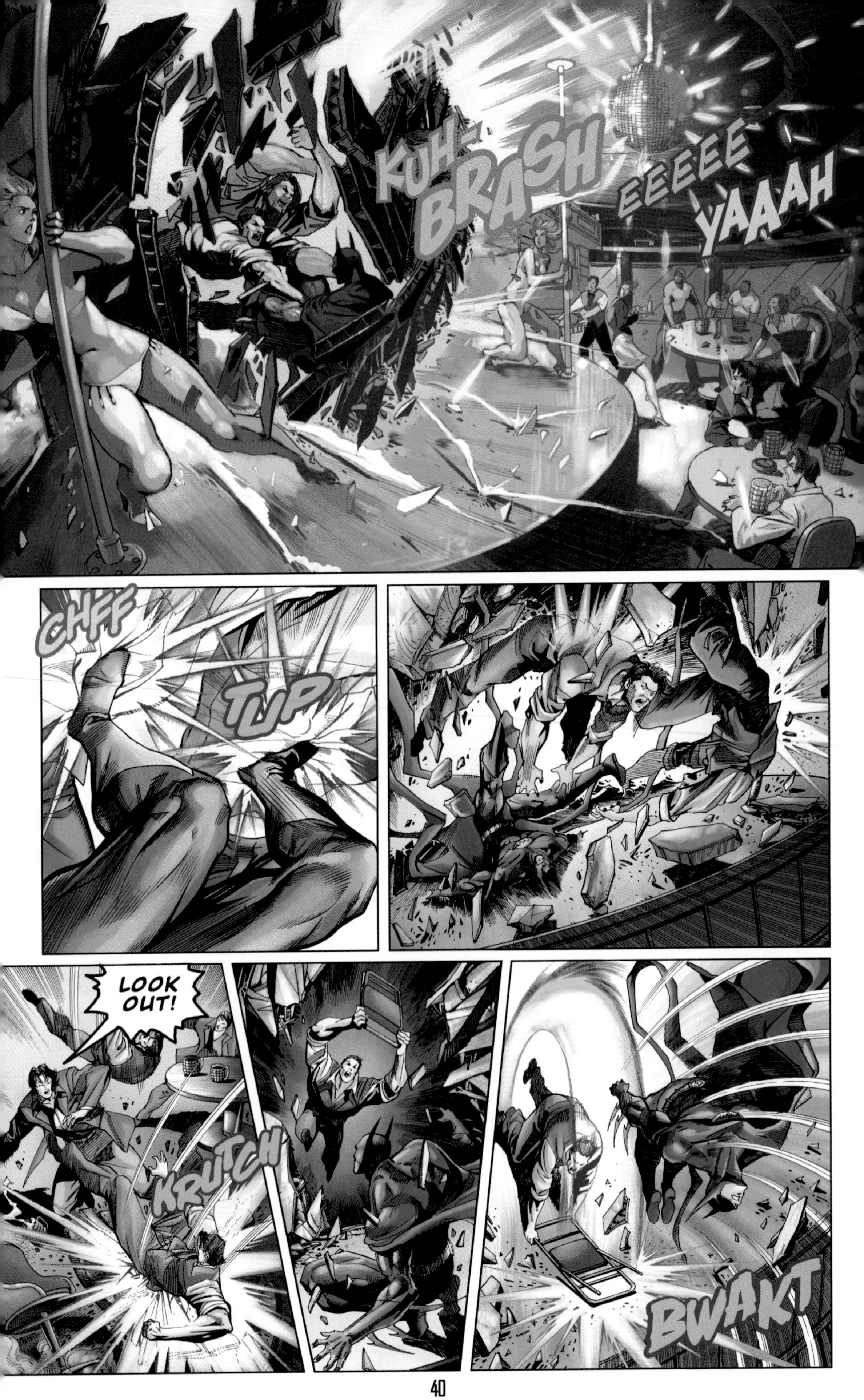
KUH-BRASH
EEEEE
YAAAH
CHFF
TUP
LOOK OUT!
KRUTCH
BWAKT

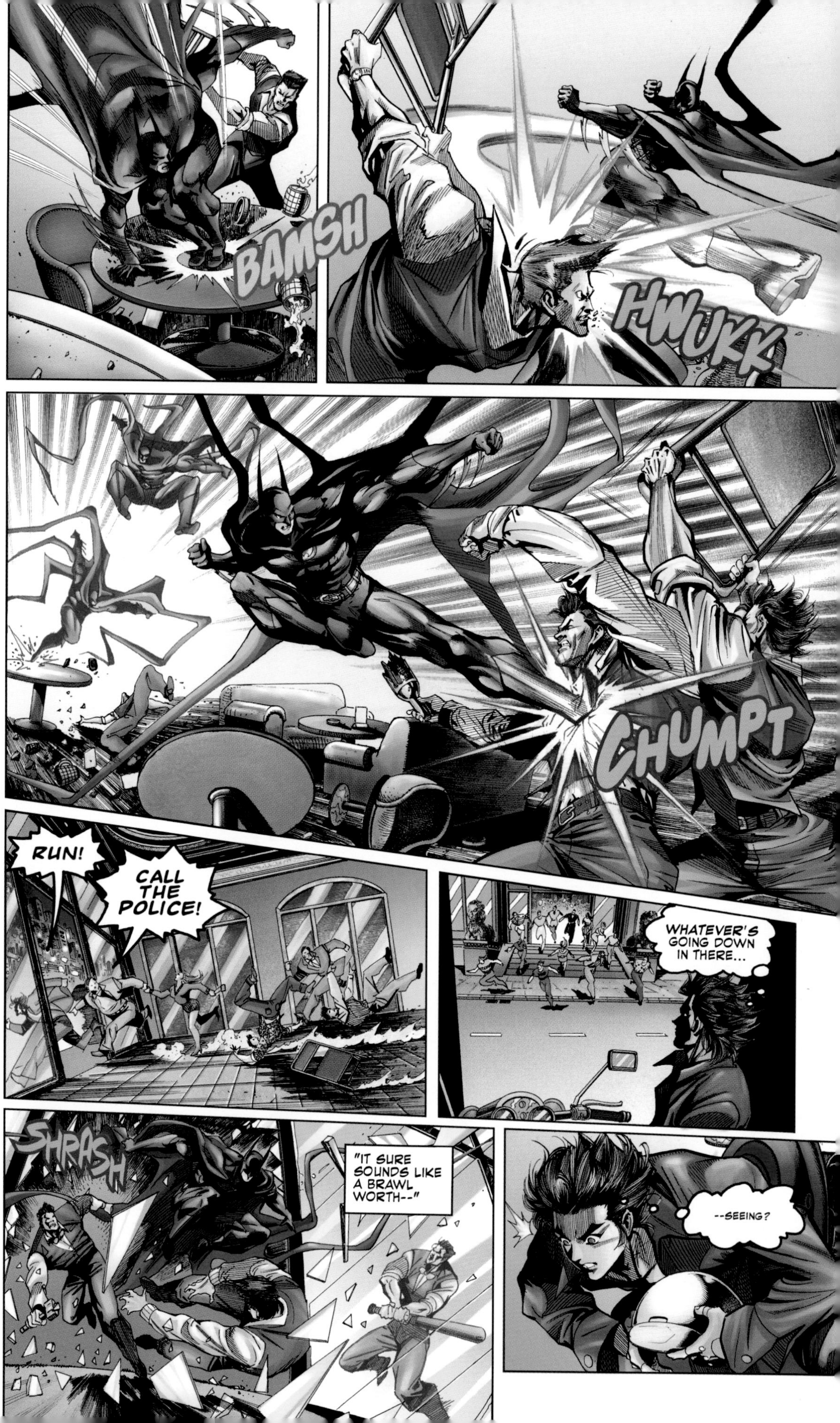
BAMSH
HWUKK
CHUMPT
RUN!
CALL THE POLICE!
WHATEVER'S GOING DOWN IN THERE...
SHRASH
"IT SURE SOUNDS LIKE A BRAWL WORTH--"
--SEEING?

HIT HIM!

HE'S TOO FAST!

EVERYONE AT THE SAME TIME!

AHN--!

SPLAMM

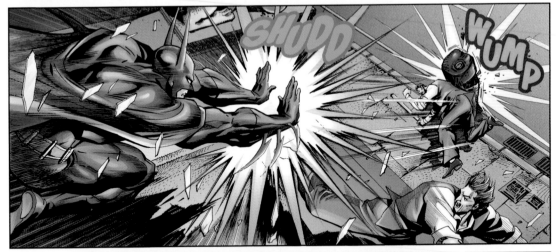

SHUDD

WUMP

NO MORE!

EEOOEEOOEEOO

...AND HERE COME THE COPS.

IT'S OVER--THE LAST TWO HAVE HAD ENOUGH...

EEOOEEOOEEOO

YOU SPOKE ENGLISH.

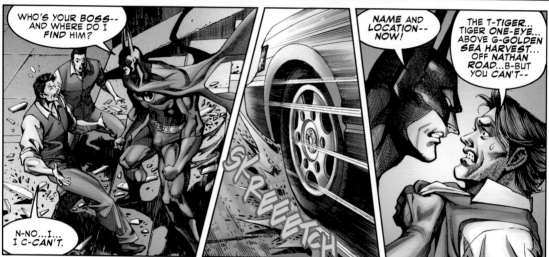

WHO'S YOUR BOSS-- AND WHERE DO I FIND HIM?

N-NO...I... I C-CAN'T.

SK-REEETCH

NAME AND LOCATION-- NOW!

THE T-TIGER... TIGER ONE-EYE... ABOVE G-GOLDEN SEA HARVEST... OFF NATHAN ROAD...B-BUT YOU CAN'T--

⟨FREEZE!⟩

THE POLICE! DON'T LET THEM SHOOT!

⟨SHOW YOUR HANDS!⟩

⟨NOW!⟩

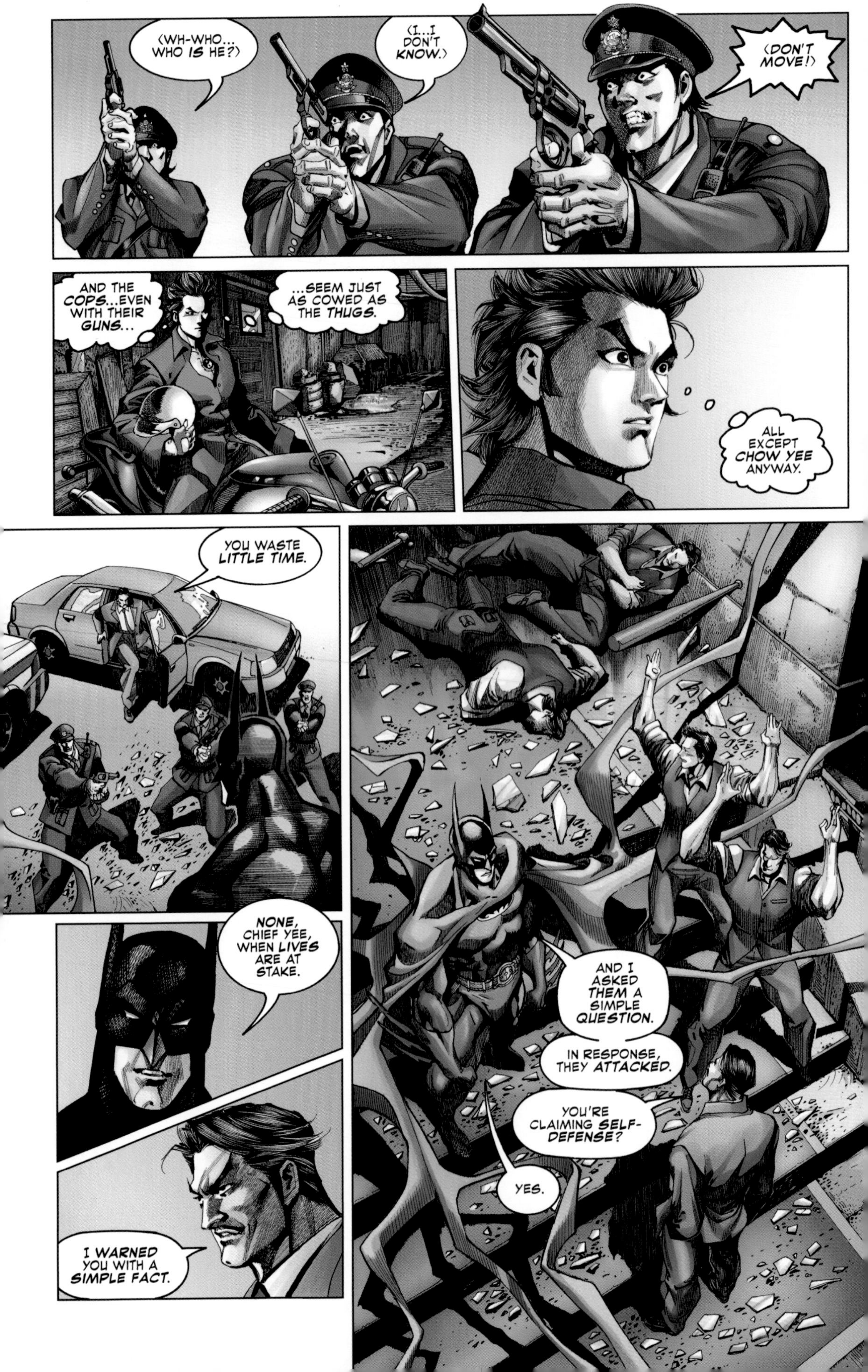
(WH-WHO... WHO IS HE?)
(I...I DON'T KNOW.)
(DON'T MOVE!)
AND THE COPS...EVEN WITH THEIR GUNS...
...SEEM JUST AS COWED AS THE THUGS.
ALL EXCEPT CHOW YEE ANYWAY.
YOU WASTE LITTLE TIME.
NONE, CHIEF YEE, WHEN LIVES ARE AT STAKE.
I WARNED YOU WITH A SIMPLE FACT.
AND I ASKED THEM A SIMPLE QUESTION.
IN RESPONSE, THEY ATTACKED.
YOU'RE CLAIMING SELF-DEFENSE?
YES.

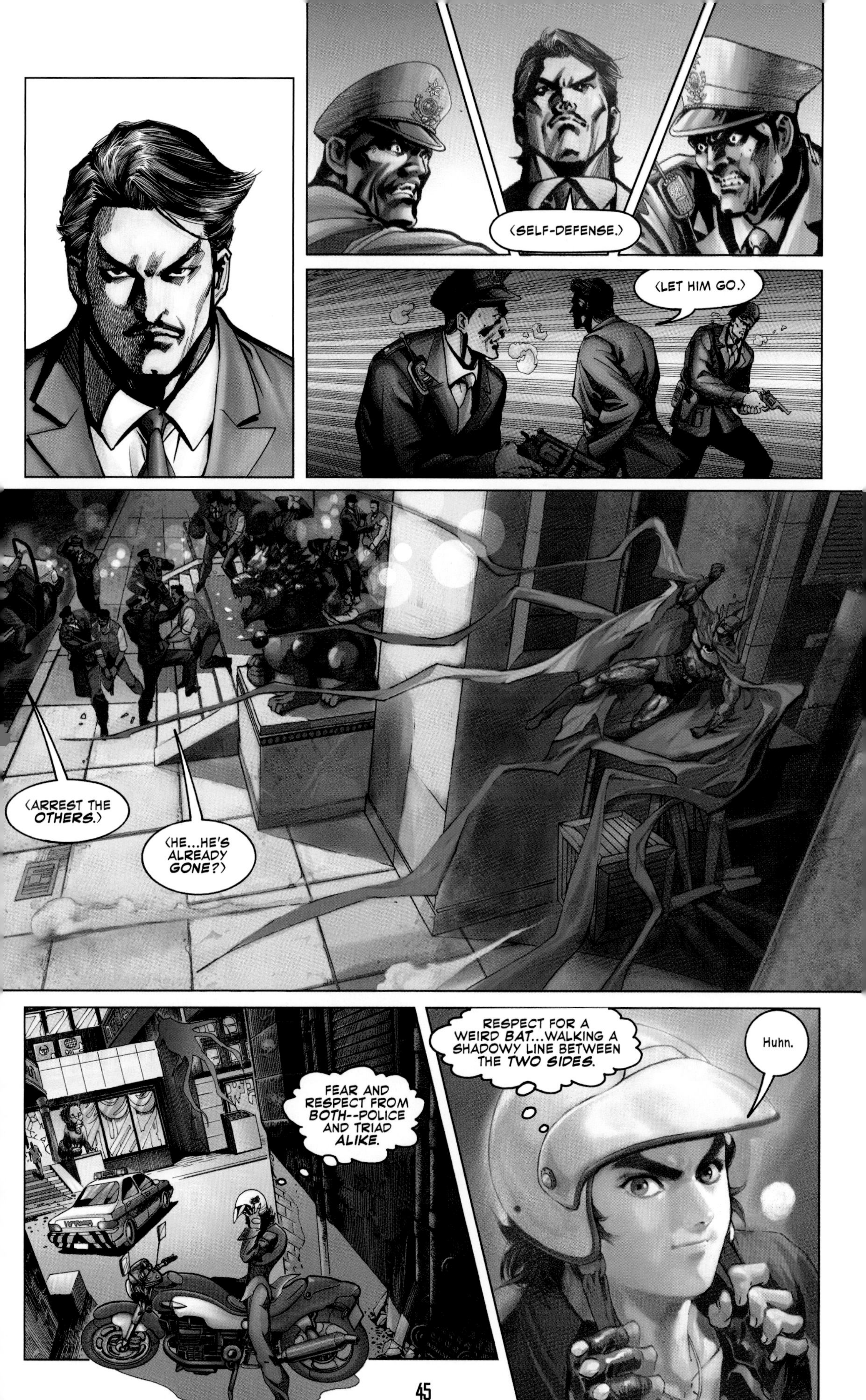
〈SELF-DEFENSE.〉
〈LET HIM GO.〉
〈ARREST THE OTHERS.〉
〈HE...HE'S ALREADY GONE?〉
FEAR AND RESPECT FROM BOTH--POLICE AND TRIAD ALIKE.
RESPECT FOR A WEIRD BAT...WALKING A SHADOWY LINE BETWEEN THE TWO SIDES.
Huhn.

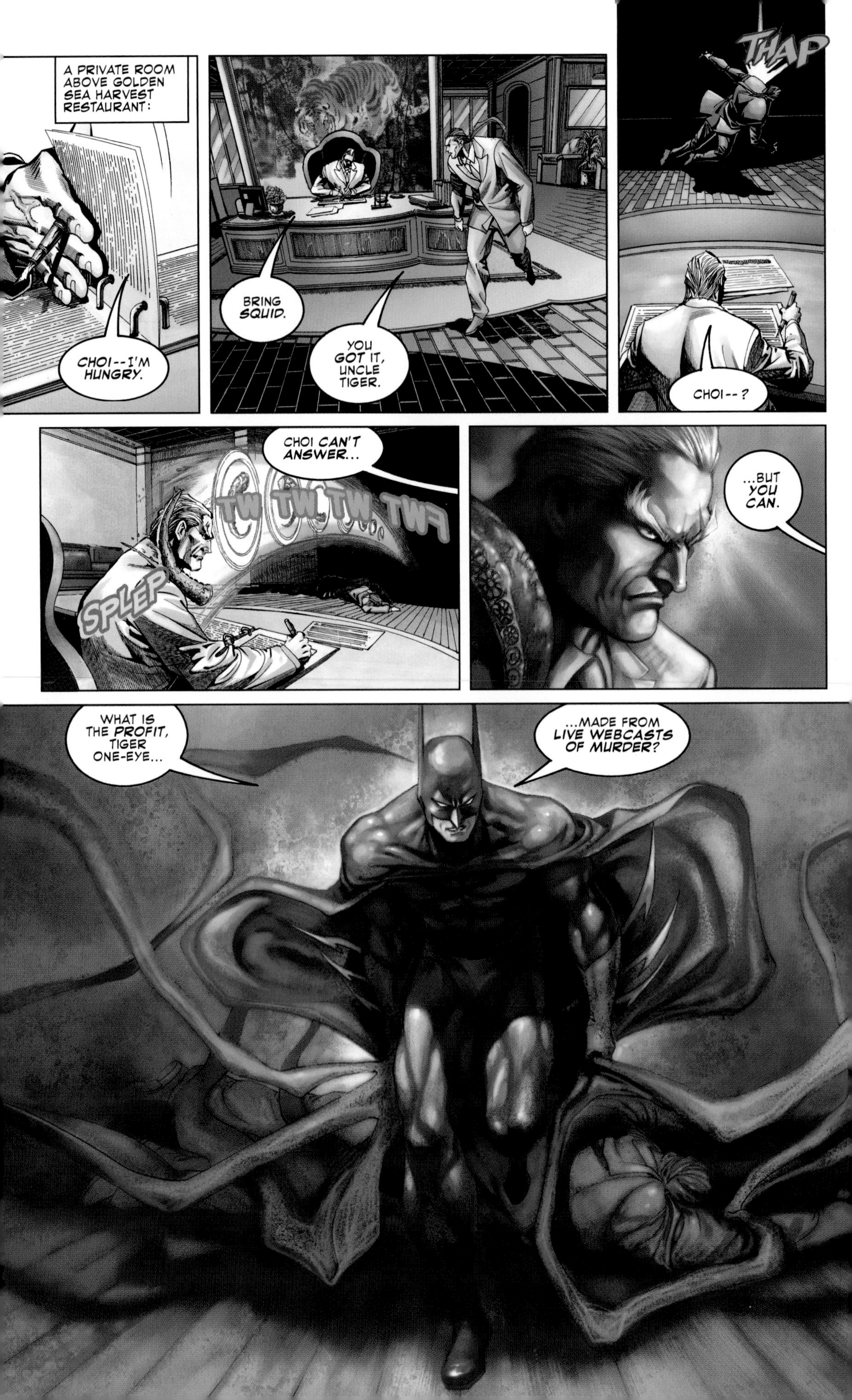
A PRIVATE ROOM ABOVE GOLDEN SEA HARVEST RESTAURANT:
CHOI--I'M HUNGRY.
BRING SQUID.
YOU GOT IT, UNCLE TIGER.
THAP
CHOI--?
CHOI CAN'T ANSWER...
FWT WT WT WT WT
SPLEP
...BUT YOU CAN.
WHAT IS THE PROFIT, TIGER ONE-EYE...
...MADE FROM LIVE WEBCASTS OF MURDER?

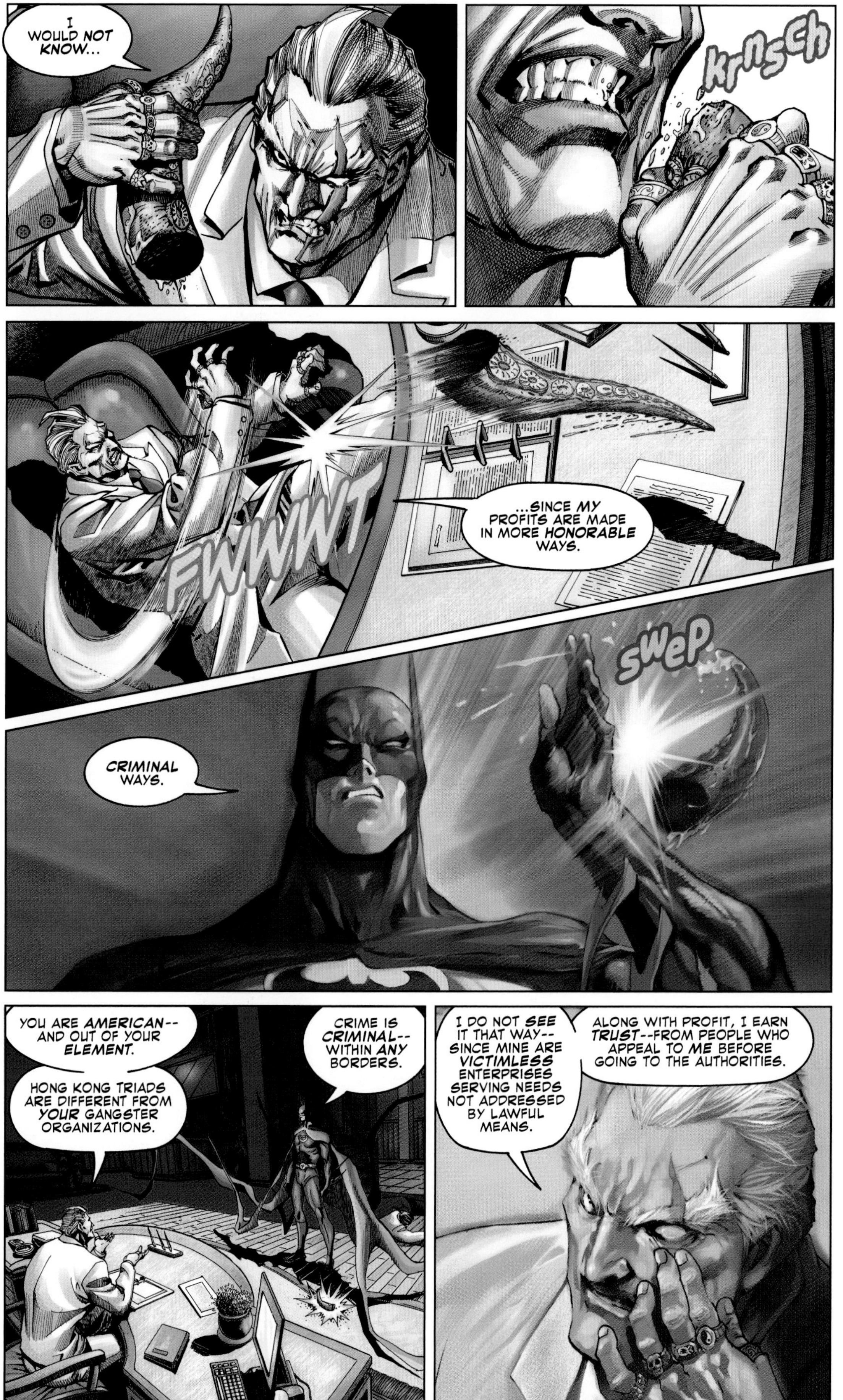
I WOULD NOT KNOW...
krnsch
FWWWT
...SINCE MY PROFITS ARE MADE IN MORE HONORABLE WAYS.
sweP
CRIMINAL WAYS.
YOU ARE AMERICAN-- AND OUT OF YOUR ELEMENT.
HONG KONG TRIADS ARE DIFFERENT FROM YOUR GANGSTER ORGANIZATIONS.
CRIME IS CRIMINAL-- WITHIN ANY BORDERS.
I DO NOT SEE IT THAT WAY-- SINCE MINE ARE VICTIMLESS ENTERPRISES SERVING NEEDS NOT ADDRESSED BY LAWFUL MEANS.
ALONG WITH PROFIT, I EARN TRUST--FROM PEOPLE WHO APPEAL TO ME BEFORE GOING TO THE AUTHORITIES.

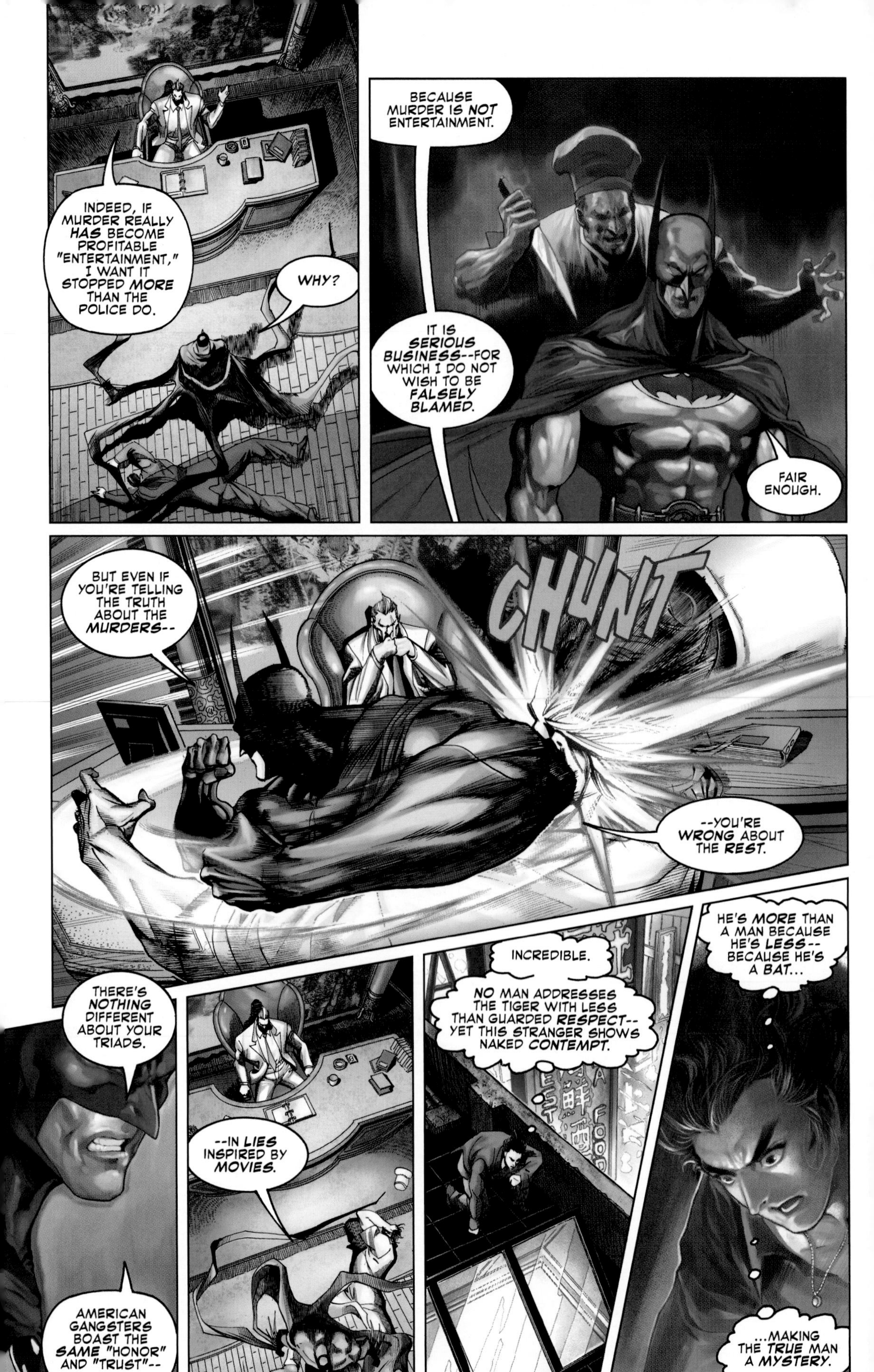
INDEED, IF MURDER REALLY HAS BECOME PROFITABLE "ENTERTAINMENT," I WANT IT STOPPED MORE THAN THE POLICE DO.
WHY?
BECAUSE MURDER IS NOT ENTERTAINMENT.
IT IS SERIOUS BUSINESS--FOR WHICH I DO NOT WISH TO BE FALSELY BLAMED.
FAIR ENOUGH.
BUT EVEN IF YOU'RE TELLING THE TRUTH ABOUT THE MURDERS--
CHUNT
--YOU'RE WRONG ABOUT THE REST.
THERE'S NOTHING DIFFERENT ABOUT YOUR TRIADS.
AMERICAN GANGSTERS BOAST THE SAME "HONOR" AND "TRUST"--
--IN LIES INSPIRED BY MOVIES.
INCREDIBLE.
NO MAN ADDRESSES THE TIGER WITH LESS THAN GUARDED RESPECT--YET THIS STRANGER SHOWS NAKED CONTEMPT.
HE'S MORE THAN A MAN BECAUSE HE'S LESS--BECAUSE HE'S A BAT...
...MAKING THE TRUE MAN A MYSTERY.

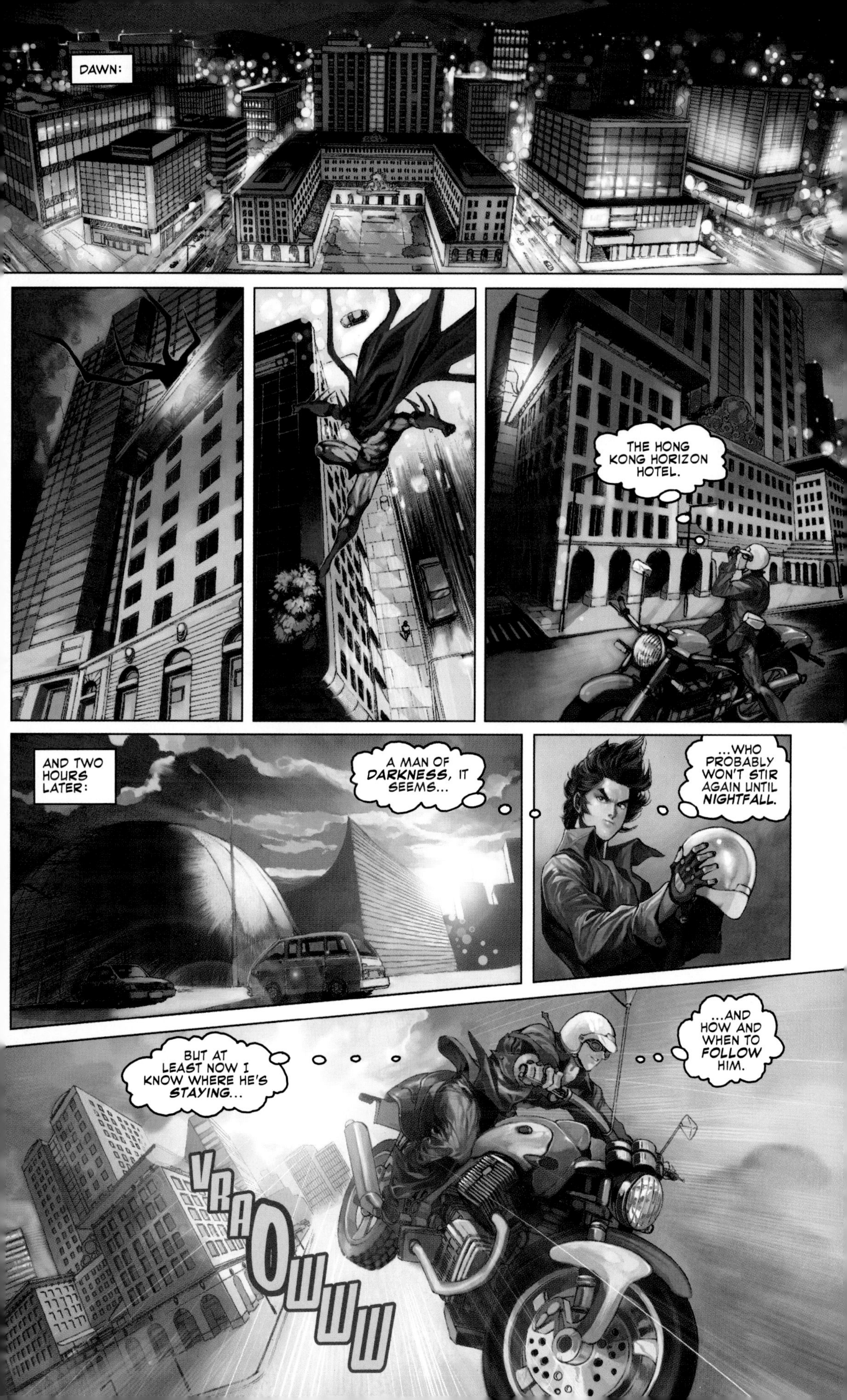
DAWN:
THE HONG KONG HORIZON HOTEL.
AND TWO HOURS LATER:
A MAN OF DARKNESS, IT SEEMS...
...WHO PROBABLY WON'T STIR AGAIN UNTIL NIGHTFALL.
BUT AT LEAST NOW I KNOW WHERE HE'S STAYING...
...AND HOW AND WHEN TO FOLLOW HIM.
VRAOWWW

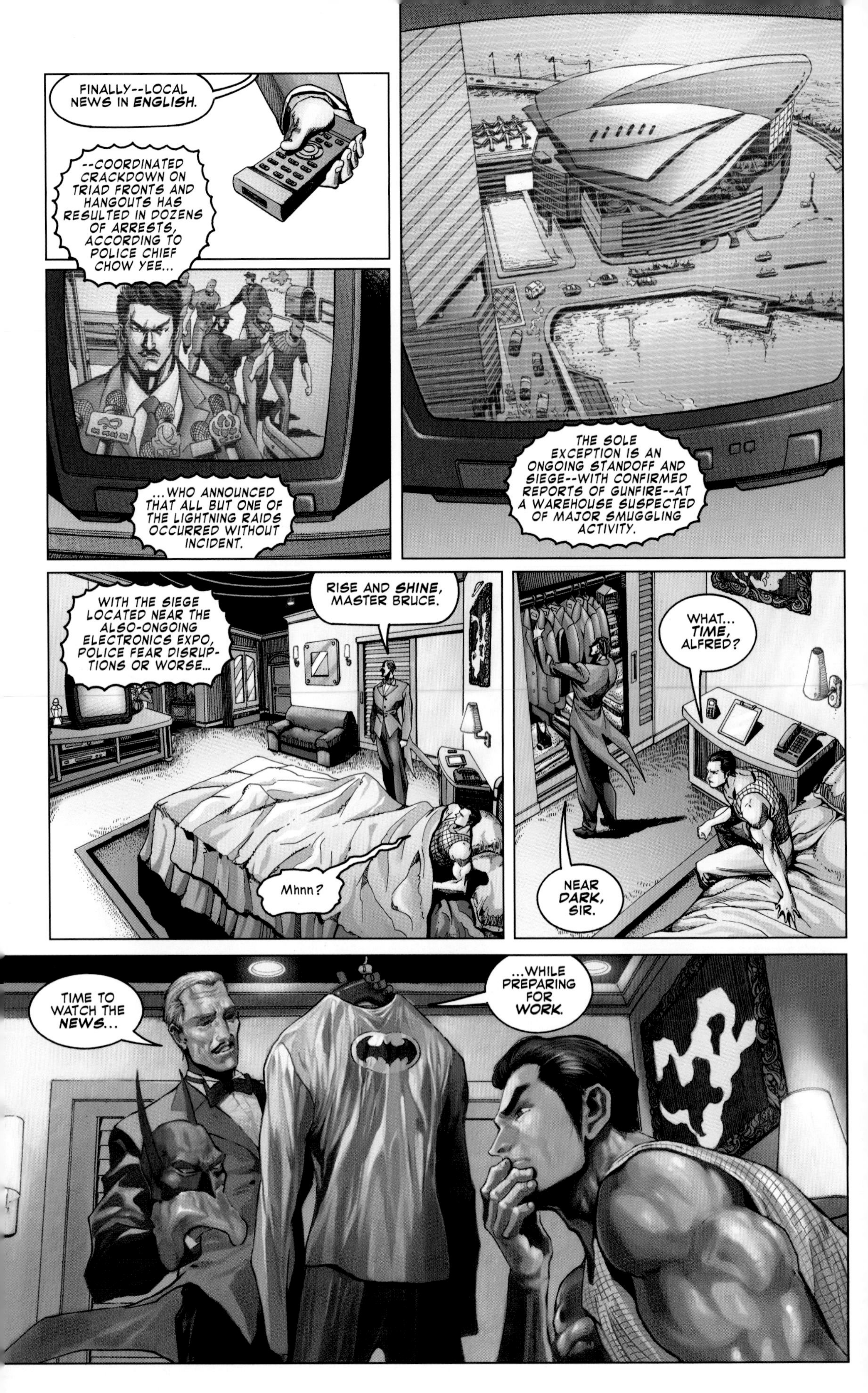
FINALLY--LOCAL NEWS IN ENGLISH.
--COORDINATED CRACKDOWN ON TRIAD FRONTS AND HANGOUTS HAS RESULTED IN DOZENS OF ARRESTS, ACCORDING TO POLICE CHIEF CHOW YEE...
...WHO ANNOUNCED THAT ALL BUT ONE OF THE LIGHTNING RAIDS OCCURRED WITHOUT INCIDENT.
THE SOLE EXCEPTION IS AN ONGOING STANDOFF AND SIEGE--WITH CONFIRMED REPORTS OF GUNFIRE--AT A WAREHOUSE SUSPECTED OF MAJOR SMUGGLING ACTIVITY.
WITH THE SIEGE LOCATED NEAR THE ALSO-ONGOING ELECTRONICS EXPO, POLICE FEAR DISRUPTIONS OR WORSE...
RISE AND SHINE, MASTER BRUCE.
Mhnn?
WHAT... TIME, ALFRED?
NEAR DARK, SIR.
TIME TO WATCH THE NEWS...
...WHILE PREPARING FOR WORK.

A LONG DAY OF PREPARATION...

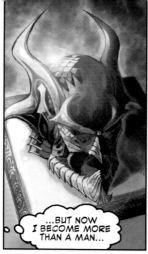

...BUT NOW I BECOME MORE THAN A MAN...

...BY MAKING MYSELF LESS...

...BY TRANSFORMING INTO A DRAGON...

K-CHAK

SHHHKT

...A WEIRD NIGHT-CREATURE TREADING THE SHADOWS BETWEEN JUSTICE AND VENGEANCE...

...WHILE THE TRUE MAN FADES TO MYSTERY.

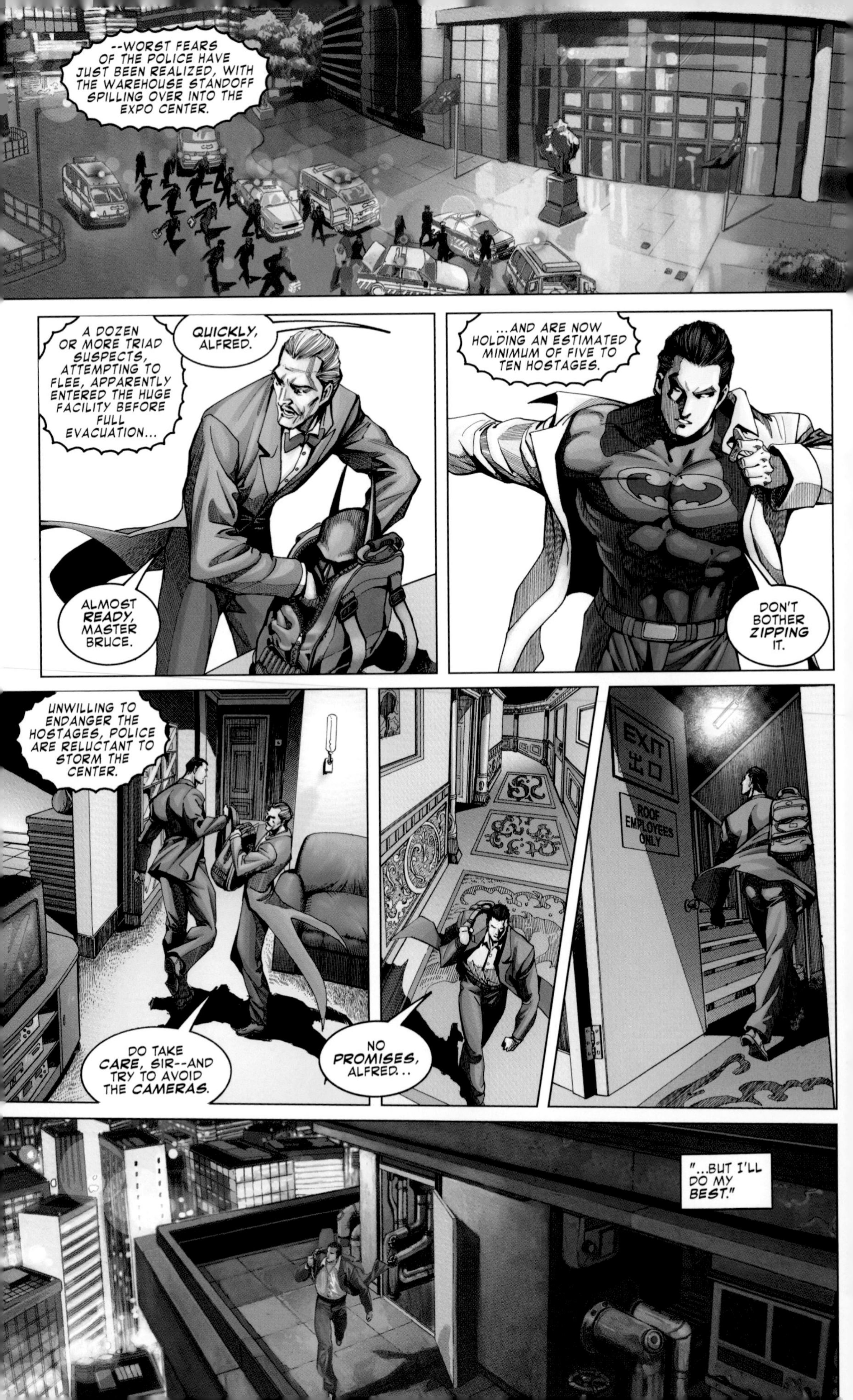
--WORST FEARS OF THE POLICE HAVE JUST BEEN REALIZED, WITH THE WAREHOUSE STANDOFF SPILLING OVER INTO THE EXPO CENTER.
A DOZEN OR MORE TRIAD SUSPECTS, ATTEMPTING TO FLEE, APPARENTLY ENTERED THE HUGE FACILITY BEFORE FULL EVACUATION...
QUICKLY, ALFRED.
ALMOST READY, MASTER BRUCE.
...AND ARE NOW HOLDING AN ESTIMATED MINIMUM OF FIVE TO TEN HOSTAGES.
DON'T BOTHER ZIPPING IT.
UNWILLING TO ENDANGER THE HOSTAGES, POLICE ARE RELUCTANT TO STORM THE CENTER.
DO TAKE CARE, SIR--AND TRY TO AVOID THE CAMERAS.
NO PROMISES, ALFRED...
EXIT
出口
ROOF EMPLOYEES ONLY
"...BUT I'LL DO MY BEST."

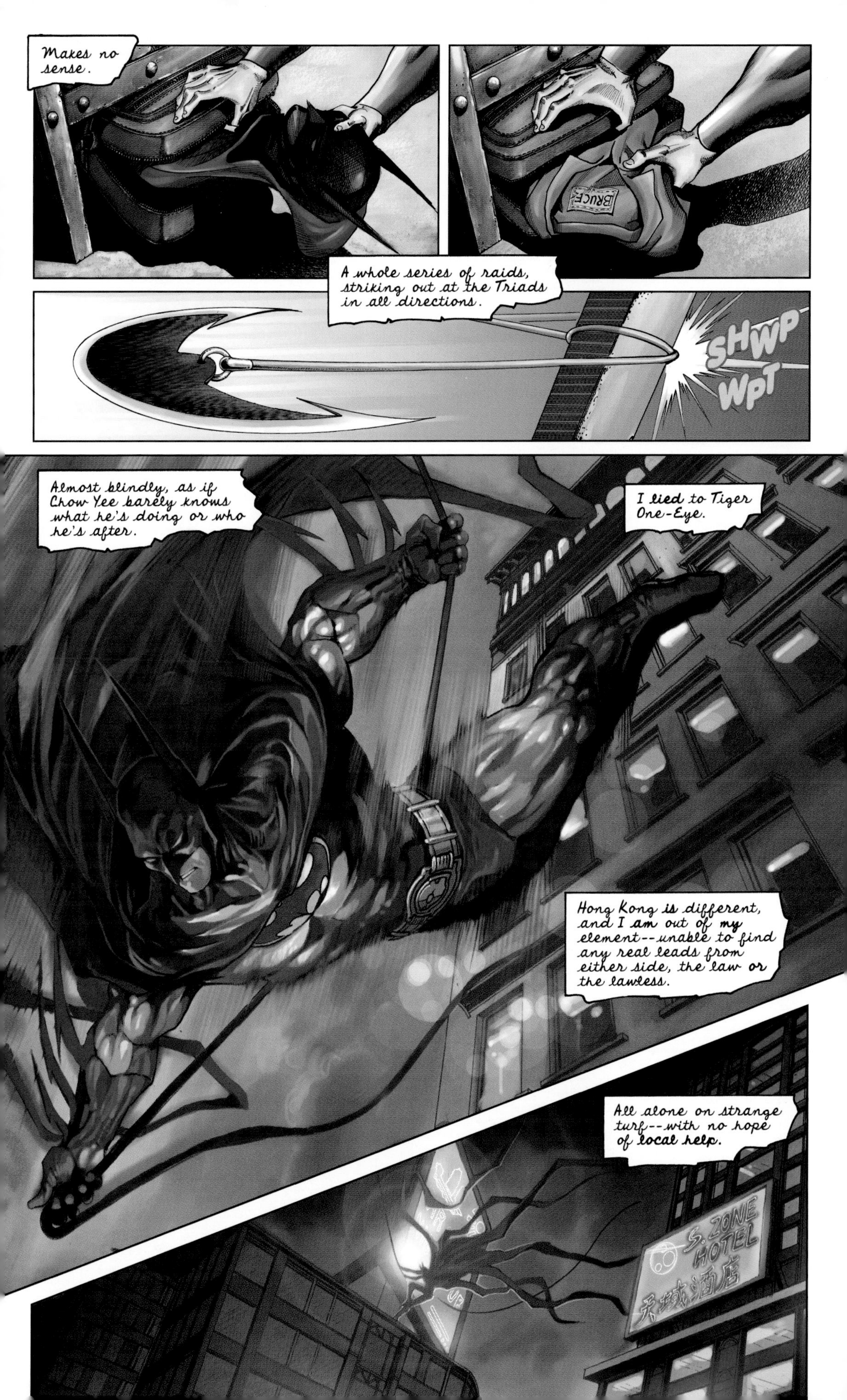

Makes no sense.
A whole series of raids, striking out at the Triads in all directions.
SHWP
WPT
Almost blindly, as if Chow Yee barely knows what he's doing or who he's after.
I lied to Tiger One-Eye.
Hong Kong is different, and I am out of my element--unable to find any real leads from either side, the law or the lawless.
All alone on strange turf--with no hope of local help.
S. ZONE HOTEL

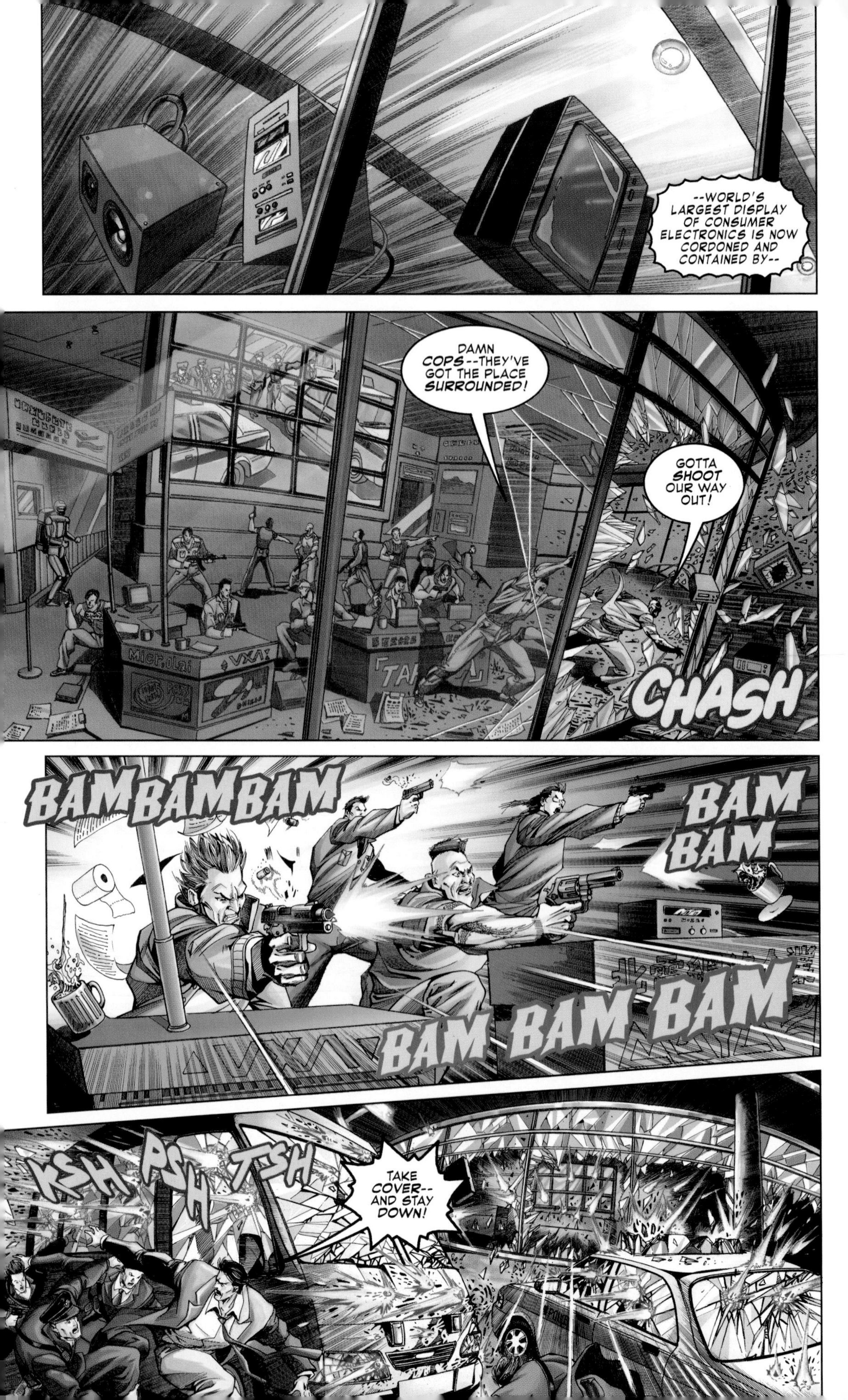
--WORLD'S LARGEST DISPLAY OF CONSUMER ELECTRONICS IS NOW CORDONED AND CONTAINED BY--
DAMN COPS--THEY'VE GOT THE PLACE SURROUNDED!
GOTTA SHOOT OUR WAY OUT!
CHASH
BAMBAMBAM
BAM BAM
BAM BAM BAM
KSH PSH TSH
TAKE COVER--AND STAY DOWN!

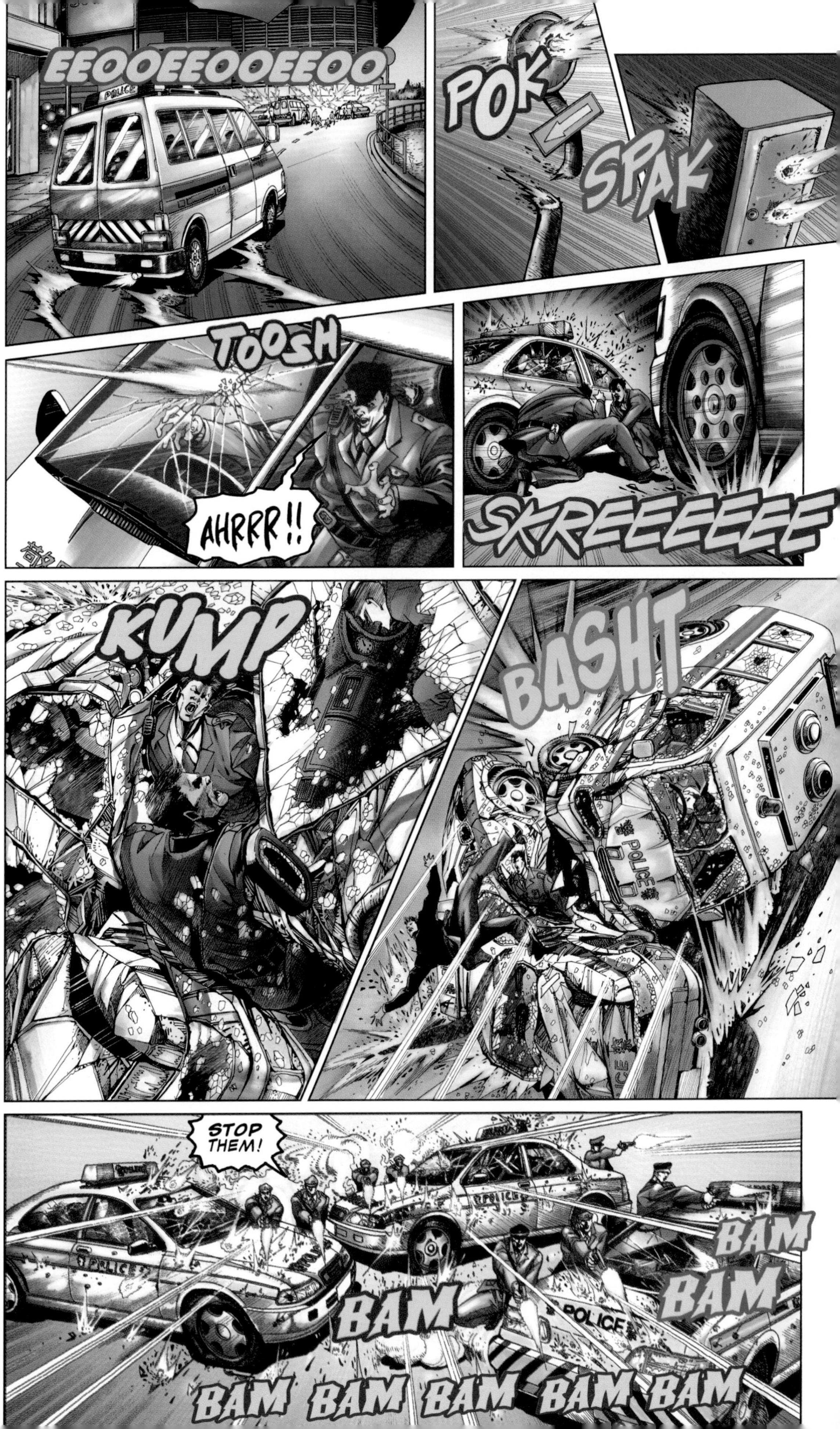
EEOOEEOOEEOO
POK
SPAK
TOOSH
AHRRR!!
SKREEEEEE
KUMP
BASHT
STOP THEM!
BAM
BAM
BAM
BAM BAM BAM BAM BAM

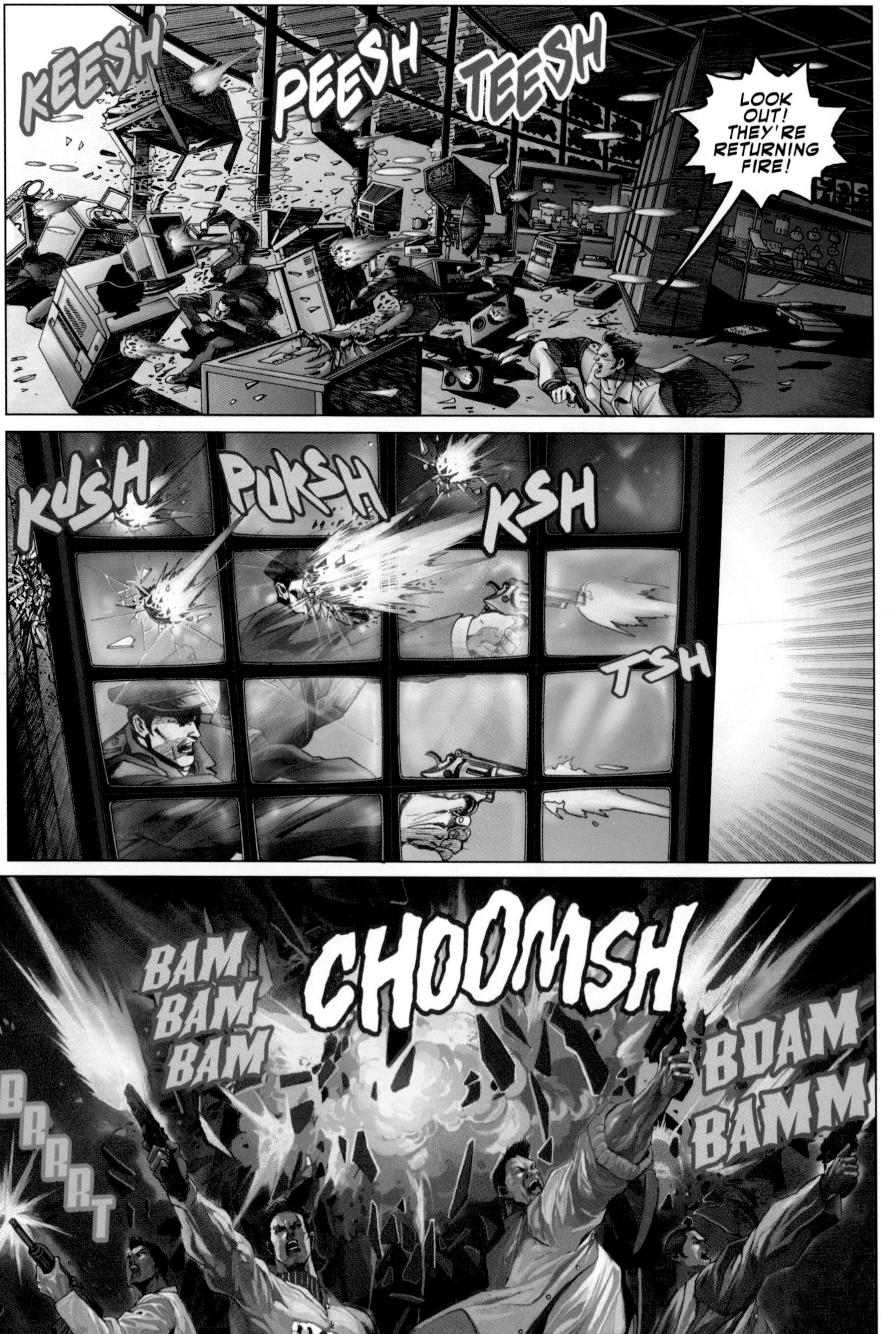
KEESH
PEESH
TEESH
LOOK OUT! THEY'RE RETURNING FIRE!
KUSH
PUKSH
KSH
TSH
BAM
BAM
BAM
CHOOMSH
BRRRRT
BDAM
BAMM

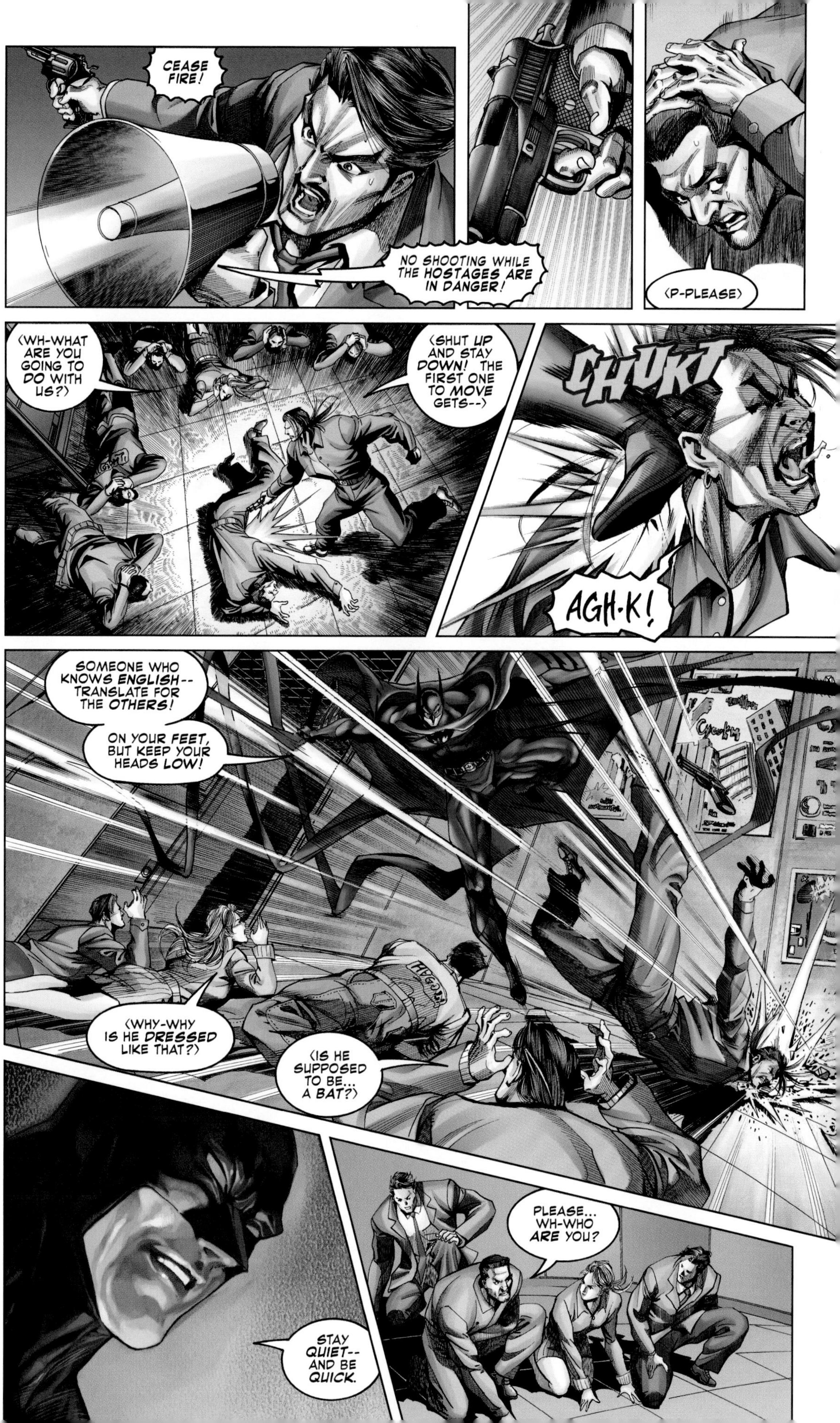
CEASE FIRE!
NO SHOOTING WHILE THE HOSTAGES ARE IN DANGER!
⟨P-PLEASE⟩
⟨WH-WHAT ARE YOU GOING TO DO WITH US?⟩
⟨SHUT UP AND STAY DOWN! THE FIRST ONE TO MOVE GETS--⟩
CHUKT
AGH-K!
SOMEONE WHO KNOWS ENGLISH-- TRANSLATE FOR THE OTHERS!
ON YOUR FEET, BUT KEEP YOUR HEADS LOW!
⟨WHY-WHY IS HE DRESSED LIKE THAT?⟩
⟨IS HE SUPPOSED TO BE... A BAT?⟩
PLEASE... WH-WHO ARE YOU?
STAY QUIET-- AND BE QUICK.

A FRIEND.

NOW JUST FOLLOW ME-- OUT THE BACK.

STAY TOGETHER AS YOU CROSS THE STREET.

FAST-- BUT DON'T PANIC.

TELL THE POLICE ALL THE HOSTAGES ARE OUT.

THEY CAN MOVE IN NOW.

BUT... WHAT ABOUT YOU?

IT'S NOT OVER YET.

I'M GOING BACK.

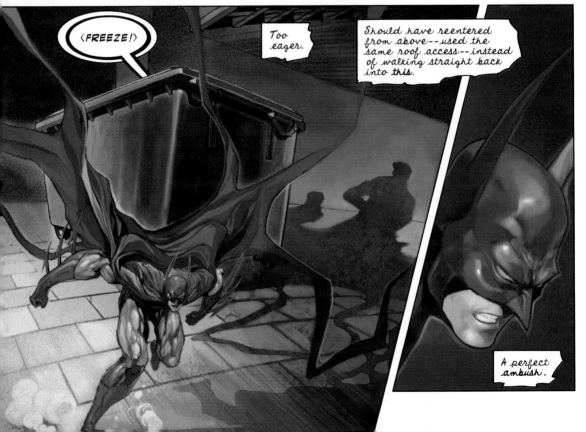

⟨FREEZE!⟩

Too eager.

Should have reentered from above--used the same roof access--instead of walking straight back into this.

A perfect ambush.

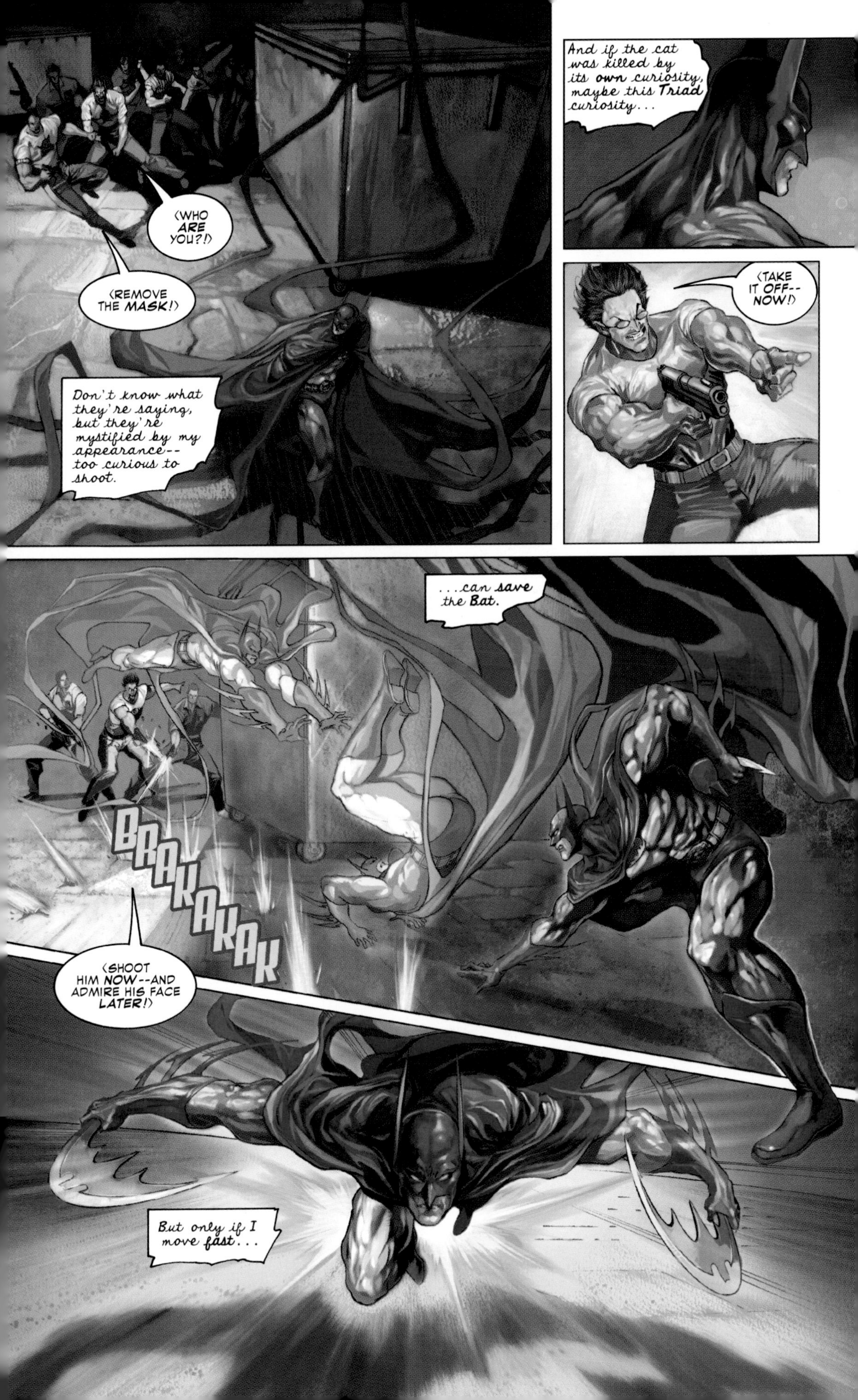
(WHO ARE YOU?!)
(REMOVE THE MASK!)
Don't know what they're saying, but they're mystified by my appearance--too curious to shoot.
And if the cat was killed by its own curiosity, maybe this Triad curiosity...
(TAKE IT OFF--NOW!)
...can save the Bat.
BRAKAKAK
(SHOOT HIM NOW--AND ADMIRE HIS FACE LATER!)
But only if I move fast...

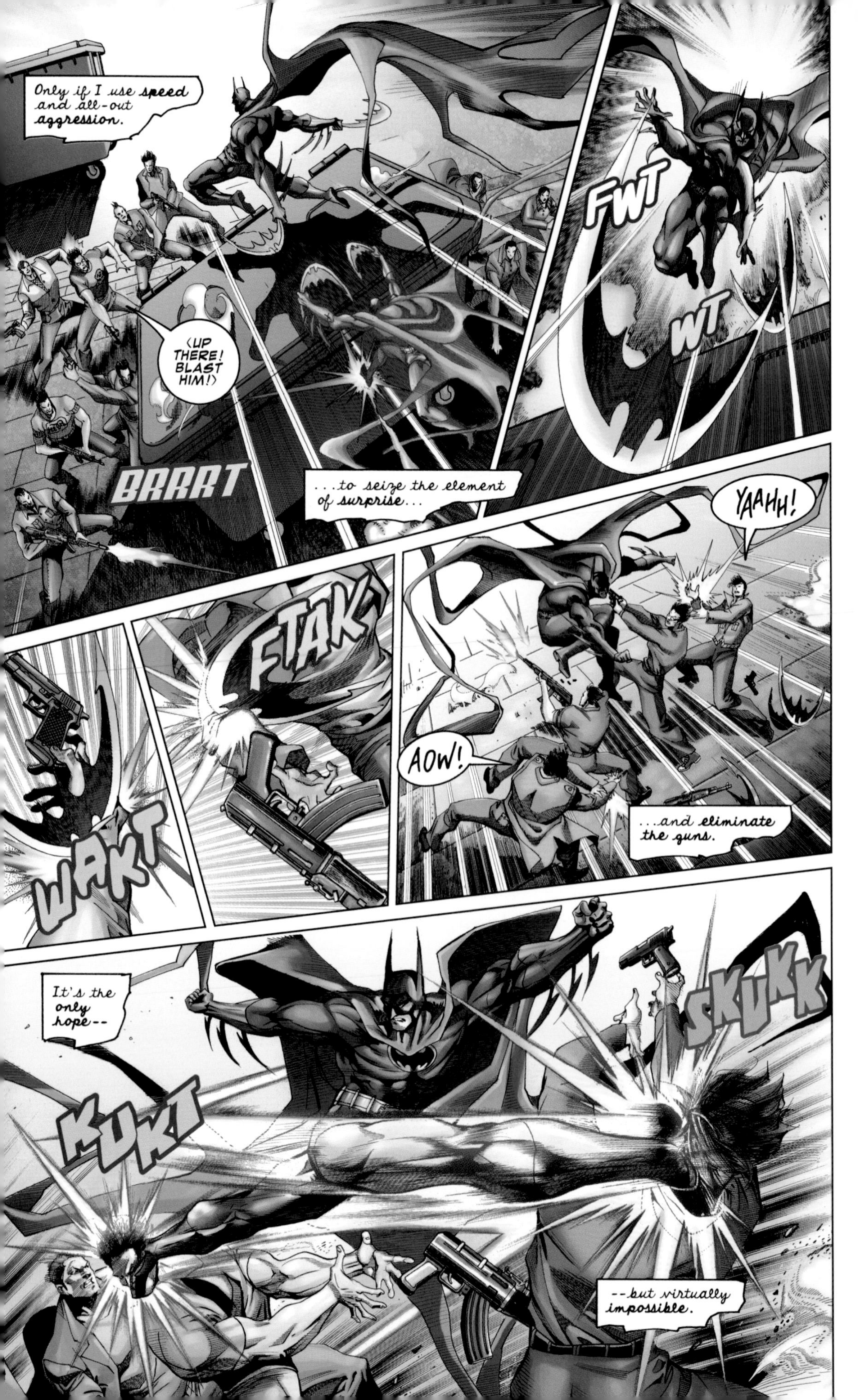

Only if I use speed and all-out aggression.
FWT
WT
(UP THERE! BLAST HIM!)
BRRRT
...to seize the element of surprise...
YAAHH!
FTAK
AOW!
...and eliminate the guns.
WAKT
It's the only hope--
SKUKK
KUKT
--but virtually impossible.

Just too many... guns.

BAM BAM BAM
BAM BAM BAM

⟨YOU GOT HIM! KEEP BLASTING!⟩

No penetration yet...but pinned down...wind knocked out...can't breathe...can't move at all...

BAM BAM BAM

BRRRT

...let alone faster than bullets.

And the outfit's Kevlar armor...can't hold up much longer.

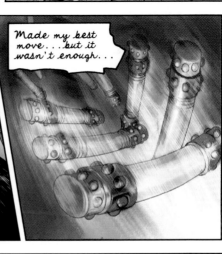

Made my best move...but it wasn't enough.

...not against so many--

K-KUKT

CHUT

TUT

TUP

WUK

DUT

CHUD

TUD

WUP

--weapons?

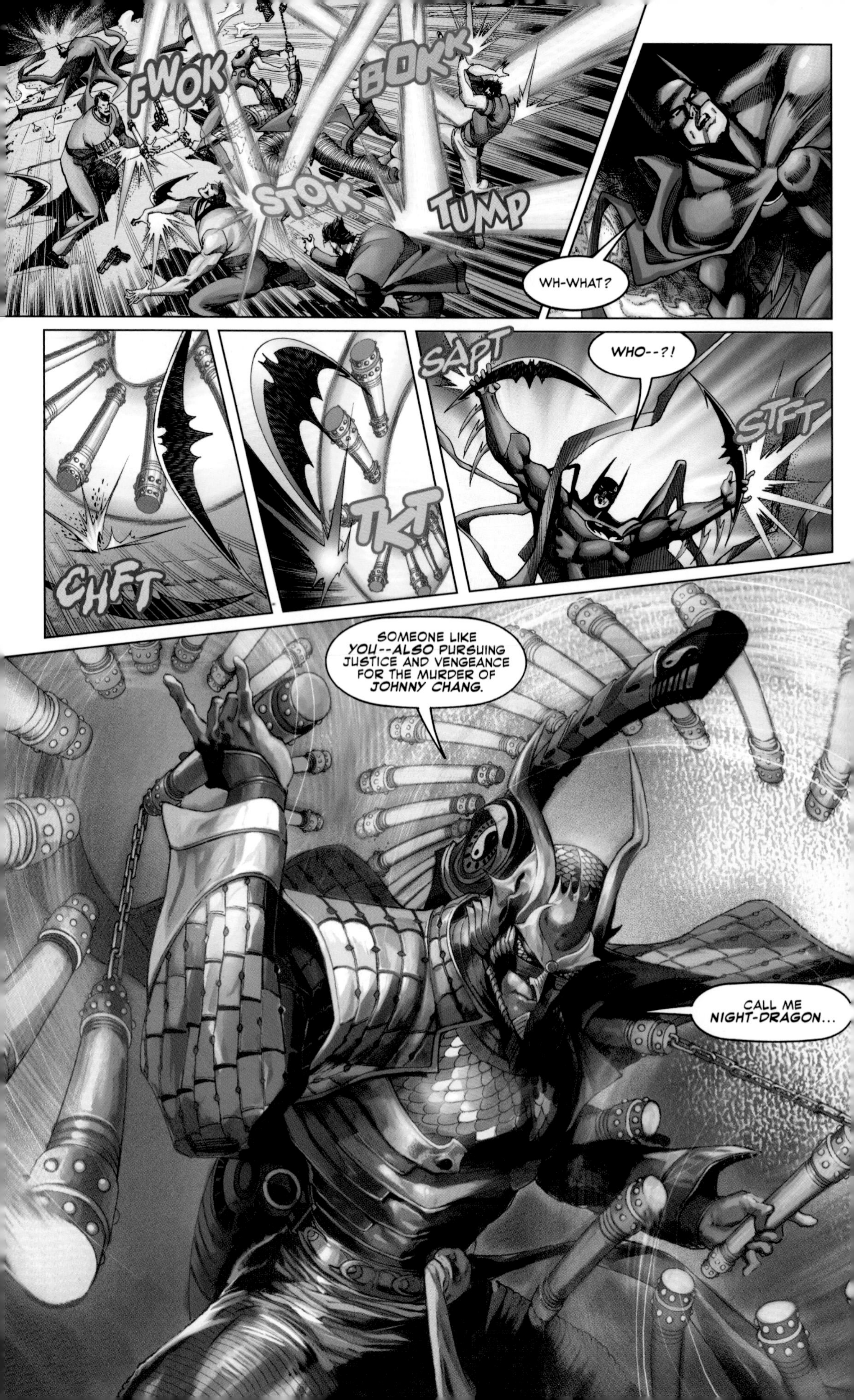
FWOK
BOKK
STOK
TUMP
WH-WHAT?
CHFT
TKT
SAPT
WHO--?!
STFT
SOMEONE LIKE YOU--ALSO PURSUING JUSTICE AND VENGEANCE FOR THE MURDER OF JOHNNY CHANG.
CALL ME NIGHT-DRAGON...

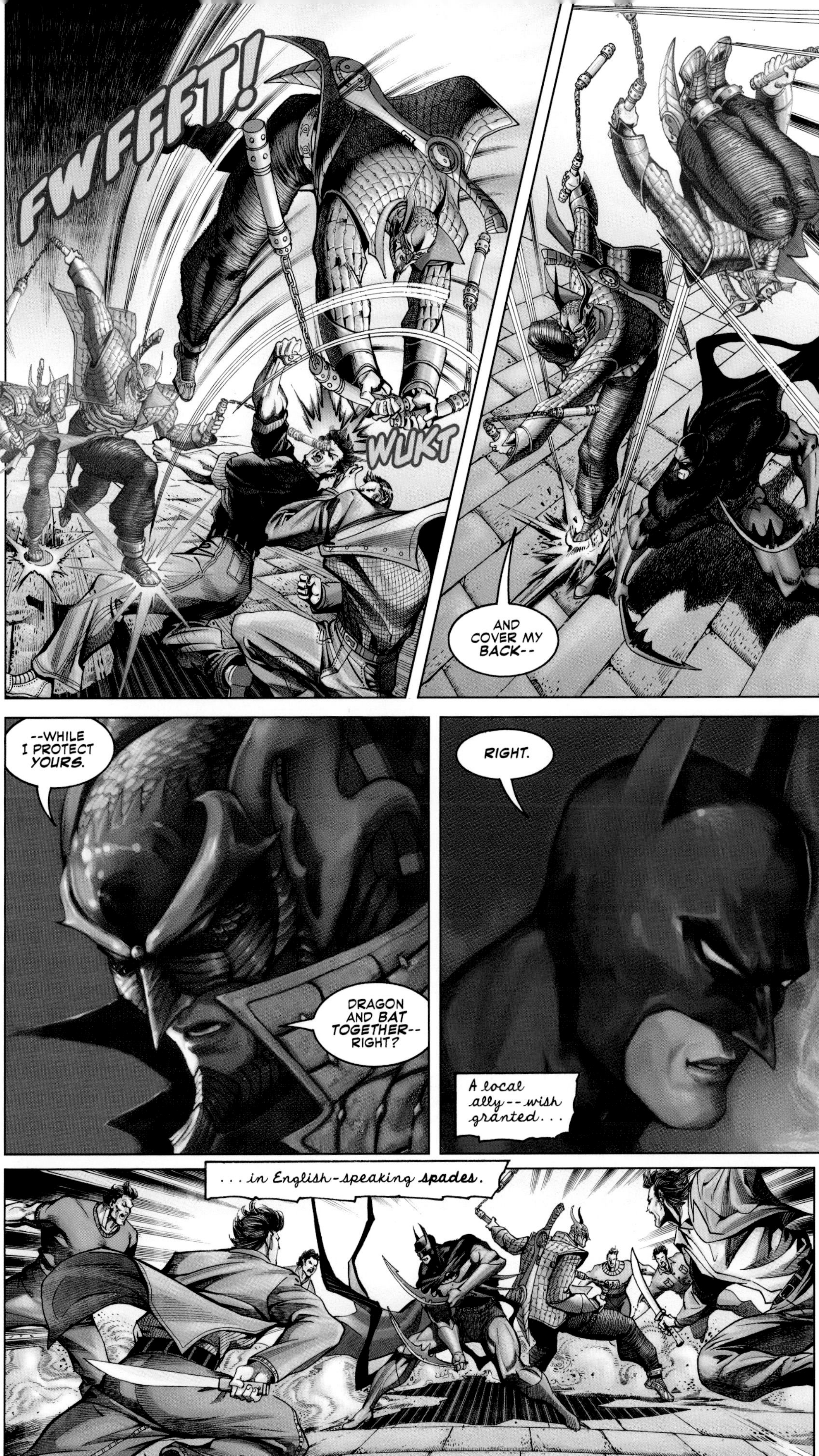
FWFFFT!
WUKT
AND COVER MY BACK--
--WHILE I PROTECT YOURS.
DRAGON AND BAT TOGETHER-- RIGHT?
RIGHT.
A local ally--wish granted...
...in English-speaking spades.

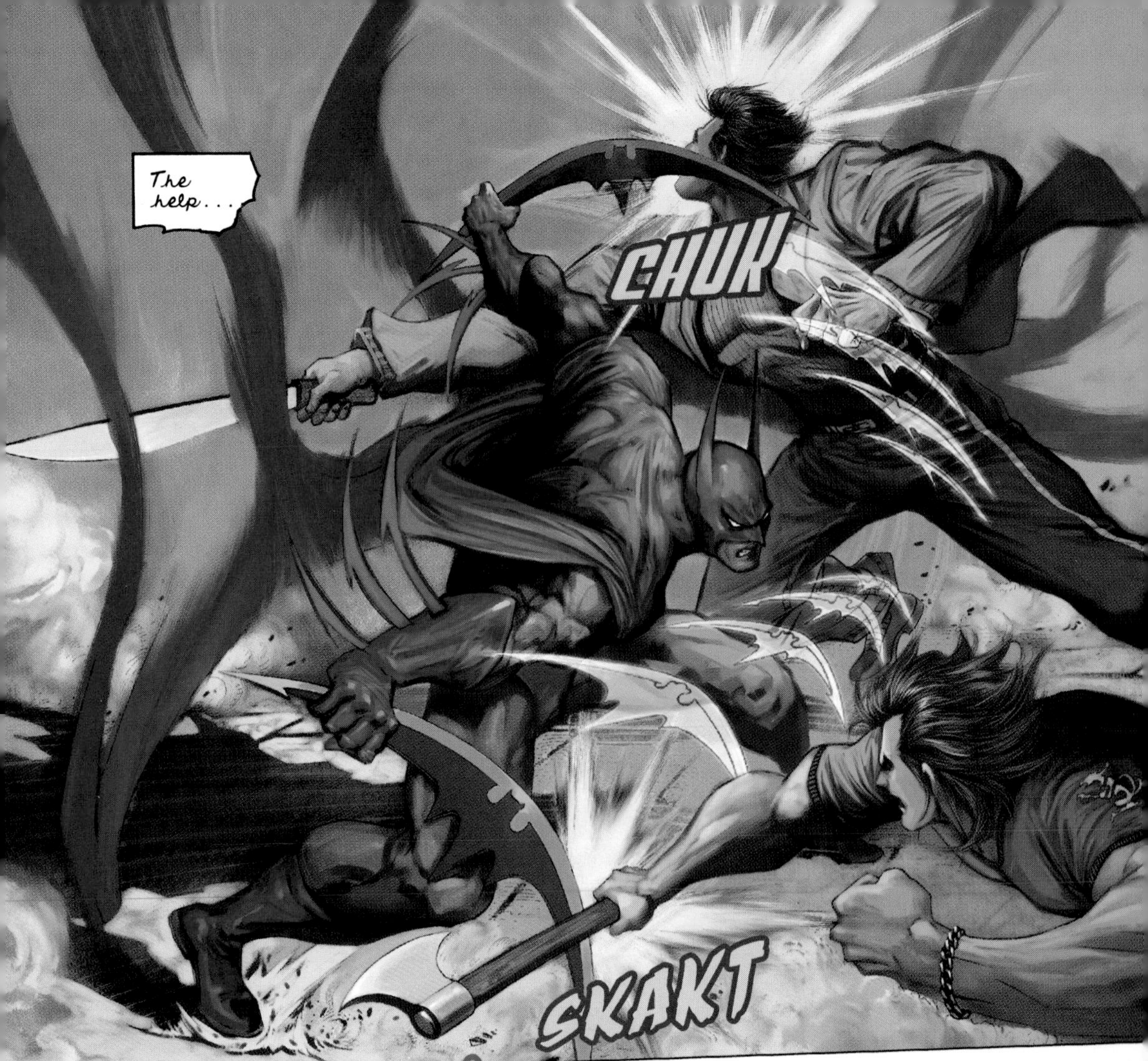
The help...
CHUK
SKAKT

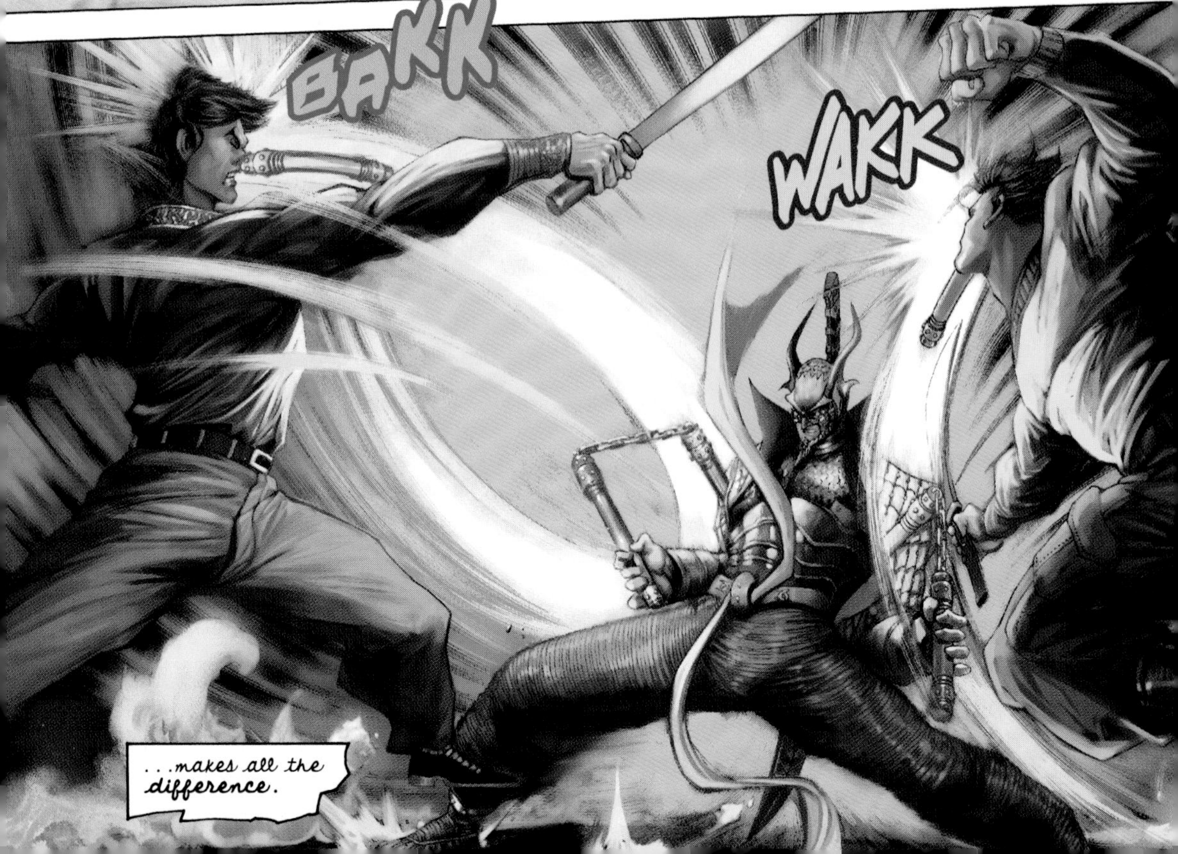
BAKK
WAKK
...makes all the difference.

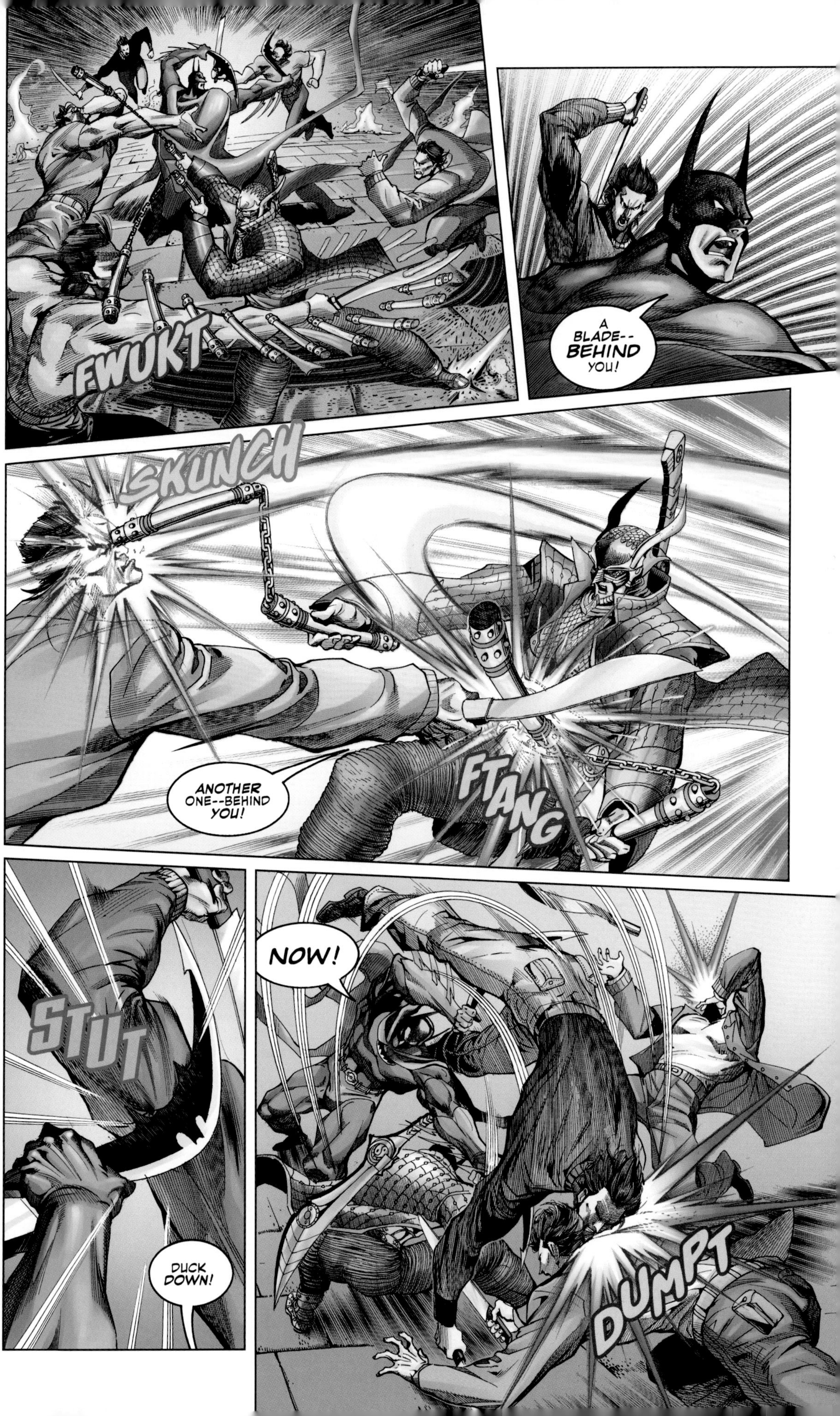

FWUKT
A BLADE--
BEHIND
YOU!
SKUNCH
ANOTHER
ONE--BEHIND
YOU!
FTANG
STUT
DUCK
DOWN!
NOW!
DUMPT

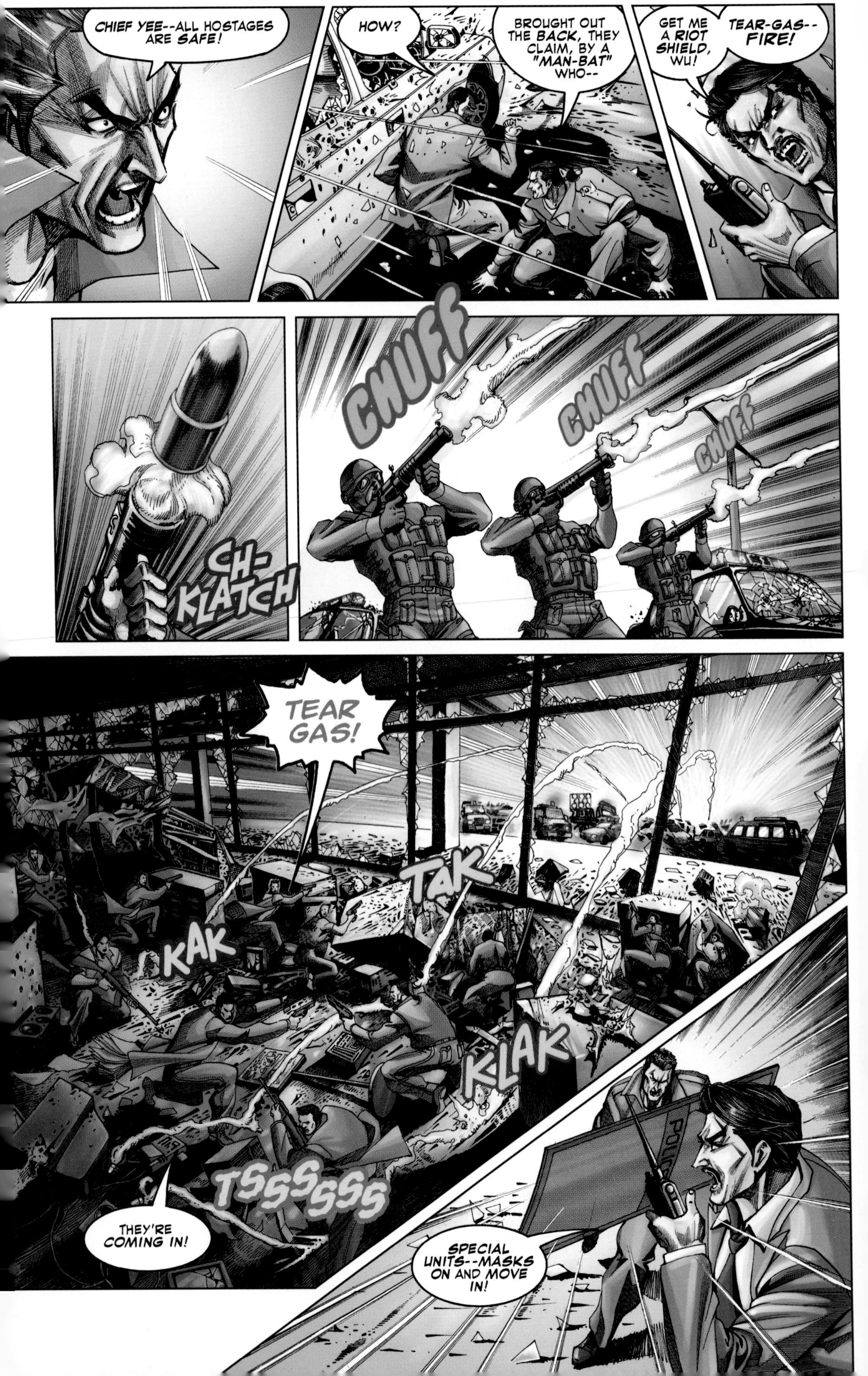
CHIEF YEE--ALL HOSTAGES ARE SAFE!
HOW?
BROUGHT OUT THE BACK, THEY CLAIM, BY A "MAN-BAT" WHO--
GET ME A RIOT SHIELD, WU!
TEAR-GAS--FIRE!
CH-KLATCH
CHUFF
CHUFF
CHUFF
TEAR GAS!
TAK
KAK
KLAK
TSSSSSS
THEY'RE COMING IN!
SPECIAL UNITS--MASKS ON AND MOVE IN!

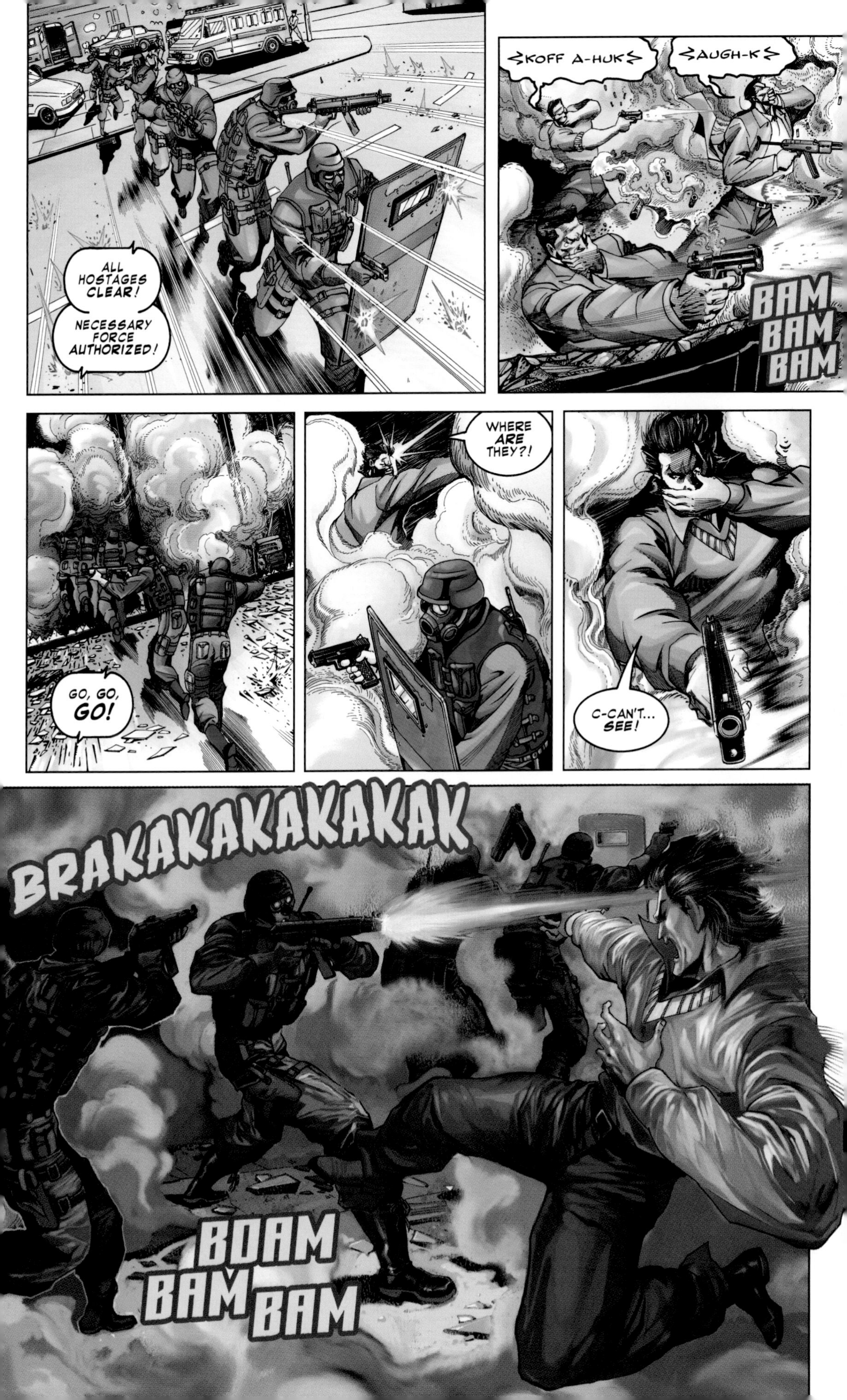
ALL HOSTAGES CLEAR!
NECESSARY FORCE AUTHORIZED!
KOFF A-HUK
AUGH-K
BAM BAM BAM
GO, GO, GO!
WHERE ARE THEY?!
C-CAN'T... SEE!
BRAKAKAKAKAKAK
BOAM BAM BAM

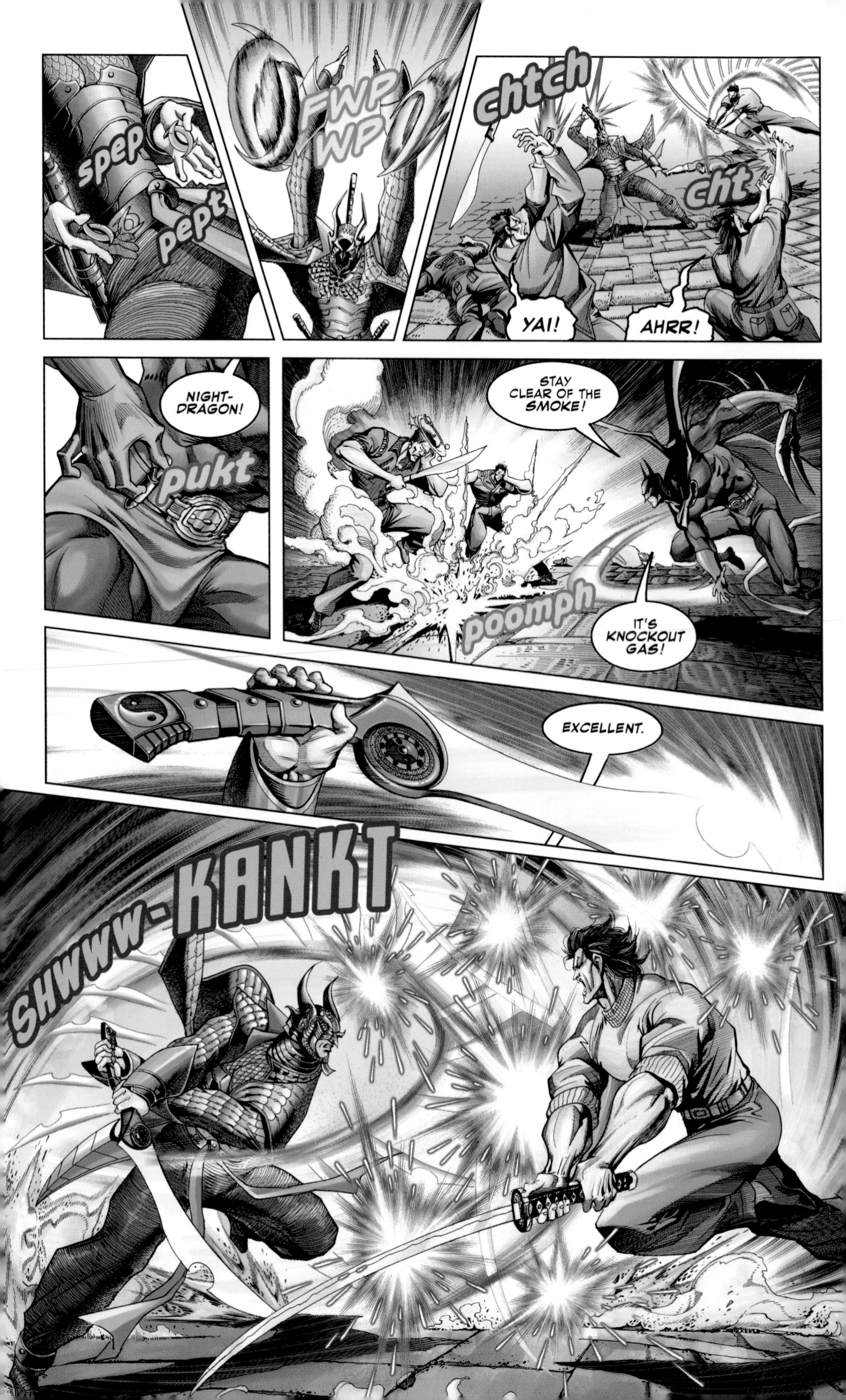
spep
pept
FWP WP
chtch
cht
YAI!
AHRR!
NIGHT-DRAGON!
pukt
STAY CLEAR OF THE SMOKE!
poomph
IT'S KNOCKOUT GAS!
EXCELLENT.
SHWWW-KANKT

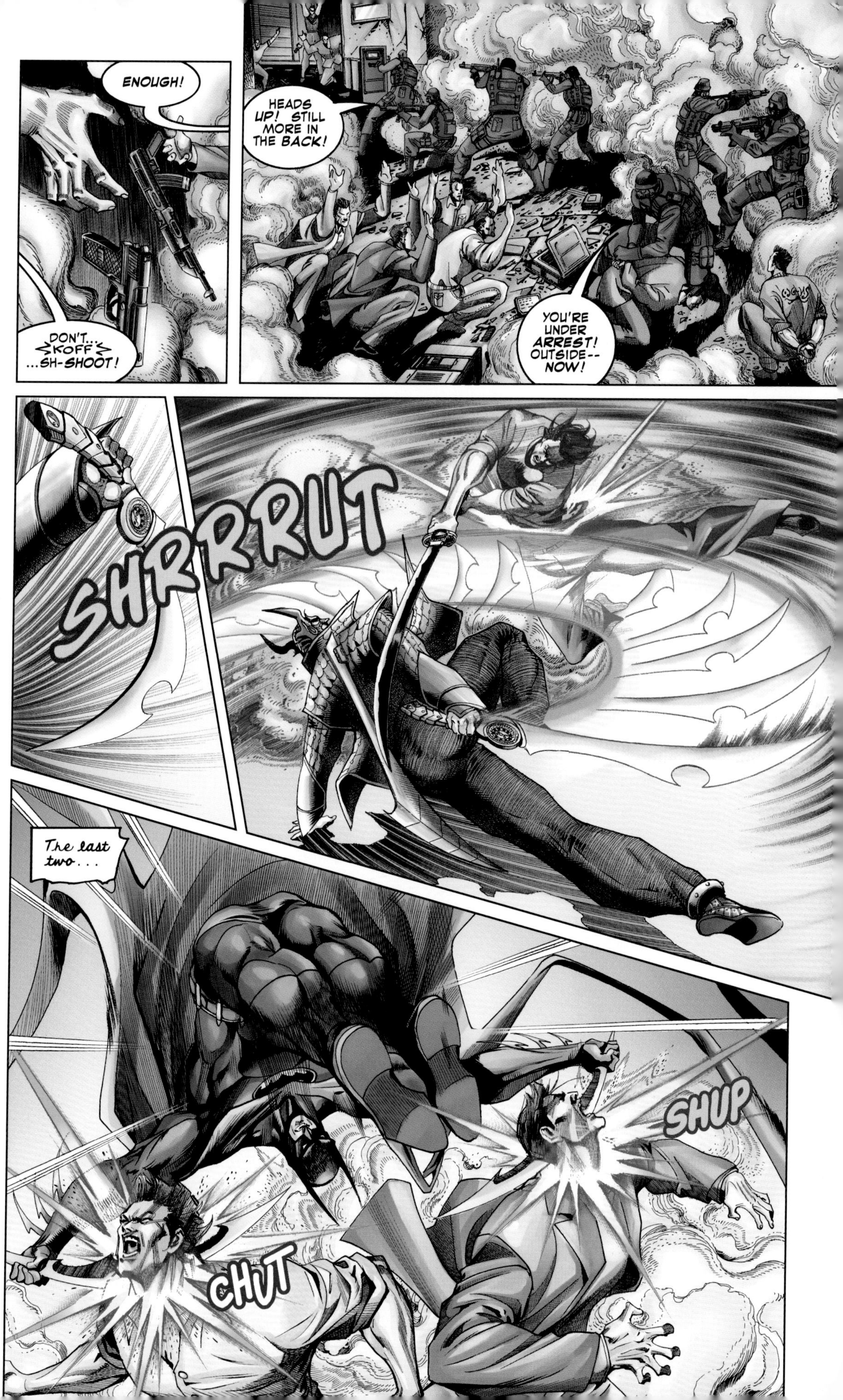
ENOUGH!
DON'T... KOFF ...SH-SHOOT!
HEADS UP! STILL MORE IN THE BACK!
YOU'RE UNDER ARREST! OUTSIDE-- NOW!
SHRRRUT
The last two...
SHUP
CHUT

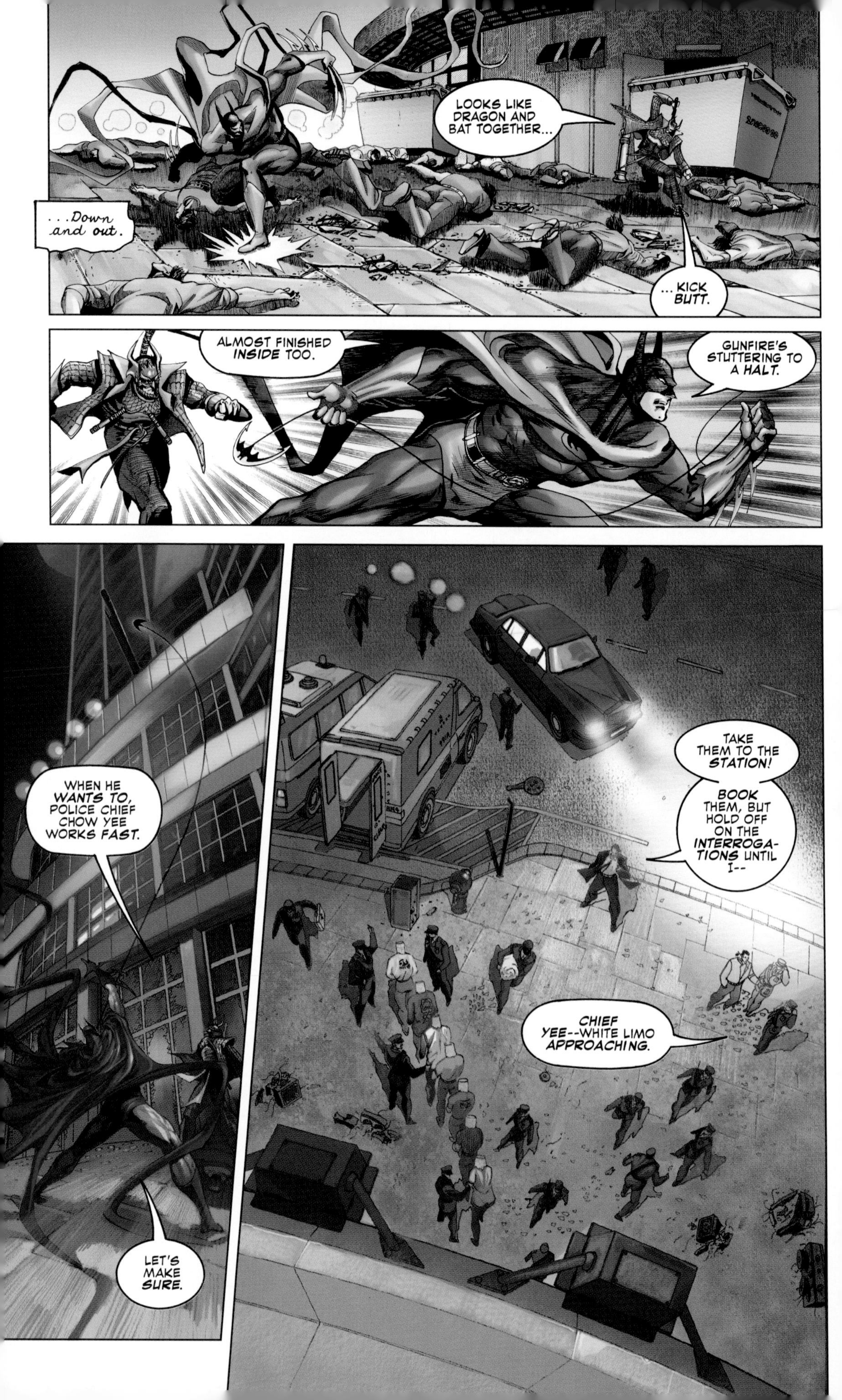

LOOKS LIKE DRAGON AND BAT TOGETHER...
...Down and out.
...KICK BUTT.
ALMOST FINISHED INSIDE TOO.
GUNFIRE'S STUTTERING TO A HALT.
WHEN HE WANTS TO, POLICE CHIEF CHOW YEE WORKS FAST.
LET'S MAKE SURE.
TAKE THEM TO THE STATION!
BOOK THEM, BUT HOLD OFF ON THE INTERROGATIONS UNTIL I--
CHIEF YEE--WHITE LIMO APPROACHING.

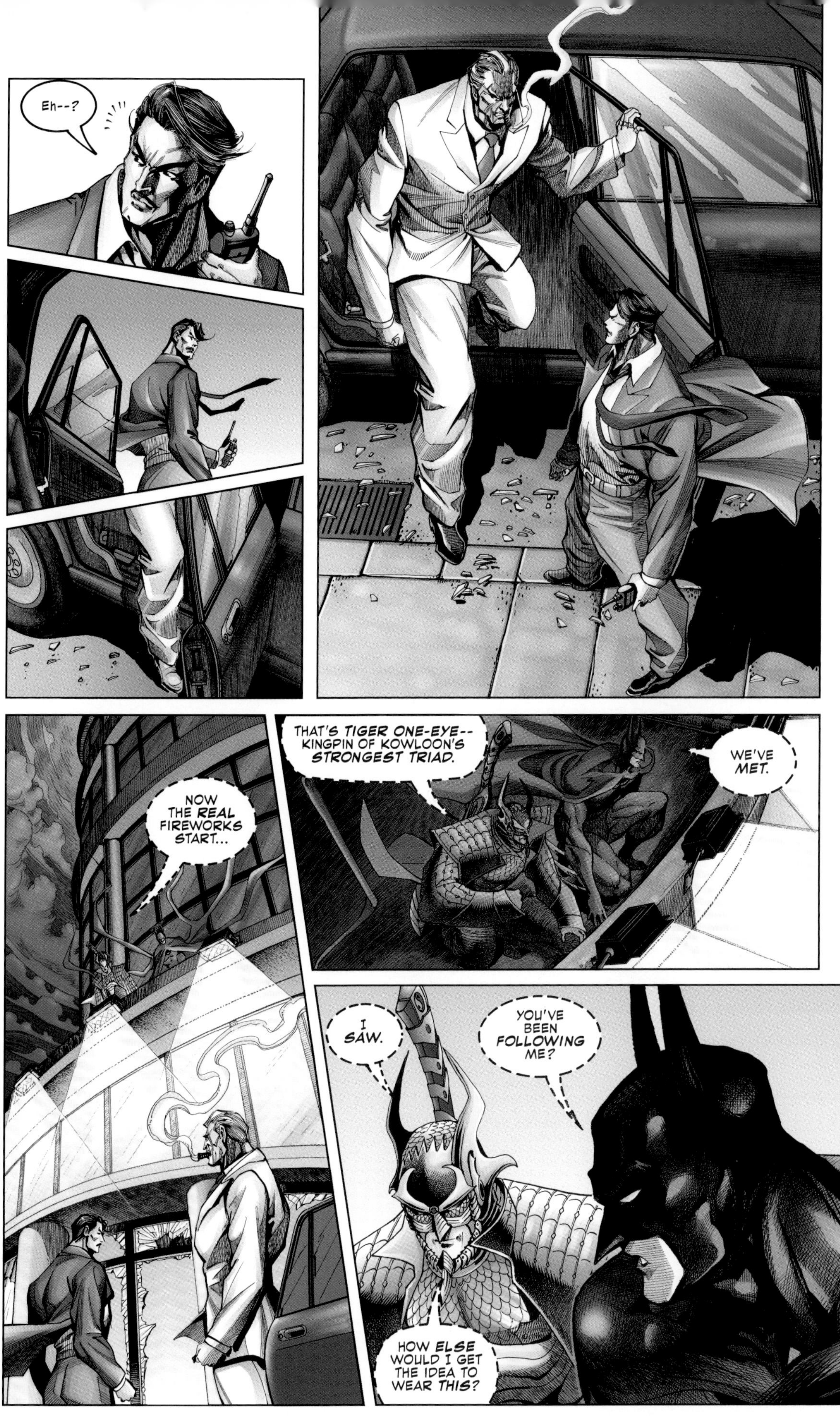
Eh--?
NOW THE REAL FIREWORKS START...
THAT'S TIGER ONE-EYE-- KINGPIN OF KOWLOON'S STRONGEST TRIAD.
WE'VE MET.
I SAW.
YOU'VE BEEN FOLLOWING ME?
HOW ELSE WOULD I GET THE IDEA TO WEAR THIS?

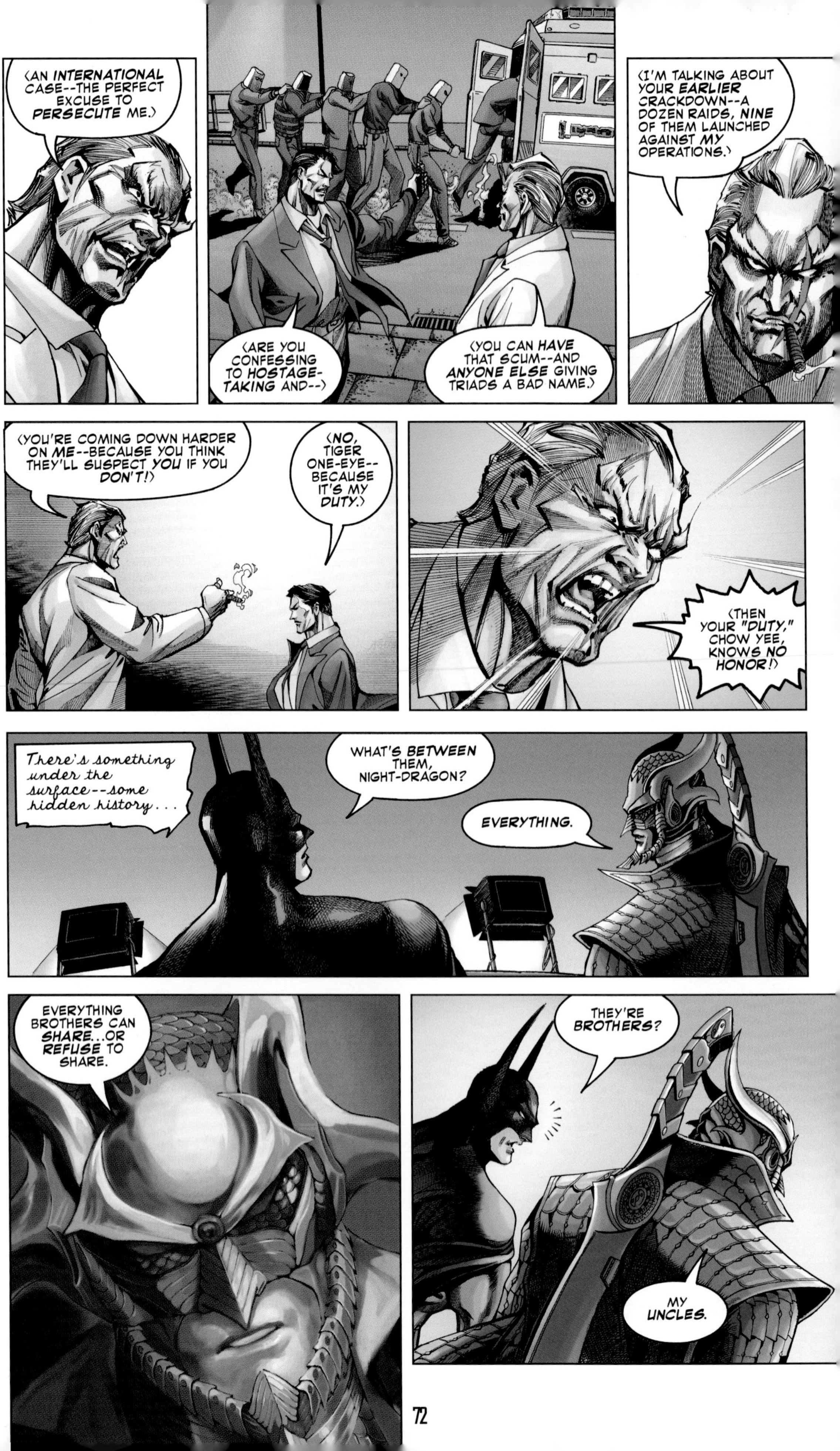

⟨AN INTERNATIONAL CASE--THE PERFECT EXCUSE TO PERSECUTE ME.⟩
⟨ARE YOU CONFESSING TO HOSTAGE-TAKING AND--⟩
⟨YOU CAN HAVE THAT SCUM--AND ANYONE ELSE GIVING TRIADS A BAD NAME.⟩
⟨I'M TALKING ABOUT YOUR EARLIER CRACKDOWN--A DOZEN RAIDS, NINE OF THEM LAUNCHED AGAINST MY OPERATIONS.⟩
⟨YOU'RE COMING DOWN HARDER ON ME--BECAUSE YOU THINK THEY'LL SUSPECT YOU IF YOU DON'T!⟩
⟨NO, TIGER ONE-EYE--BECAUSE IT'S MY DUTY.⟩
⟨THEN YOUR "DUTY," CHOW YEE, KNOWS NO HONOR!⟩
There's something under the surface--some hidden history...
WHAT'S BETWEEN THEM, NIGHT-DRAGON?
EVERYTHING.
EVERYTHING BROTHERS CAN SHARE...OR REFUSE TO SHARE.
THEY'RE BROTHERS?
MY UNCLES.

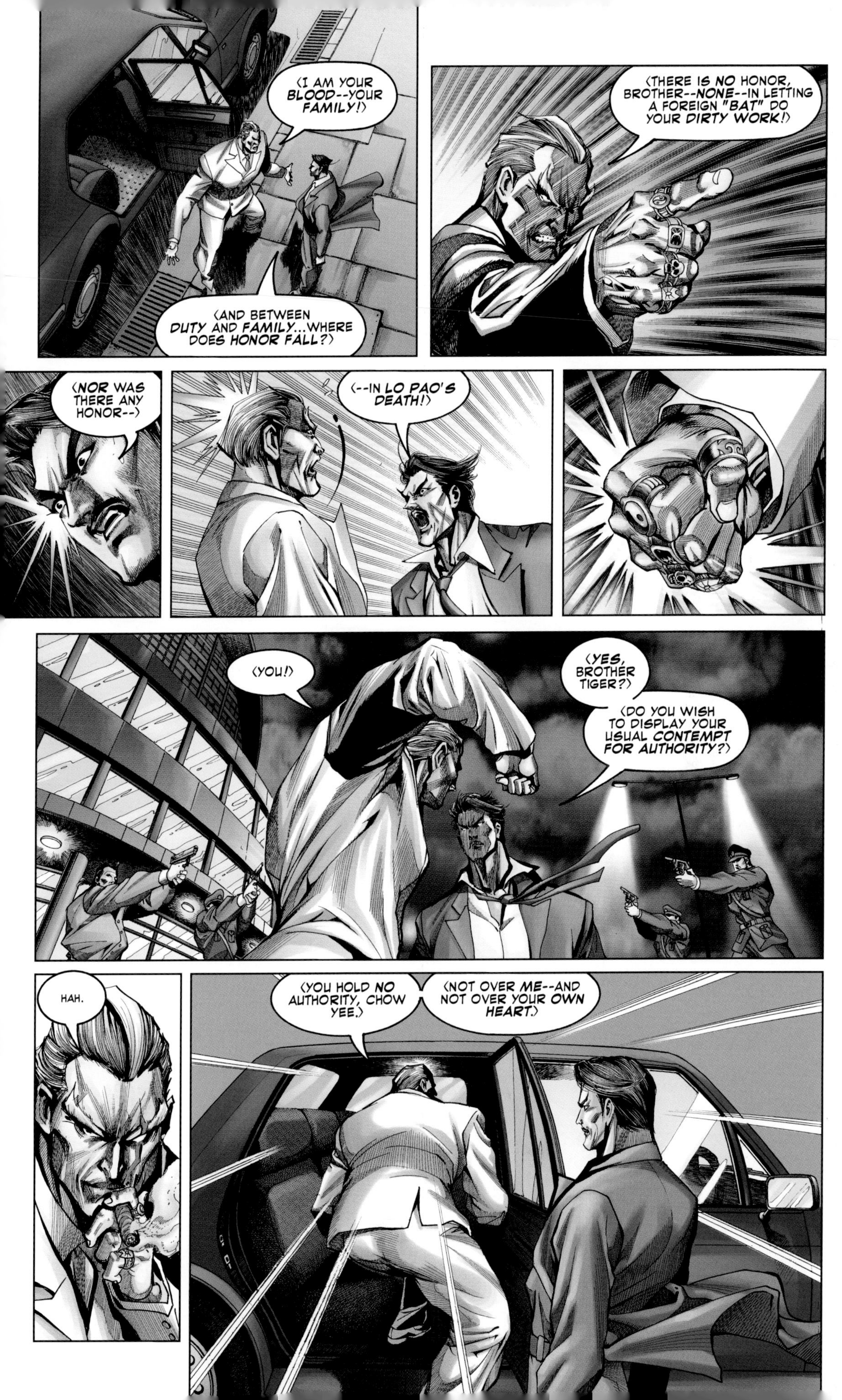
(I AM YOUR BLOOD--YOUR FAMILY!)
(AND BETWEEN DUTY AND FAMILY...WHERE DOES HONOR FALL?)
(THERE IS NO HONOR, BROTHER--NONE--IN LETTING A FOREIGN "BAT" DO YOUR DIRTY WORK!)
(NOR WAS THERE ANY HONOR--)
(--IN LO PAO'S DEATH!)
(YOU!)
(YES, BROTHER TIGER?)
(DO YOU WISH TO DISPLAY YOUR USUAL CONTEMPT FOR AUTHORITY?)
HAH.
(YOU HOLD NO AUTHORITY, CHOW YEE.)
(NOT OVER ME--AND NOT OVER YOUR OWN HEART.)

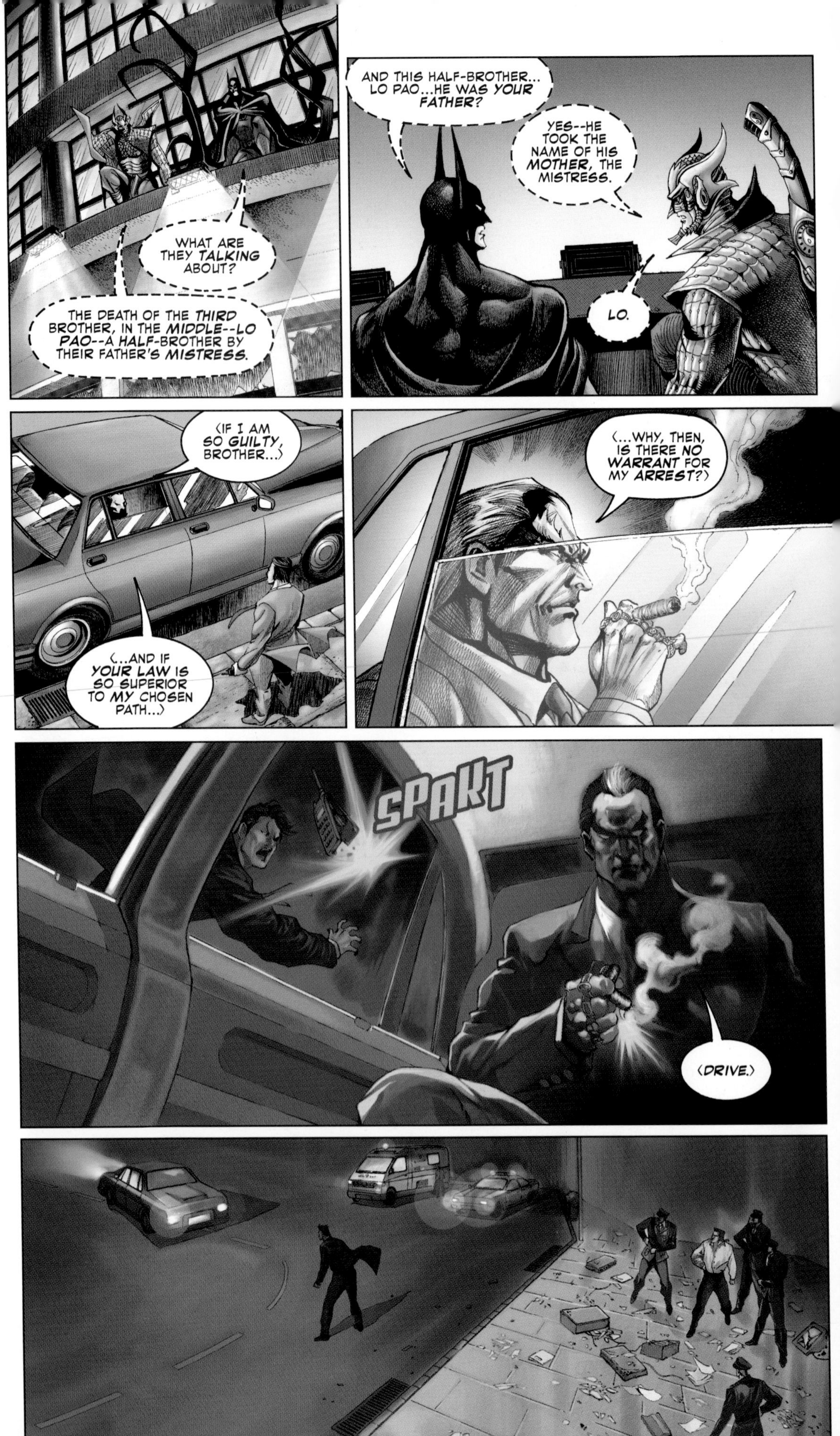
WHAT ARE THEY TALKING ABOUT?
THE DEATH OF THE THIRD BROTHER, IN THE MIDDLE--LO PAO--A HALF-BROTHER BY THEIR FATHER'S MISTRESS.
AND THIS HALF-BROTHER... LO PAO...HE WAS YOUR FATHER?
YES--HE TOOK THE NAME OF HIS MOTHER, THE MISTRESS.
LO.
(IF I AM SO GUILTY, BROTHER...)
(...AND IF YOUR LAW IS SO SUPERIOR TO MY CHOSEN PATH...)
(...WHY, THEN, IS THERE NO WARRANT FOR MY ARREST?)
SPAKT
(DRIVE.)

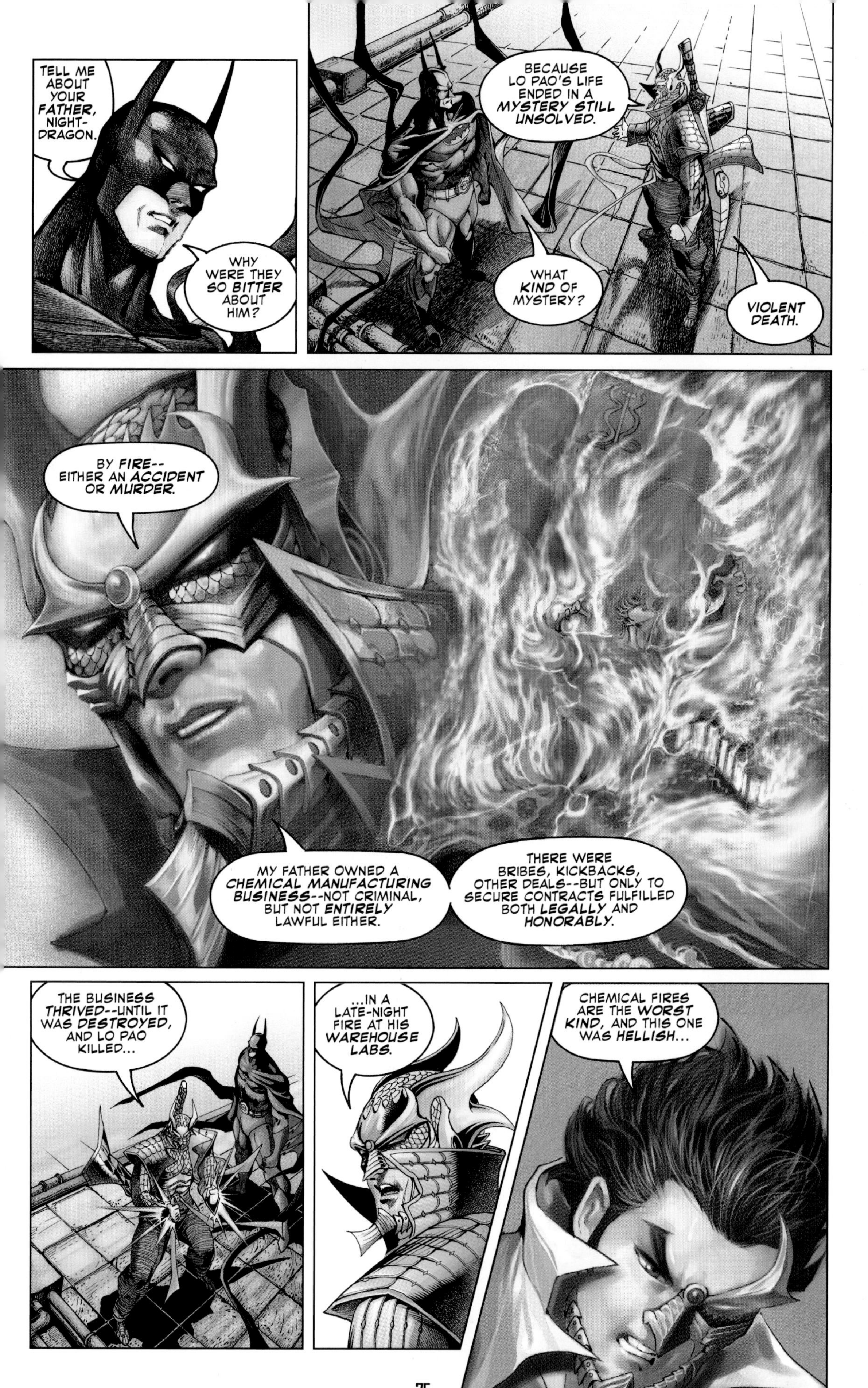
TELL ME ABOUT YOUR FATHER, NIGHT-DRAGON.
WHY WERE THEY SO BITTER ABOUT HIM?
BECAUSE LO PAO'S LIFE ENDED IN A MYSTERY STILL UNSOLVED.
WHAT KIND OF MYSTERY?
VIOLENT DEATH.
BY FIRE-- EITHER AN ACCIDENT OR MURDER.
MY FATHER OWNED A CHEMICAL MANUFACTURING BUSINESS--NOT CRIMINAL, BUT NOT ENTIRELY LAWFUL EITHER.
THERE WERE BRIBES, KICKBACKS, OTHER DEALS--BUT ONLY TO SECURE CONTRACTS FULFILLED BOTH LEGALLY AND HONORABLY.
THE BUSINESS THRIVED--UNTIL IT WAS DESTROYED, AND LO PAO KILLED...
...IN A LATE-NIGHT FIRE AT HIS WAREHOUSE LABS.
CHEMICAL FIRES ARE THE WORST KIND, AND THIS ONE WAS HELLISH...

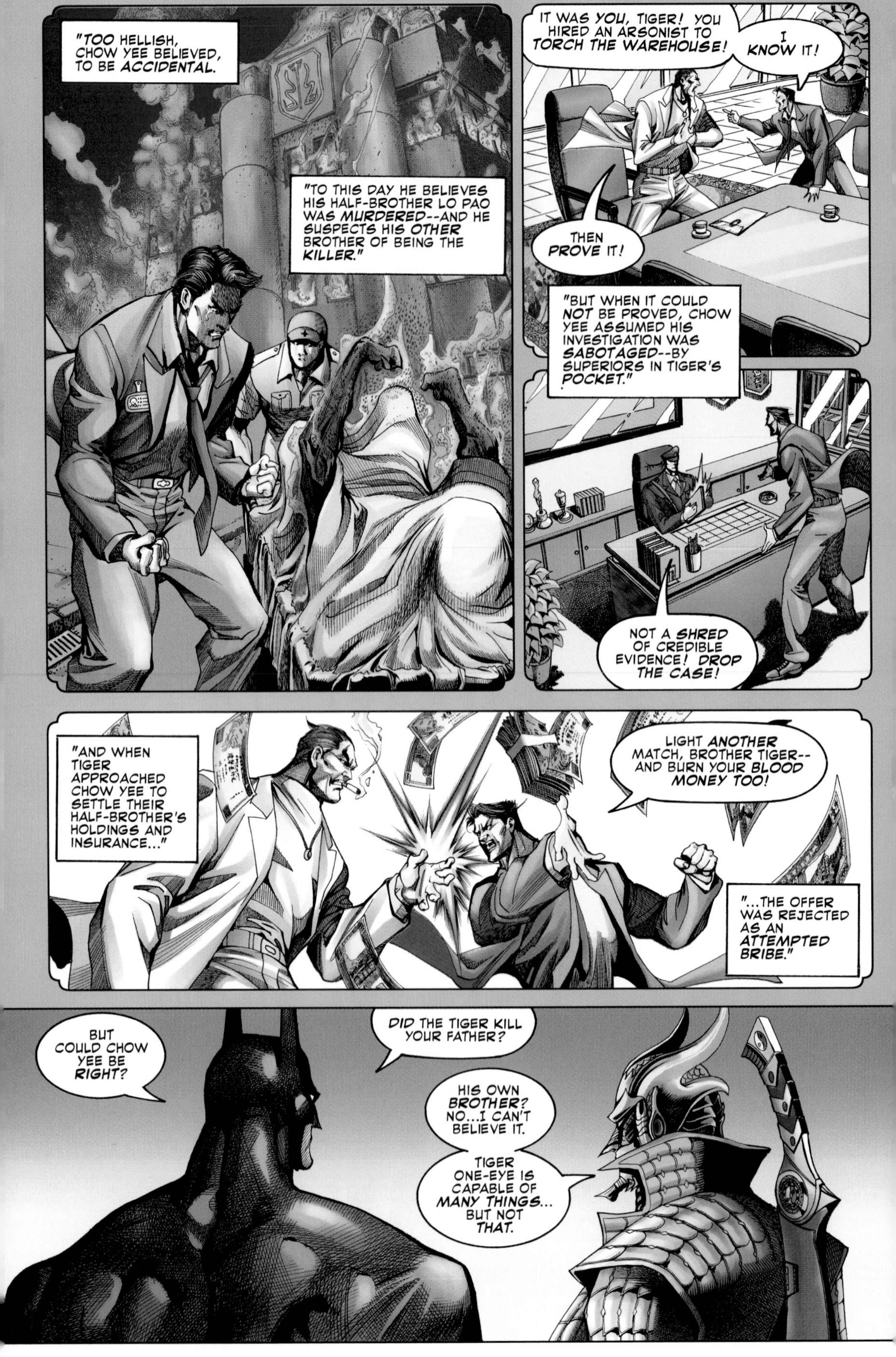
"TOO HELLISH, CHOW YEE BELIEVED, TO BE ACCIDENTAL.
"TO THIS DAY HE BELIEVES HIS HALF-BROTHER LO PAO WAS MURDERED--AND HE SUSPECTS HIS OTHER BROTHER OF BEING THE KILLER."
IT WAS YOU, TIGER! YOU HIRED AN ARSONIST TO TORCH THE WAREHOUSE!
I KNOW IT!
THEN PROVE IT!
"BUT WHEN IT COULD NOT BE PROVED, CHOW YEE ASSUMED HIS INVESTIGATION WAS SABOTAGED--BY SUPERIORS IN TIGER'S POCKET."
NOT A SHRED OF CREDIBLE EVIDENCE! DROP THE CASE!
"AND WHEN TIGER APPROACHED CHOW YEE TO SETTLE THEIR HALF-BROTHER'S HOLDINGS AND INSURANCE..."
LIGHT ANOTHER MATCH, BROTHER TIGER--AND BURN YOUR BLOOD MONEY TOO!
"...THE OFFER WAS REJECTED AS AN ATTEMPTED BRIBE."
BUT COULD CHOW YEE BE RIGHT?
DID THE TIGER KILL YOUR FATHER?
HIS OWN BROTHER? NO...I CAN'T BELIEVE IT.
TIGER ONE-EYE IS CAPABLE OF MANY THINGS... BUT NOT THAT.

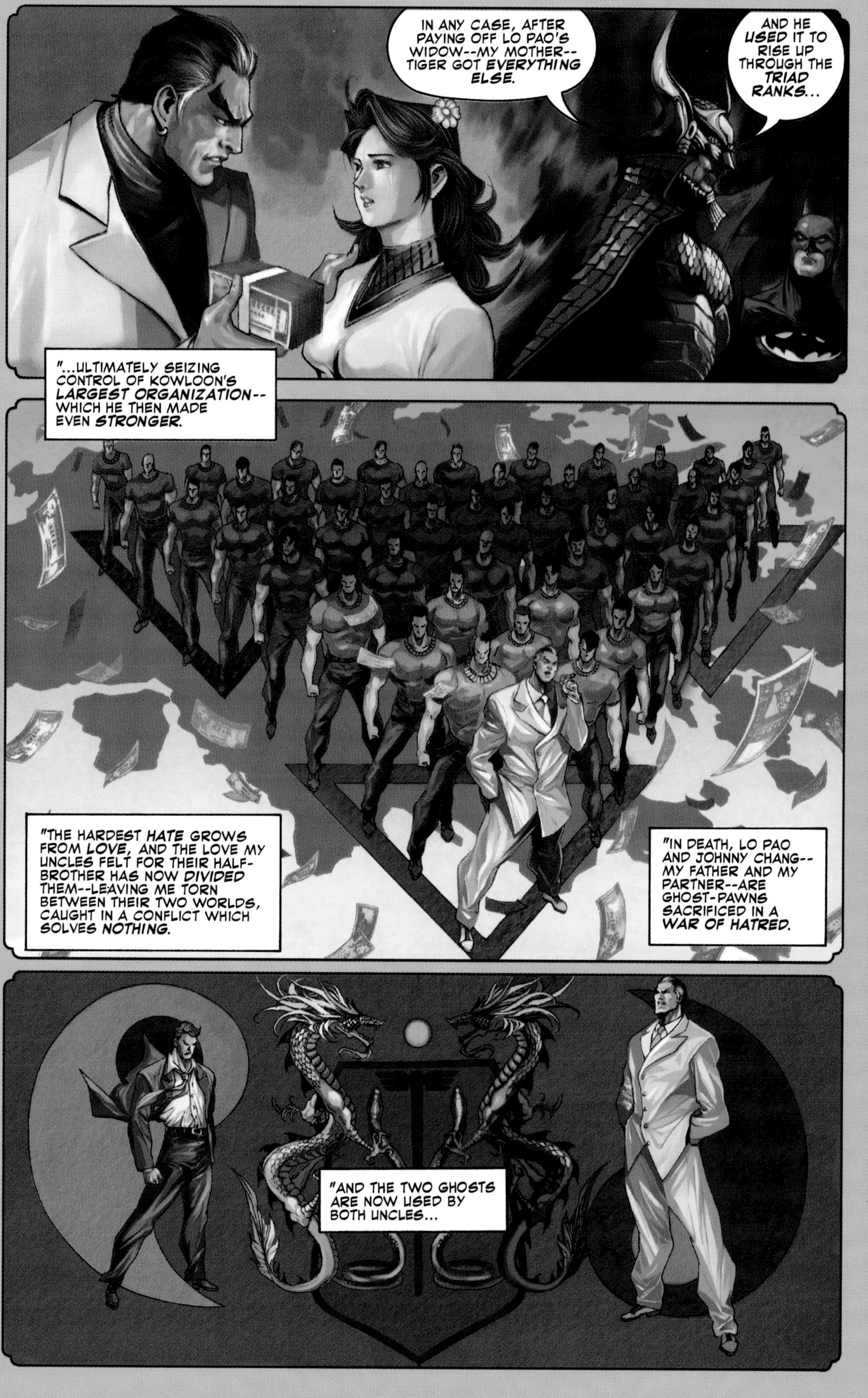
IN ANY CASE, AFTER PAYING OFF LO PAO'S WIDOW--MY MOTHER--TIGER GOT EVERYTHING ELSE.
AND HE USED IT TO RISE UP THROUGH THE TRIAD RANKS...
"...ULTIMATELY SEIZING CONTROL OF KOWLOON'S LARGEST ORGANIZATION--WHICH HE THEN MADE EVEN STRONGER.
"THE HARDEST HATE GROWS FROM LOVE, AND THE LOVE MY UNCLES FELT FOR THEIR HALF-BROTHER HAS NOW DIVIDED THEM--LEAVING ME TORN BETWEEN THEIR TWO WORLDS, CAUGHT IN A CONFLICT WHICH SOLVES NOTHING.
"IN DEATH, LO PAO AND JOHNNY CHANG--MY FATHER AND MY PARTNER--ARE GHOST-PAWNS SACRIFICED IN A WAR OF HATRED.
"AND THE TWO GHOSTS ARE NOW USED BY BOTH UNCLES...

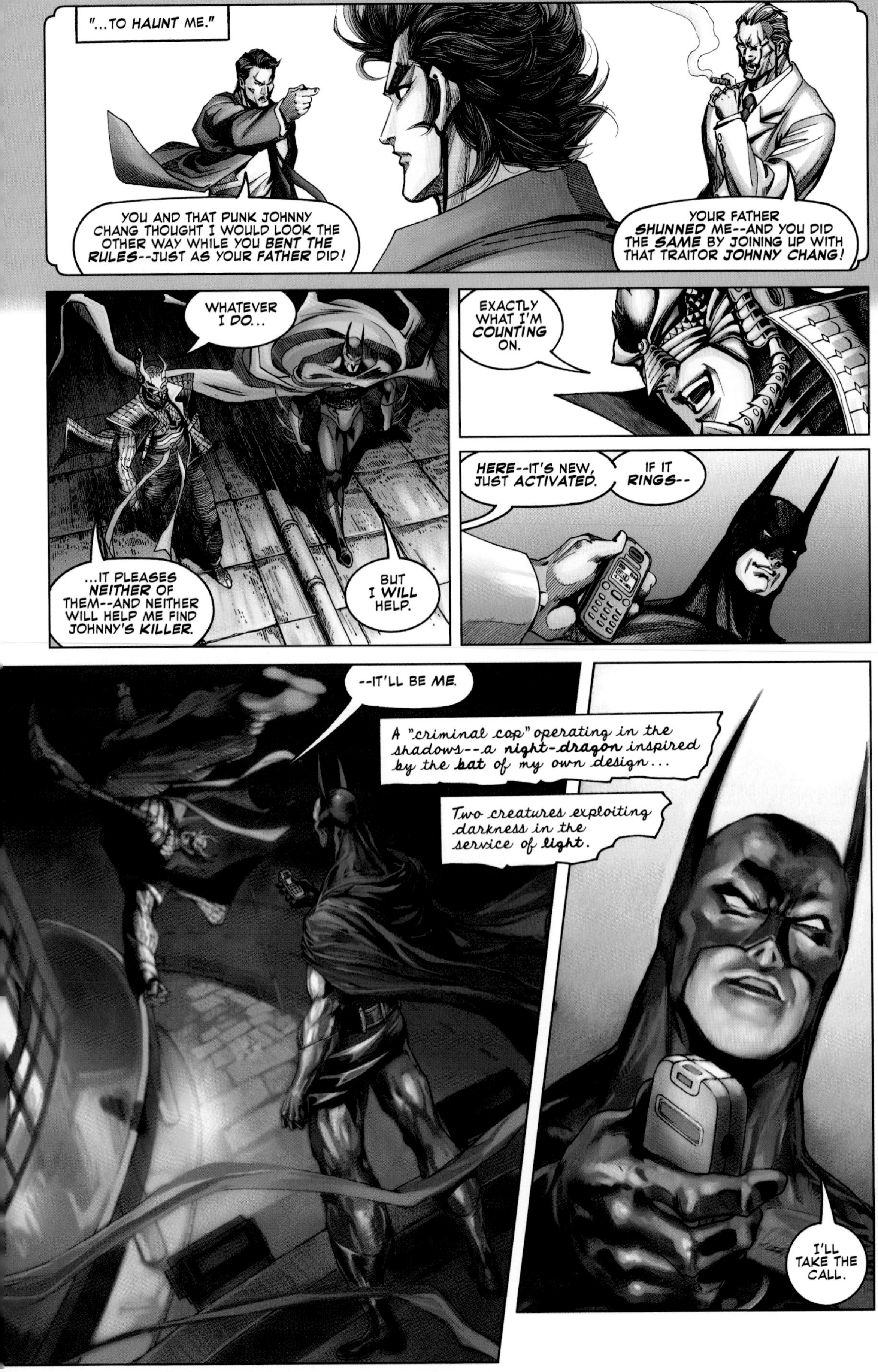

"...TO HAUNT ME."
YOU AND THAT PUNK JOHNNY CHANG THOUGHT I WOULD LOOK THE OTHER WAY WHILE YOU BENT THE RULES--JUST AS YOUR FATHER DID!
YOUR FATHER SHUNNED ME--AND YOU DID THE SAME BY JOINING UP WITH THAT TRAITOR JOHNNY CHANG!
WHATEVER I DO...
...IT PLEASES NEITHER OF THEM--AND NEITHER WILL HELP ME FIND JOHNNY'S KILLER.
BUT I WILL HELP.
EXACTLY WHAT I'M COUNTING ON.
HERE--IT'S NEW, JUST ACTIVATED.
IF IT RINGS--
--IT'LL BE ME.
A "criminal cop" operating in the shadows--a night-dragon inspired by the bat of my own design...
Two creatures exploiting darkness in the service of light.
I'LL TAKE THE CALL.

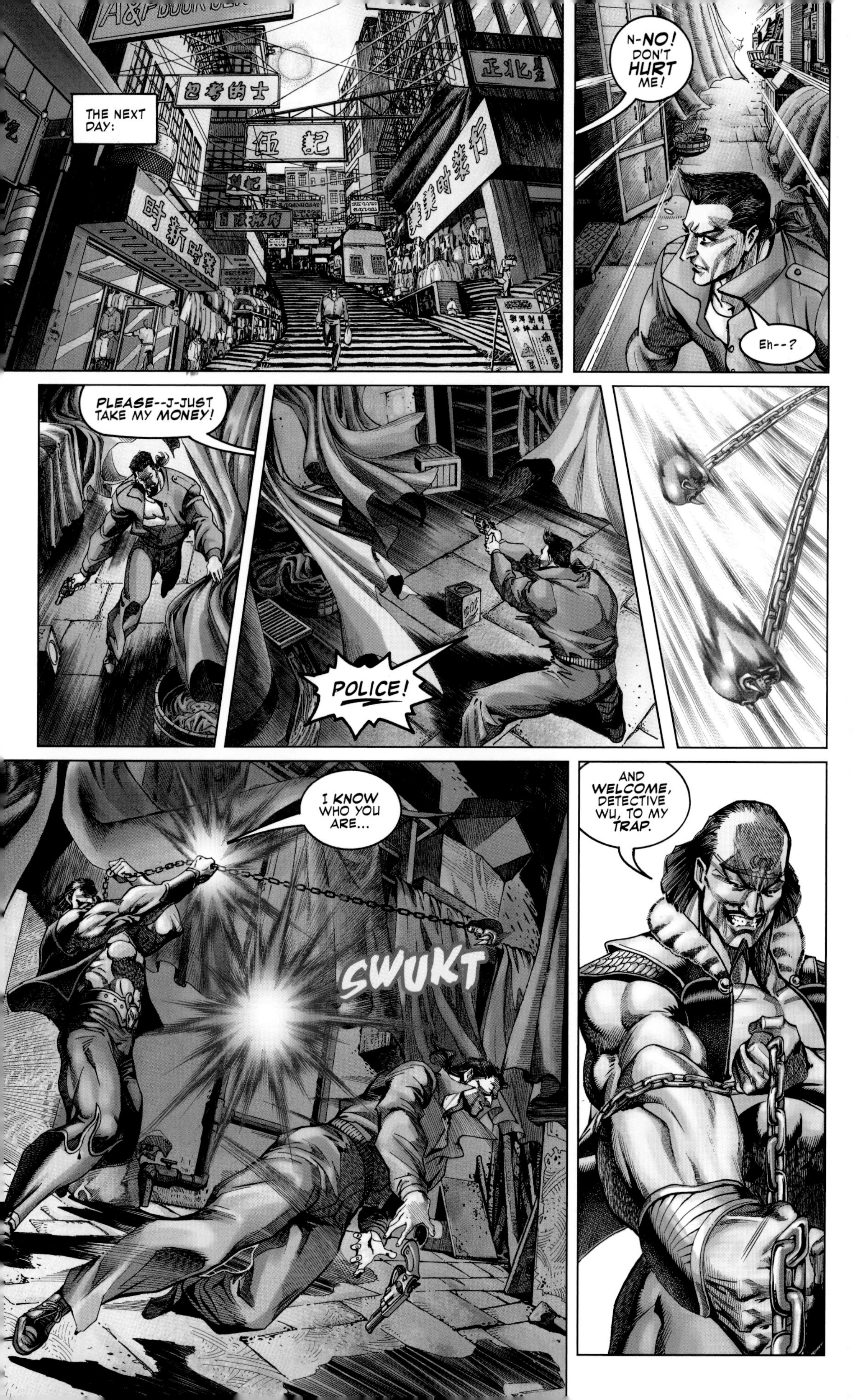
THE NEXT DAY:
N-NO! DON'T HURT ME!
Eh--?
PLEASE--J-JUST TAKE MY MONEY!
POLICE!
I KNOW WHO YOU ARE...
SWUKT
AND WELCOME, DETECTIVE WU, TO MY TRAP.

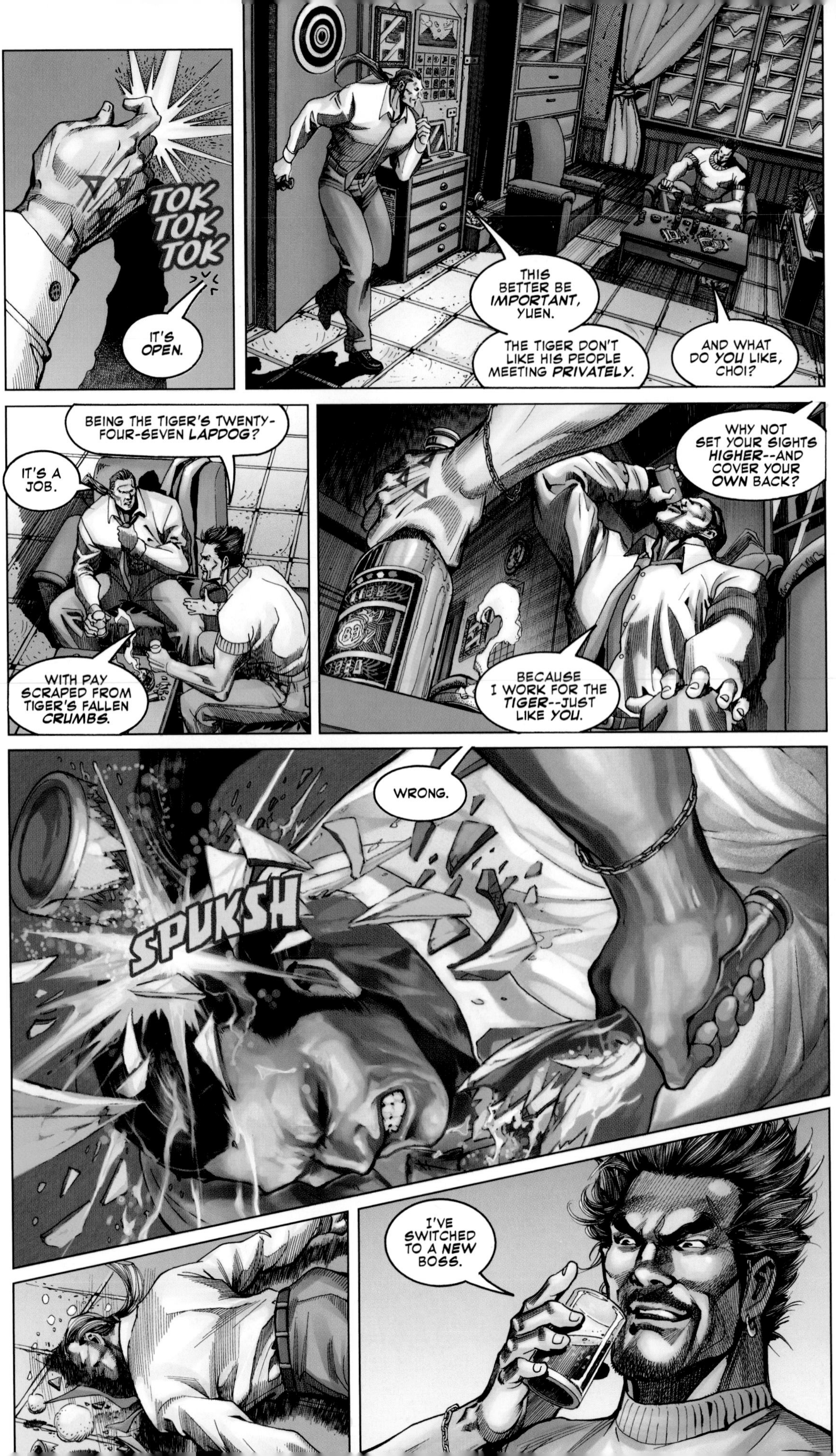
TOK TOK TOK
IT'S OPEN.
THIS BETTER BE IMPORTANT, YUEN.
THE TIGER DON'T LIKE HIS PEOPLE MEETING PRIVATELY.
AND WHAT DO YOU LIKE, CHOI?
BEING THE TIGER'S TWENTY-FOUR-SEVEN LAPDOG?
IT'S A JOB.
WITH PAY SCRAPED FROM TIGER'S FALLEN CRUMBS.
WHY NOT SET YOUR SIGHTS HIGHER--AND COVER YOUR OWN BACK?
BECAUSE I WORK FOR THE TIGER--JUST LIKE YOU.
WRONG.
SPUKSH
I'VE SWITCHED TO A NEW BOSS.

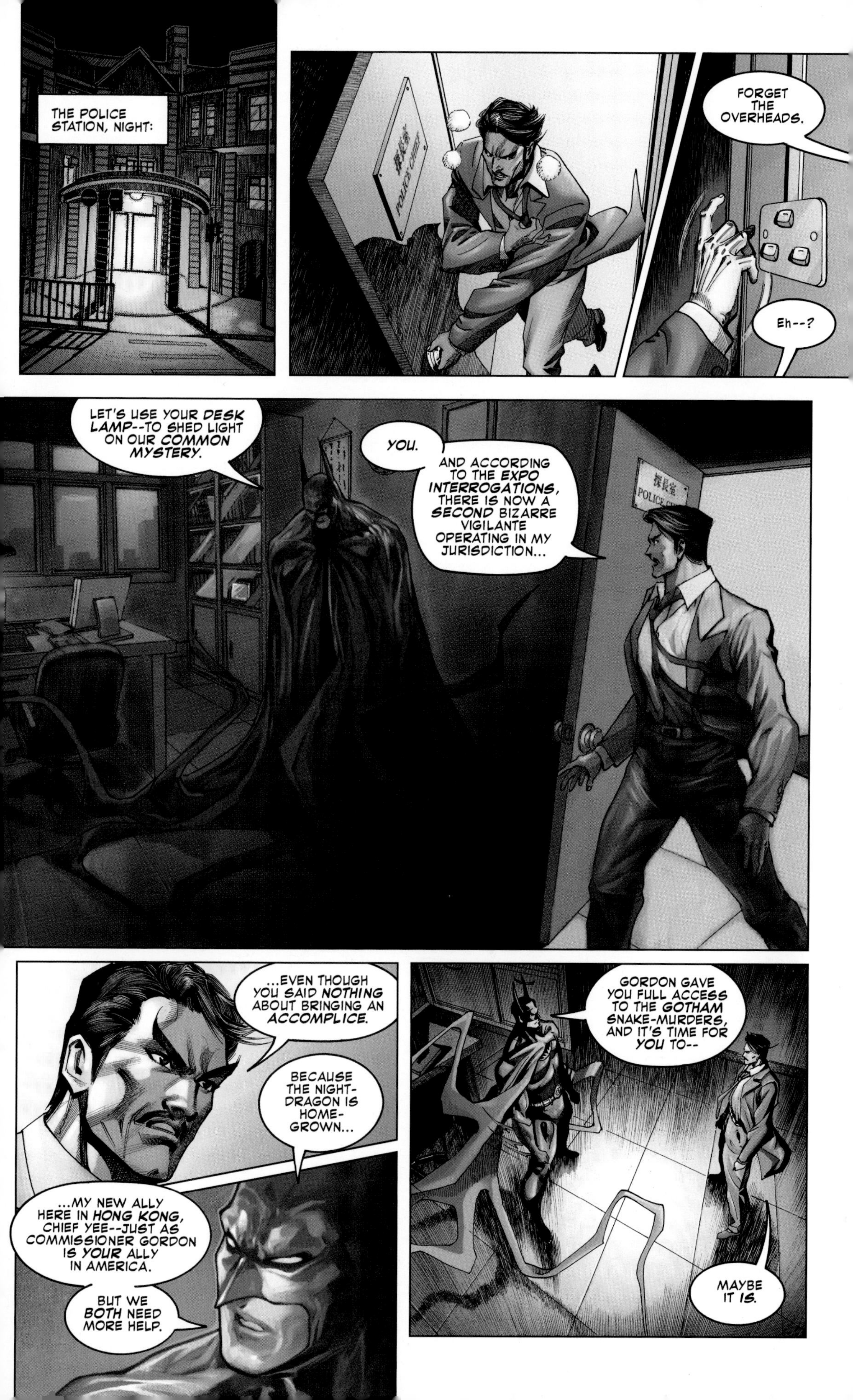
THE POLICE STATION, NIGHT:
探長室
POLICE CHIEF
FORGET THE OVERHEADS.
Eh--?
LET'S USE YOUR DESK LAMP--TO SHED LIGHT ON OUR COMMON MYSTERY.
YOU.
AND ACCORDING TO THE EXPO INTERROGATIONS, THERE IS NOW A SECOND BIZARRE VIGILANTE OPERATING IN MY JURISDICTION...
探長室
POLICE CH
...EVEN THOUGH YOU SAID NOTHING ABOUT BRINGING AN ACCOMPLICE.
BECAUSE THE NIGHT-DRAGON IS HOME-GROWN...
...MY NEW ALLY HERE IN HONG KONG, CHIEF YEE--JUST AS COMMISSIONER GORDON IS YOUR ALLY IN AMERICA.
BUT WE BOTH NEED MORE HELP.
GORDON GAVE YOU FULL ACCESS TO THE GOTHAM SNAKE-MURDERS, AND IT'S TIME FOR YOU TO--
MAYBE IT IS.

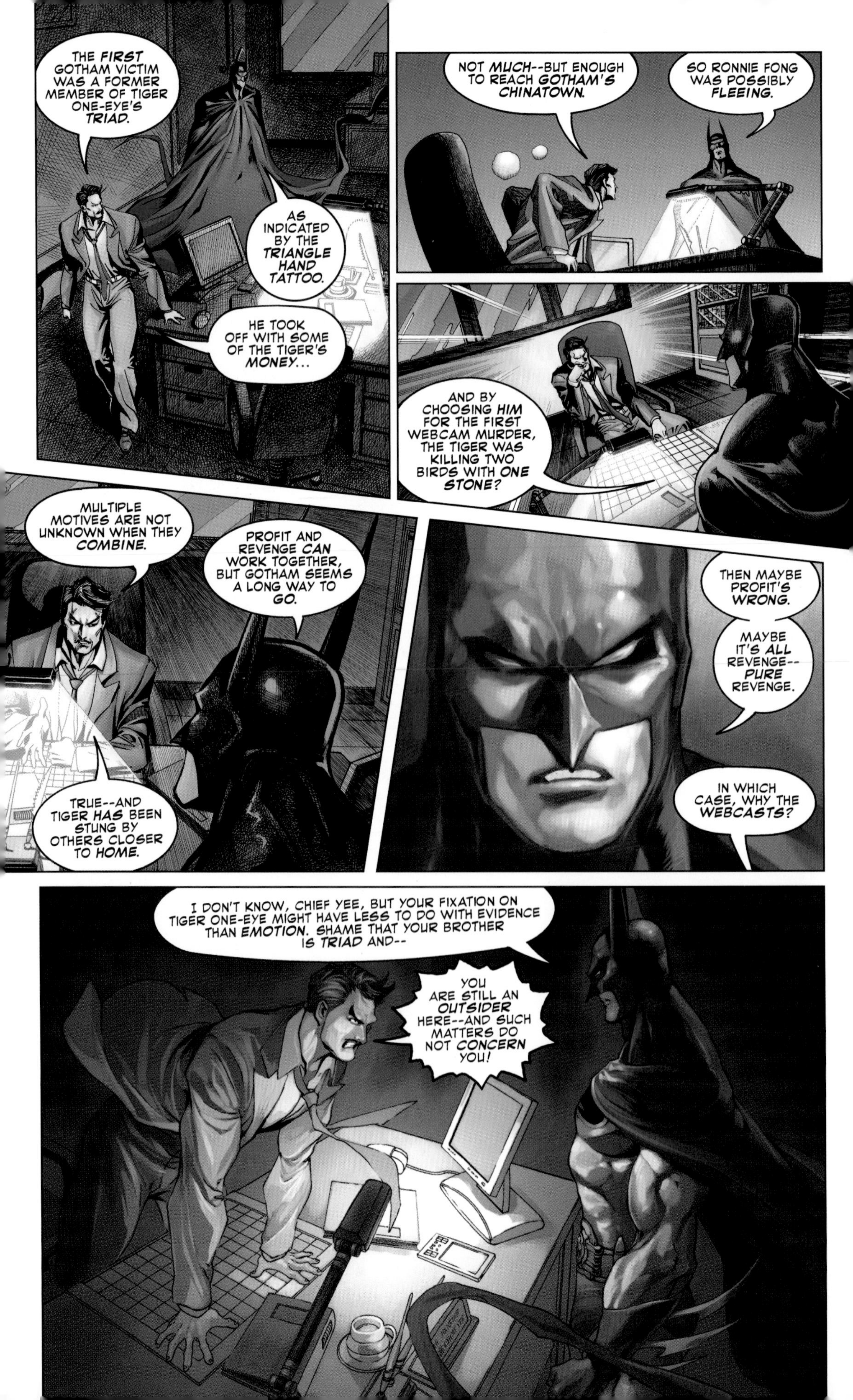
THE FIRST GOTHAM VICTIM WAS A FORMER MEMBER OF TIGER ONE-EYE'S TRIAD.
AS INDICATED BY THE TRIANGLE HAND TATTOO.
HE TOOK OFF WITH SOME OF THE TIGER'S MONEY...
NOT MUCH--BUT ENOUGH TO REACH GOTHAM'S CHINATOWN.
SO RONNIE FONG WAS POSSIBLY FLEEING.
AND BY CHOOSING HIM FOR THE FIRST WEBCAM MURDER, THE TIGER WAS KILLING TWO BIRDS WITH ONE STONE?
MULTIPLE MOTIVES ARE NOT UNKNOWN WHEN THEY COMBINE.
PROFIT AND REVENGE CAN WORK TOGETHER, BUT GOTHAM SEEMS A LONG WAY TO GO.
TRUE--AND TIGER HAS BEEN STUNG BY OTHERS CLOSER TO HOME.
THEN MAYBE PROFIT'S WRONG.
MAYBE IT'S ALL REVENGE--PURE REVENGE.
IN WHICH CASE, WHY THE WEBCASTS?
I DON'T KNOW, CHIEF YEE, BUT YOUR FIXATION ON TIGER ONE-EYE MIGHT HAVE LESS TO DO WITH EVIDENCE THAN EMOTION. SHAME THAT YOUR BROTHER IS TRIAD AND--
YOU ARE STILL AN OUTSIDER HERE--AND SUCH MATTERS DO NOT CONCERN YOU!

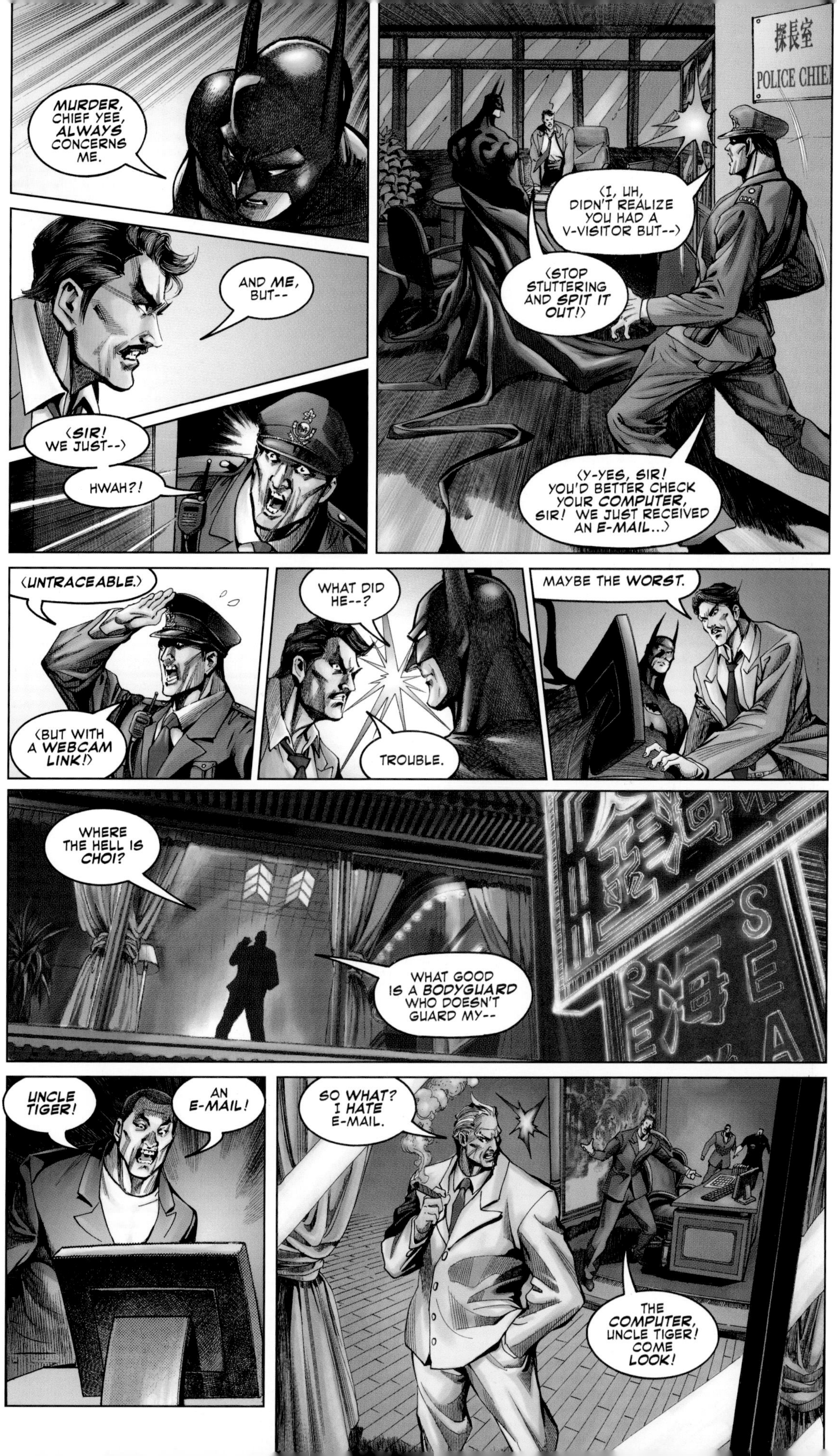
MURDER, CHIEF YEE, ALWAYS CONCERNS ME.
AND ME, BUT--
‹SIR! WE JUST--›
HWAH?!
探長室
‹I, UH, DIDN'T REALIZE YOU HAD A V-VISITOR BUT--›
‹STOP STUTTERING AND SPIT IT OUT!›
‹Y-YES, SIR! YOU'D BETTER CHECK YOUR COMPUTER, SIR! WE JUST RECEIVED AN E-MAIL...›
‹UNTRACEABLE.›
‹BUT WITH A WEBCAM LINK!›
WHAT DID HE--?
TROUBLE.
MAYBE THE WORST.
WHERE THE HELL IS CHOI?
WHAT GOOD IS A BODYGUARD WHO DOESN'T GUARD MY--
UNCLE TIGER!
AN E-MAIL!
SO WHAT? I HATE E-MAIL.
THE COMPUTER, UNCLE TIGER! COME LOOK!

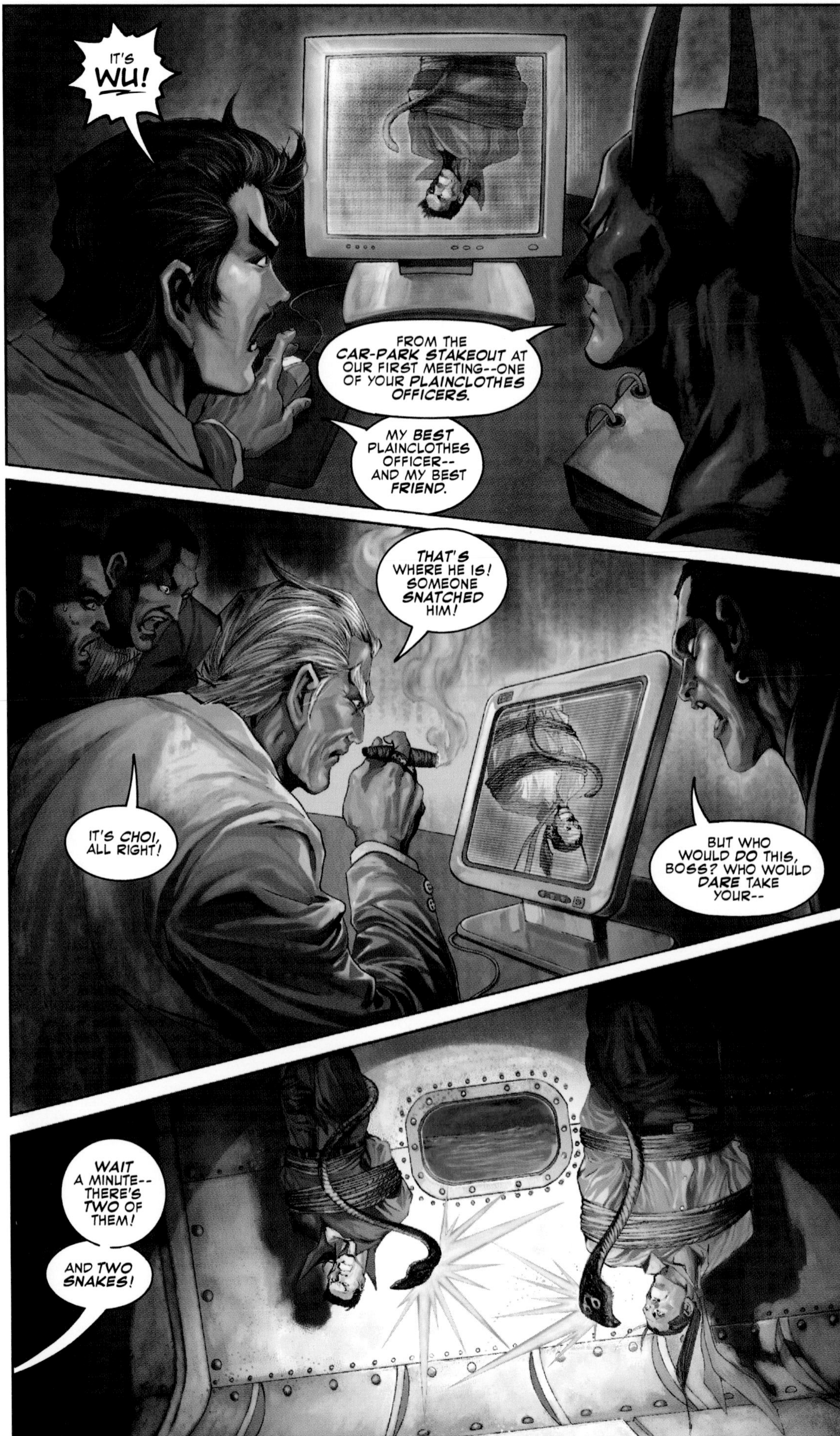
IT'S WU!
FROM THE CAR-PARK STAKEOUT AT OUR FIRST MEETING--ONE OF YOUR PLAINCLOTHES OFFICERS.
MY BEST PLAINCLOTHES OFFICER-- AND MY BEST FRIEND.
THAT'S WHERE HE IS! SOMEONE SNATCHED HIM!
IT'S CHOI, ALL RIGHT!
BUT WHO WOULD DO THIS, BOSS? WHO WOULD DARE TAKE YOUR--
WAIT A MINUTE-- THERE'S TWO OF THEM!
AND TWO SNAKES!

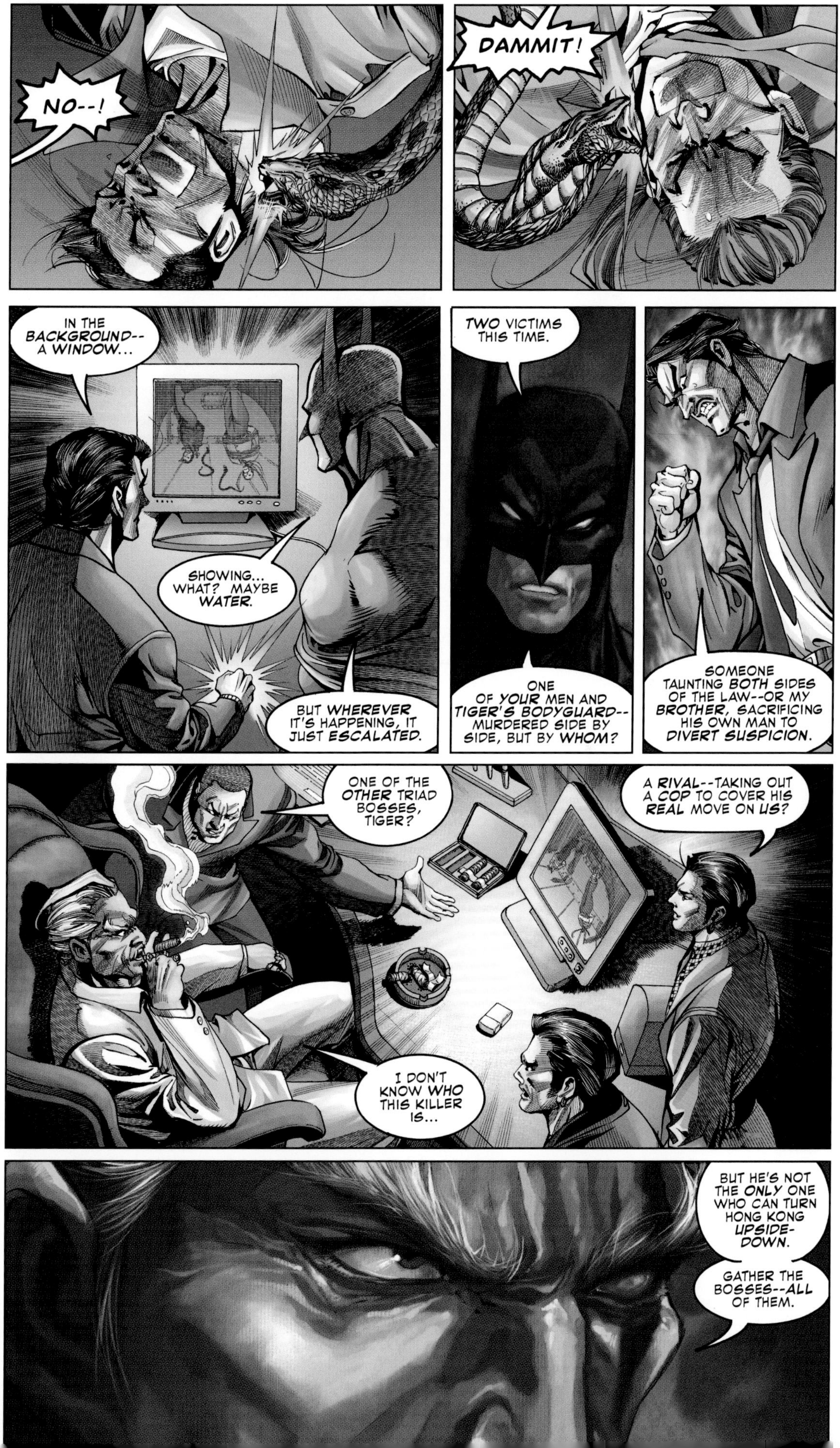

NO--!
DAMMIT!
IN THE BACKGROUND-- A WINDOW...
SHOWING... WHAT? MAYBE WATER.
BUT WHEREVER IT'S HAPPENING, IT JUST ESCALATED.
TWO VICTIMS THIS TIME.
ONE OF YOUR MEN AND TIGER'S BODYGUARD-- MURDERED SIDE BY SIDE, BUT BY WHOM?
SOMEONE TAUNTING BOTH SIDES OF THE LAW--OR MY BROTHER, SACRIFICING HIS OWN MAN TO DIVERT SUSPICION.
ONE OF THE OTHER TRIAD BOSSES, TIGER?
A RIVAL--TAKING OUT A COP TO COVER HIS REAL MOVE ON US?
I DON'T KNOW WHO THIS KILLER IS...
BUT HE'S NOT THE ONLY ONE WHO CAN TURN HONG KONG UPSIDE-DOWN.
GATHER THE BOSSES--ALL OF THEM.

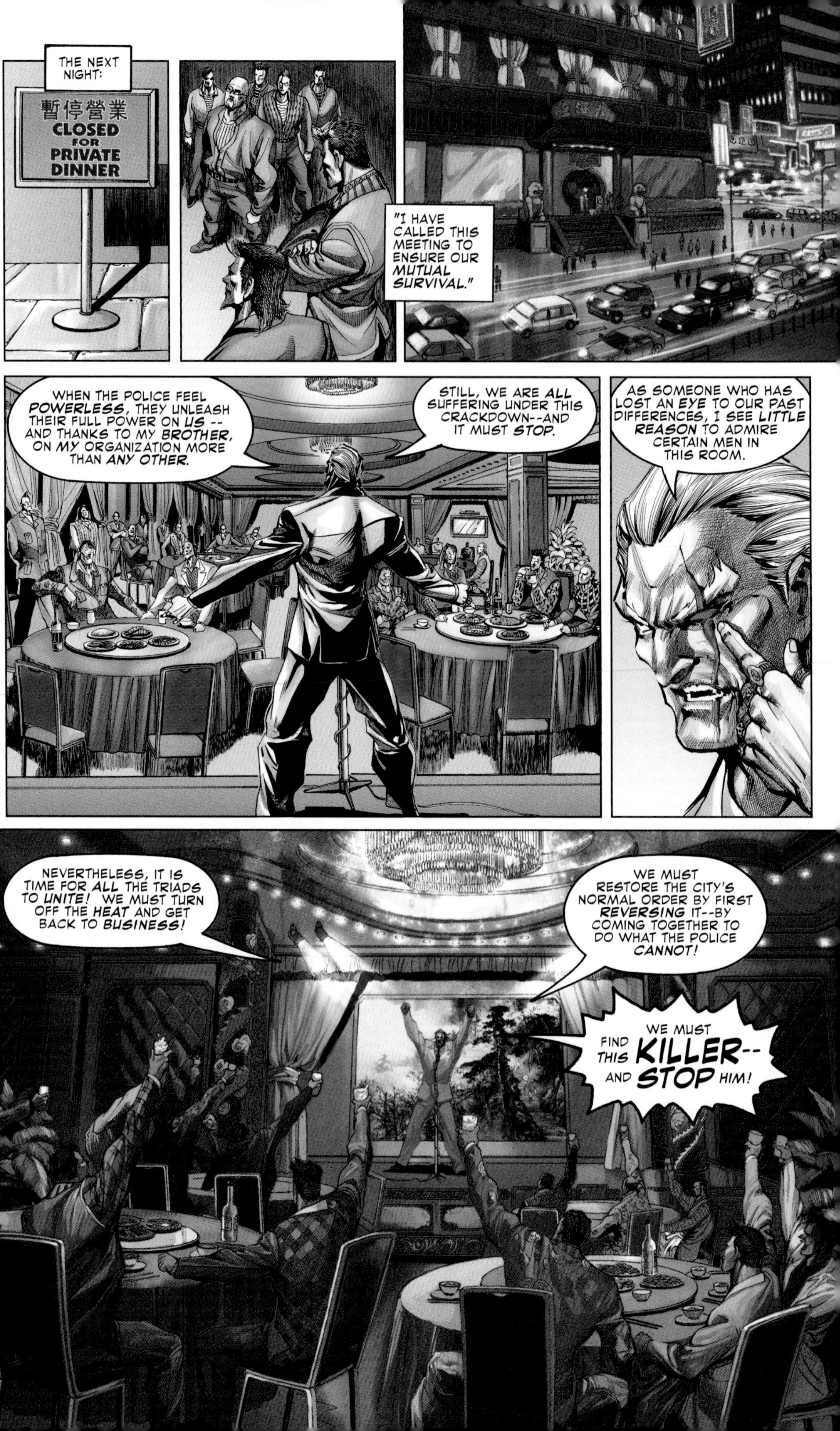
THE NEXT NIGHT:
暫停營業
CLOSED FOR PRIVATE DINNER
"I HAVE CALLED THIS MEETING TO ENSURE OUR MUTUAL SURVIVAL."
WHEN THE POLICE FEEL POWERLESS, THEY UNLEASH THEIR FULL POWER ON US -- AND THANKS TO MY BROTHER, ON MY ORGANIZATION MORE THAN ANY OTHER.
STILL, WE ARE ALL SUFFERING UNDER THIS CRACKDOWN--AND IT MUST STOP.
AS SOMEONE WHO HAS LOST AN EYE TO OUR PAST DIFFERENCES, I SEE LITTLE REASON TO ADMIRE CERTAIN MEN IN THIS ROOM.
NEVERTHELESS, IT IS TIME FOR ALL THE TRIADS TO UNITE! WE MUST TURN OFF THE HEAT AND GET BACK TO BUSINESS!
WE MUST RESTORE THE CITY'S NORMAL ORDER BY FIRST REVERSING IT--BY COMING TOGETHER TO DO WHAT THE POLICE CANNOT!
WE MUST FIND THIS KILLER-- AND STOP HIM!

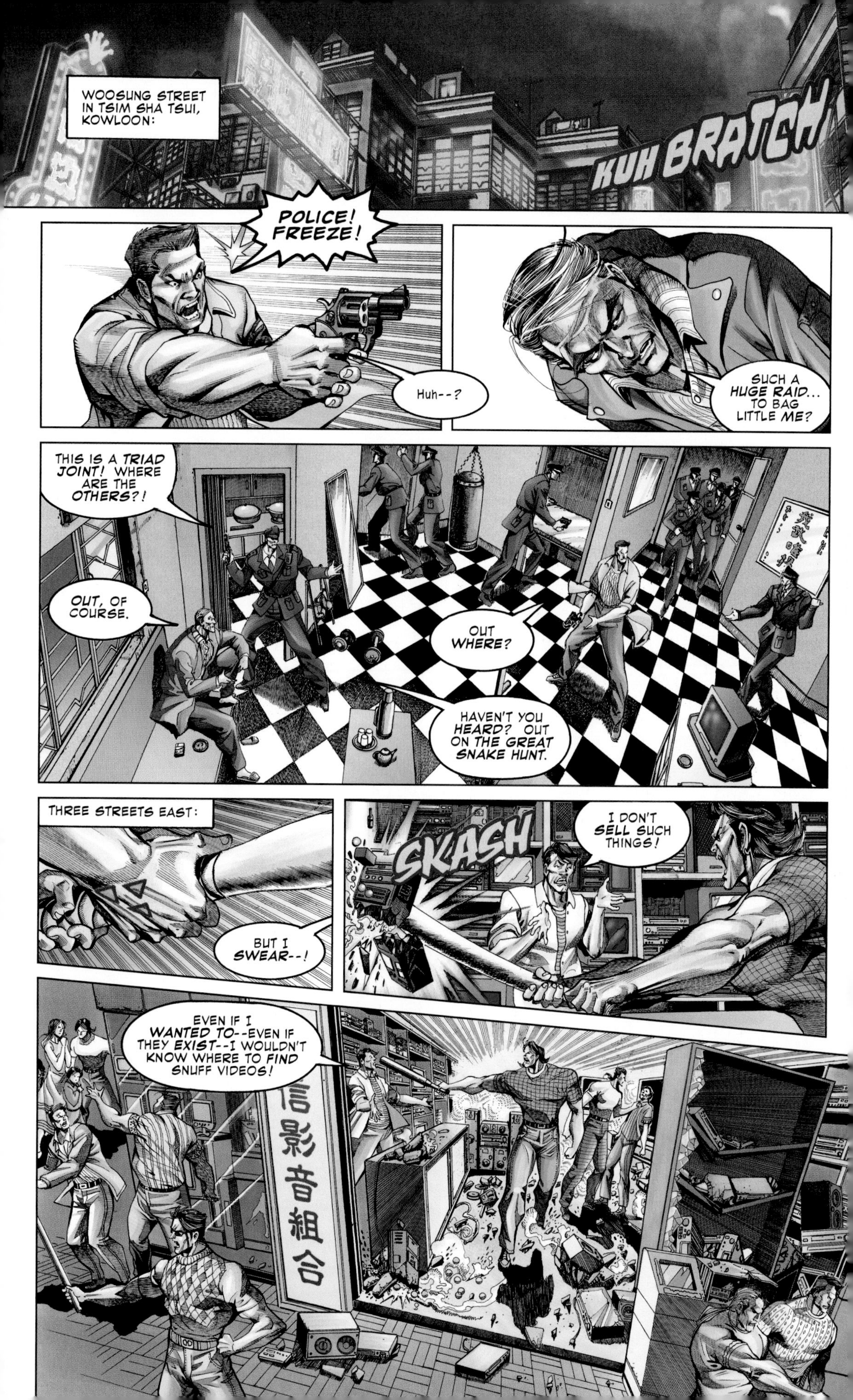
WOOSUNG STREET IN TSIM SHA TSUI, KOWLOON:
KUH BRATCH
POLICE! FREEZE!
Huh--?
SUCH A HUGE RAID... TO BAG LITTLE ME?
THIS IS A TRIAD JOINT! WHERE ARE THE OTHERS?!
OUT, OF COURSE.
OUT WHERE?
HAVEN'T YOU HEARD? OUT ON THE GREAT SNAKE HUNT.
THREE STREETS EAST:
BUT I SWEAR--!
SKASH
I DON'T SELL SUCH THINGS!
EVEN IF I WANTED TO--EVEN IF THEY EXIST--I WOULDN'T KNOW WHERE TO FIND SNUFF VIDEOS!
信影音組合

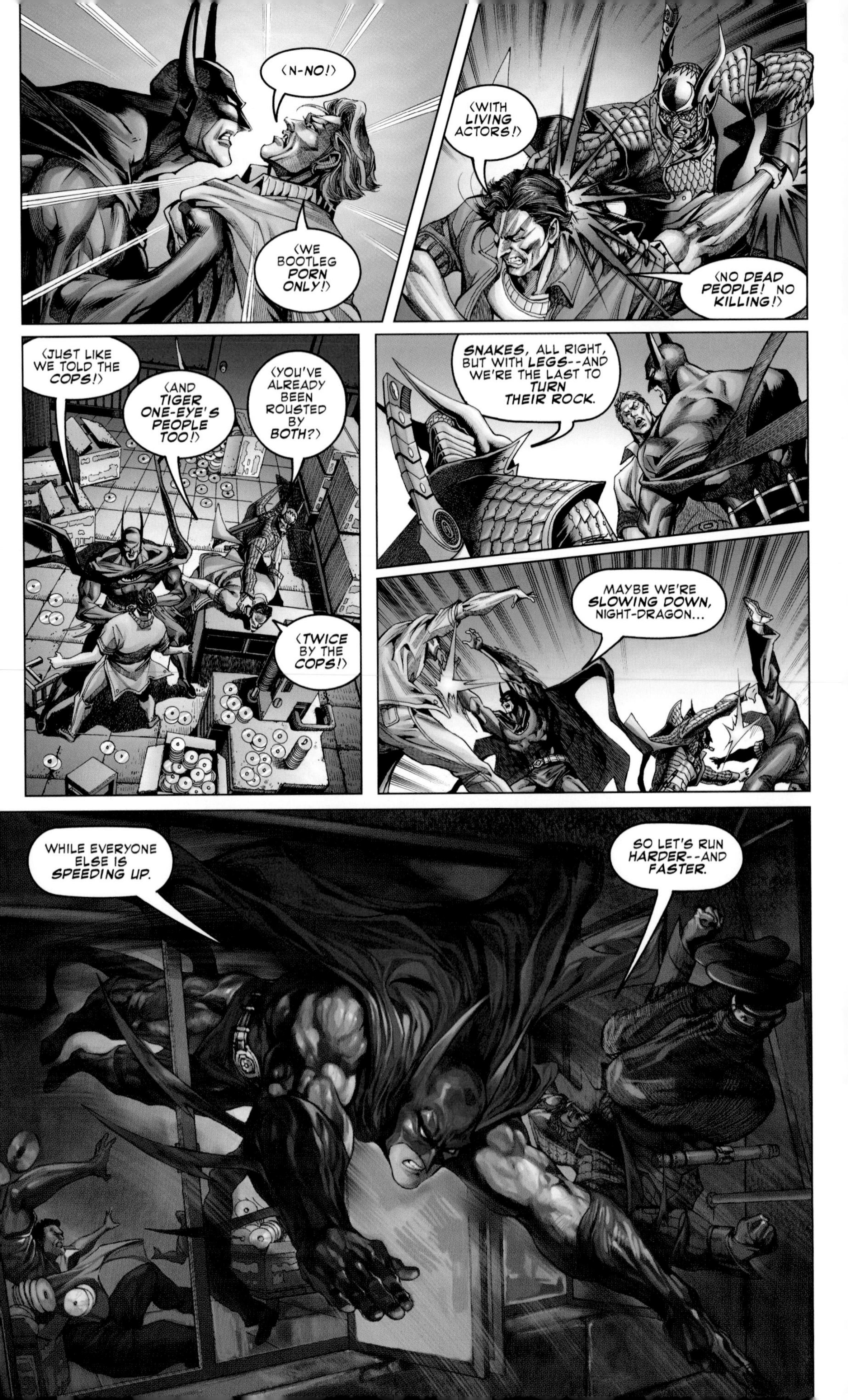
〈N-NO!〉
〈WE BOOTLEG PORN ONLY!〉
〈WITH LIVING ACTORS!〉
〈NO DEAD PEOPLE! NO KILLING!〉
〈JUST LIKE WE TOLD THE COPS!〉
〈AND TIGER ONE-EYE'S PEOPLE TOO!〉
〈YOU'VE ALREADY BEEN ROUSTED BY BOTH?〉
〈TWICE BY THE COPS!〉
SNAKES, ALL RIGHT, BUT WITH LEGS--AND WE'RE THE LAST TO TURN THEIR ROCK.
MAYBE WE'RE SLOWING DOWN, NIGHT-DRAGON...
WHILE EVERYONE ELSE IS SPEEDING UP.
SO LET'S RUN HARDER--AND FASTER.

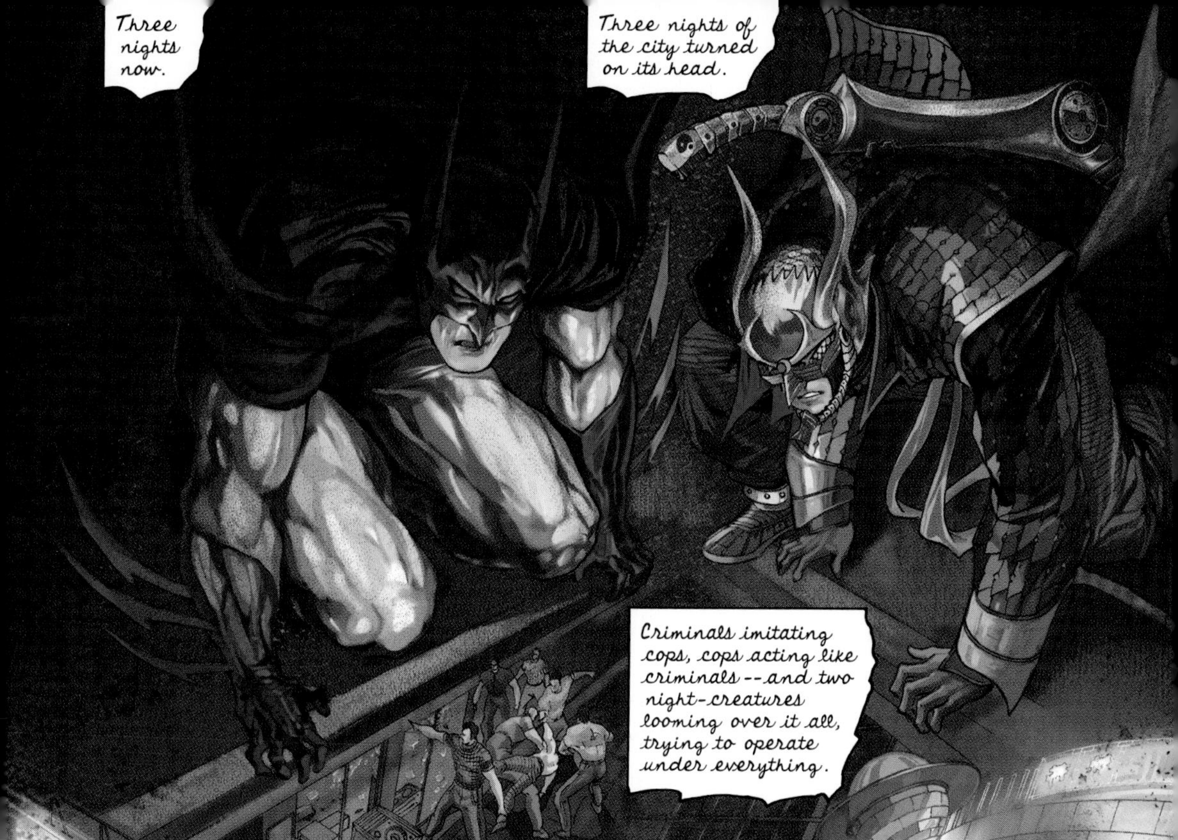
Three nights now.
Three nights of the city turned on its head.
Criminals imitating cops, cops acting like criminals --and two night-creatures looming over it all, trying to operate under everything.
Even with a local at my side, Hong Kong remains a mystery-- haunted by an elusive ghost always one step ahead.

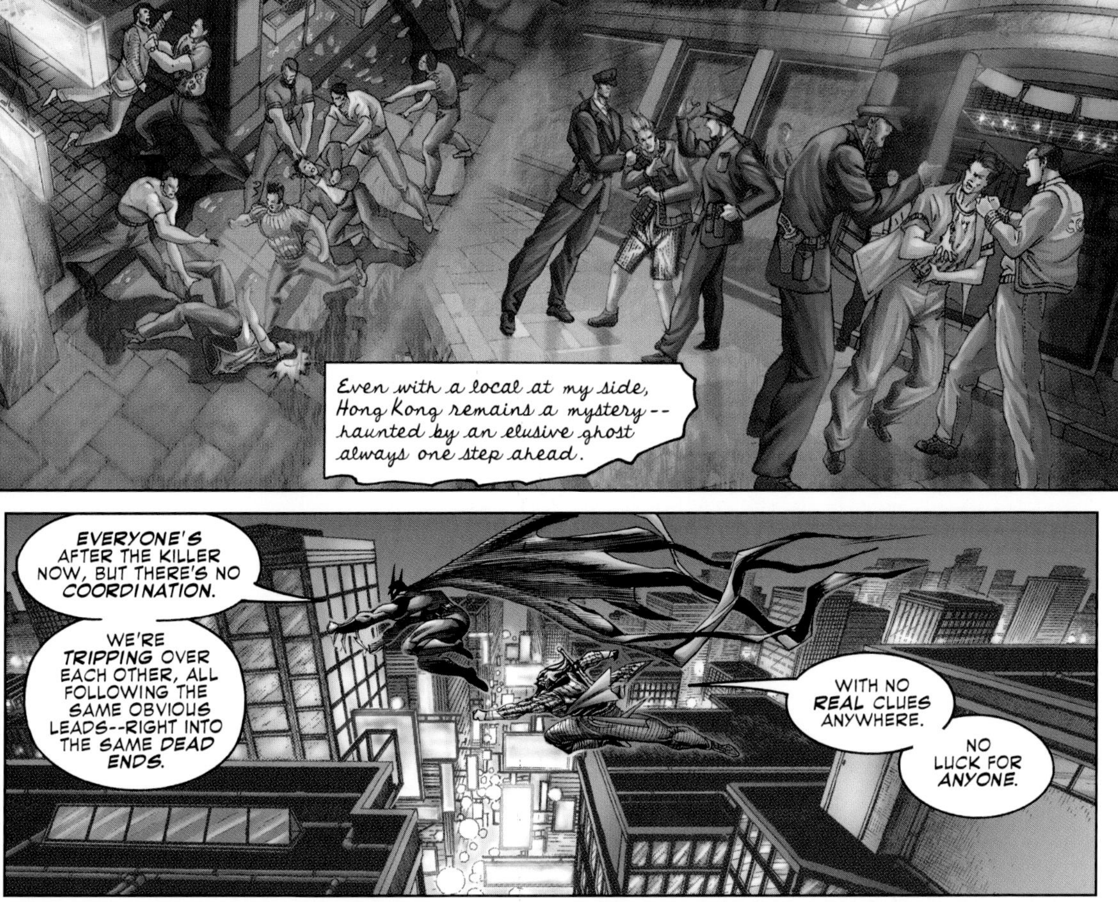
EVERYONE'S AFTER THE KILLER NOW, BUT THERE'S NO COORDINATION.
WE'RE TRIPPING OVER EACH OTHER, ALL FOLLOWING THE SAME OBVIOUS LEADS--RIGHT INTO THE SAME DEAD ENDS.
WITH NO REAL CLUES ANYWHERE.
NO LUCK FOR ANYONE.

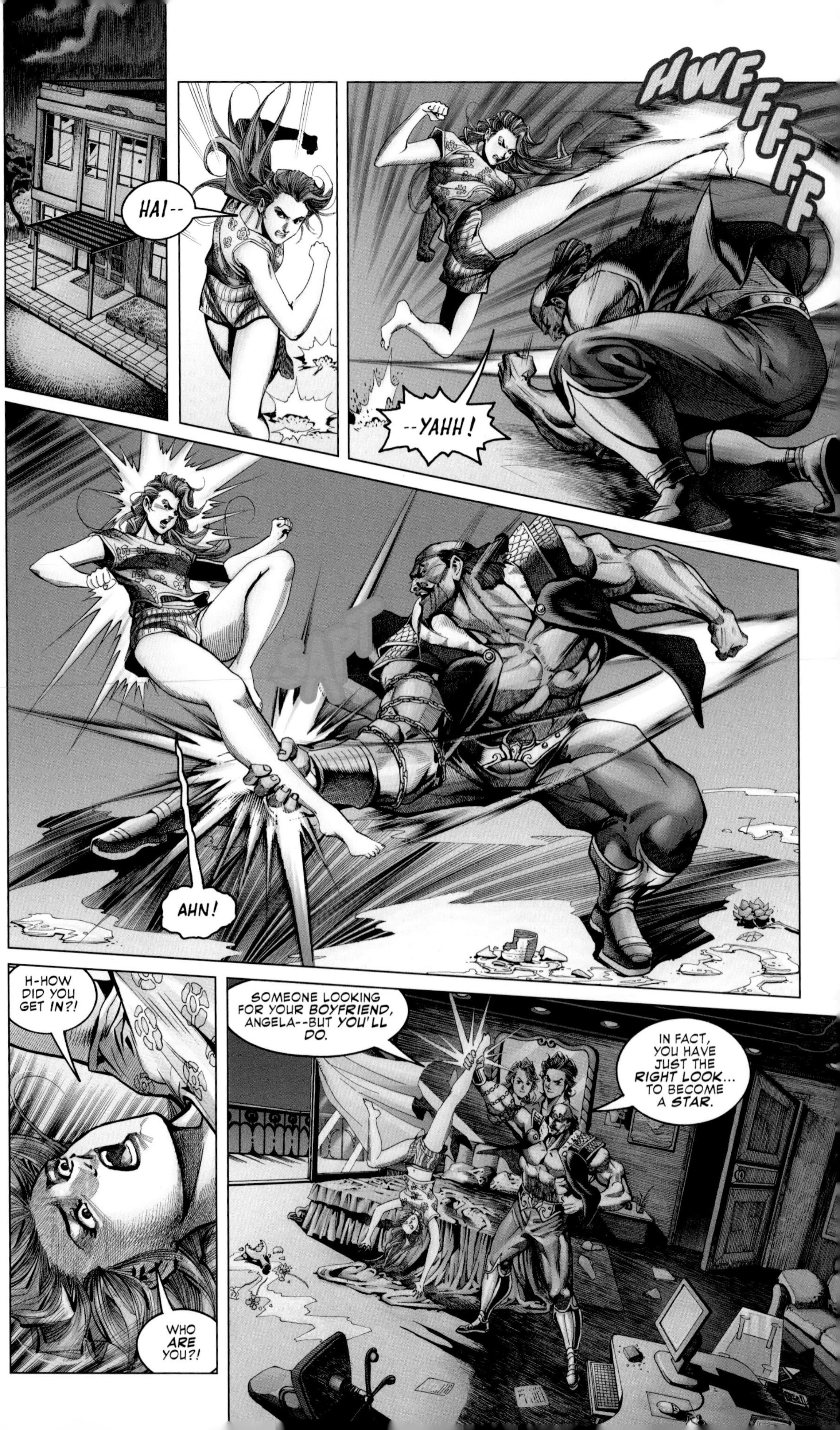

HAI--
HWFFFFF
--YAHH!
SAPT
AHN!
H-HOW DID YOU GET IN?!
WHO ARE YOU?!
SOMEONE LOOKING FOR YOUR BOYFRIEND, ANGELA--BUT YOU'LL DO.
IN FACT, YOU HAVE JUST THE RIGHT LOOK... TO BECOME A STAR.

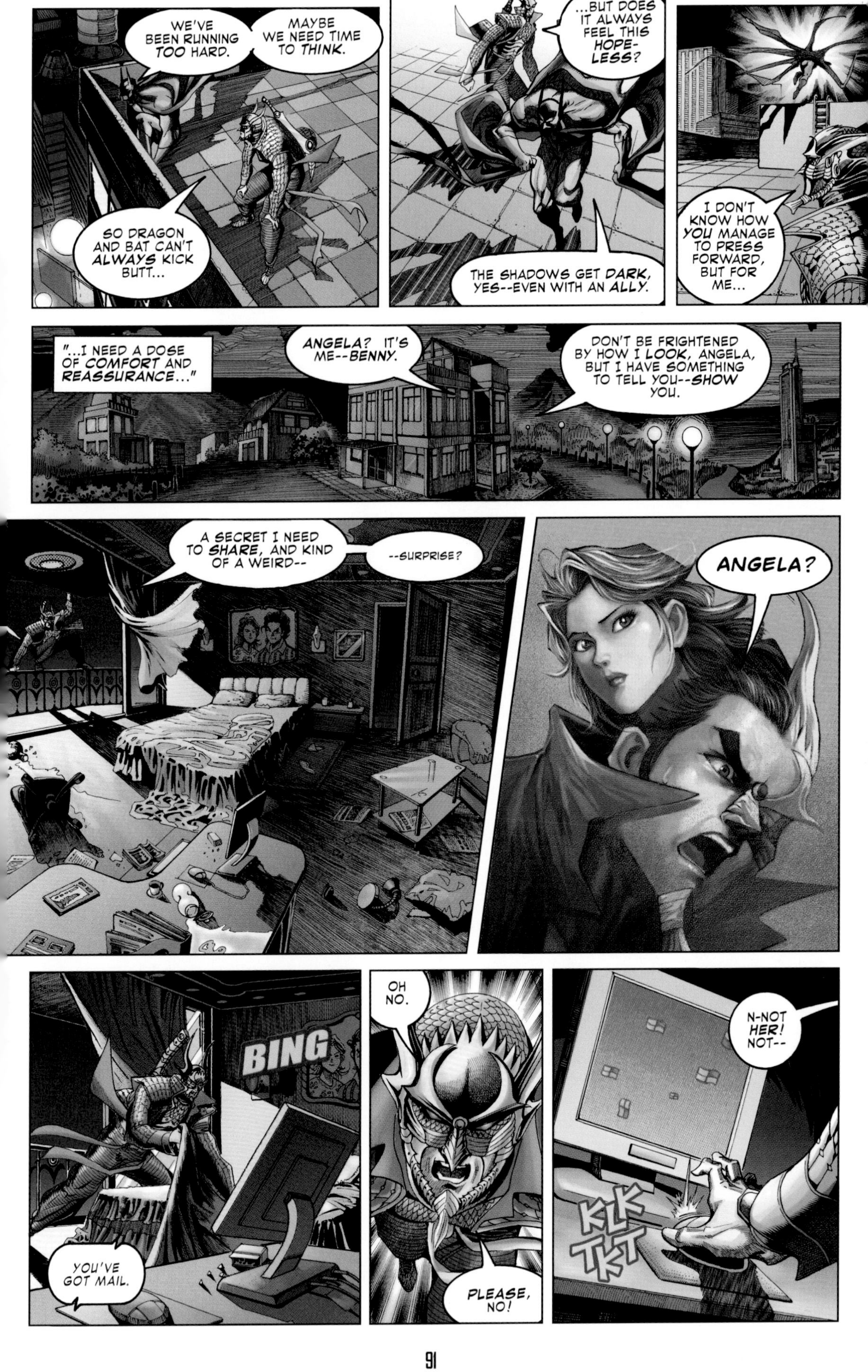

WE'VE BEEN RUNNING TOO HARD.
MAYBE WE NEED TIME TO THINK.
SO DRAGON AND BAT CAN'T ALWAYS KICK BUTT...
...BUT DOES IT ALWAYS FEEL THIS HOPE-LESS?
THE SHADOWS GET DARK, YES--EVEN WITH AN ALLY.
I DON'T KNOW HOW YOU MANAGE TO PRESS FORWARD, BUT FOR ME...
"...I NEED A DOSE OF COMFORT AND REASSURANCE..."
ANGELA? IT'S ME--BENNY.
DON'T BE FRIGHTENED BY HOW I LOOK, ANGELA, BUT I HAVE SOMETHING TO TELL YOU--SHOW YOU.
A SECRET I NEED TO SHARE, AND KIND OF A WEIRD--
--SURPRISE?
ANGELA?
BING
YOU'VE GOT MAIL.
OH NO.
PLEASE, NO!
N-NOT HER! NOT--
KLK TKT

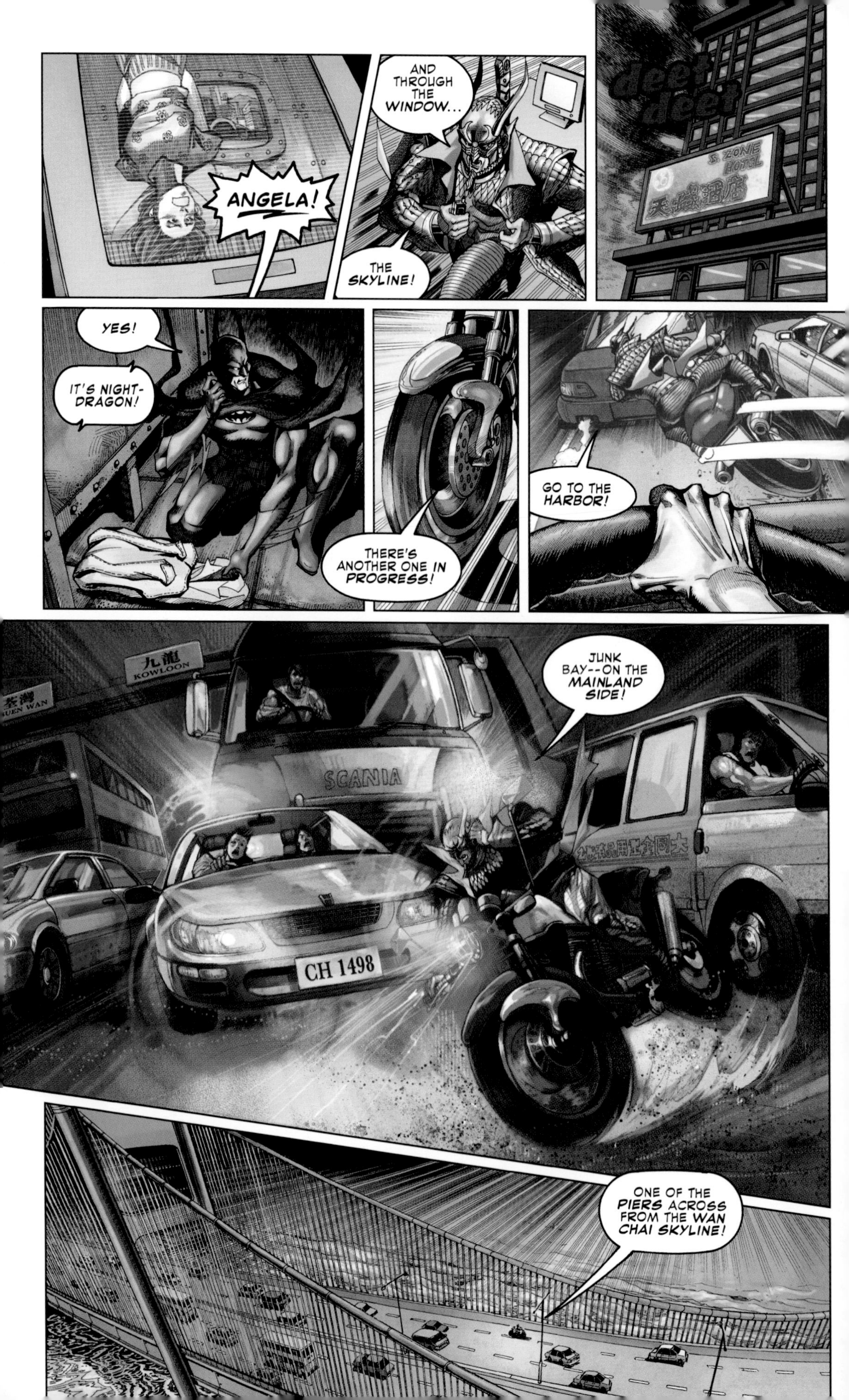
ANGELA!
AND THROUGH THE WINDOW...
THE SKYLINE!
deet deet
S. ZONE HOTEL
YES!
IT'S NIGHT-DRAGON!
THERE'S ANOTHER ONE IN PROGRESS!
GO TO THE HARBOR!
九龍
KOWLOON
JUNK BAY--ON THE MAINLAND SIDE!
SCANIA
CH 1498
ONE OF THE PIERS ACROSS FROM THE WAN CHAI SKYLINE!

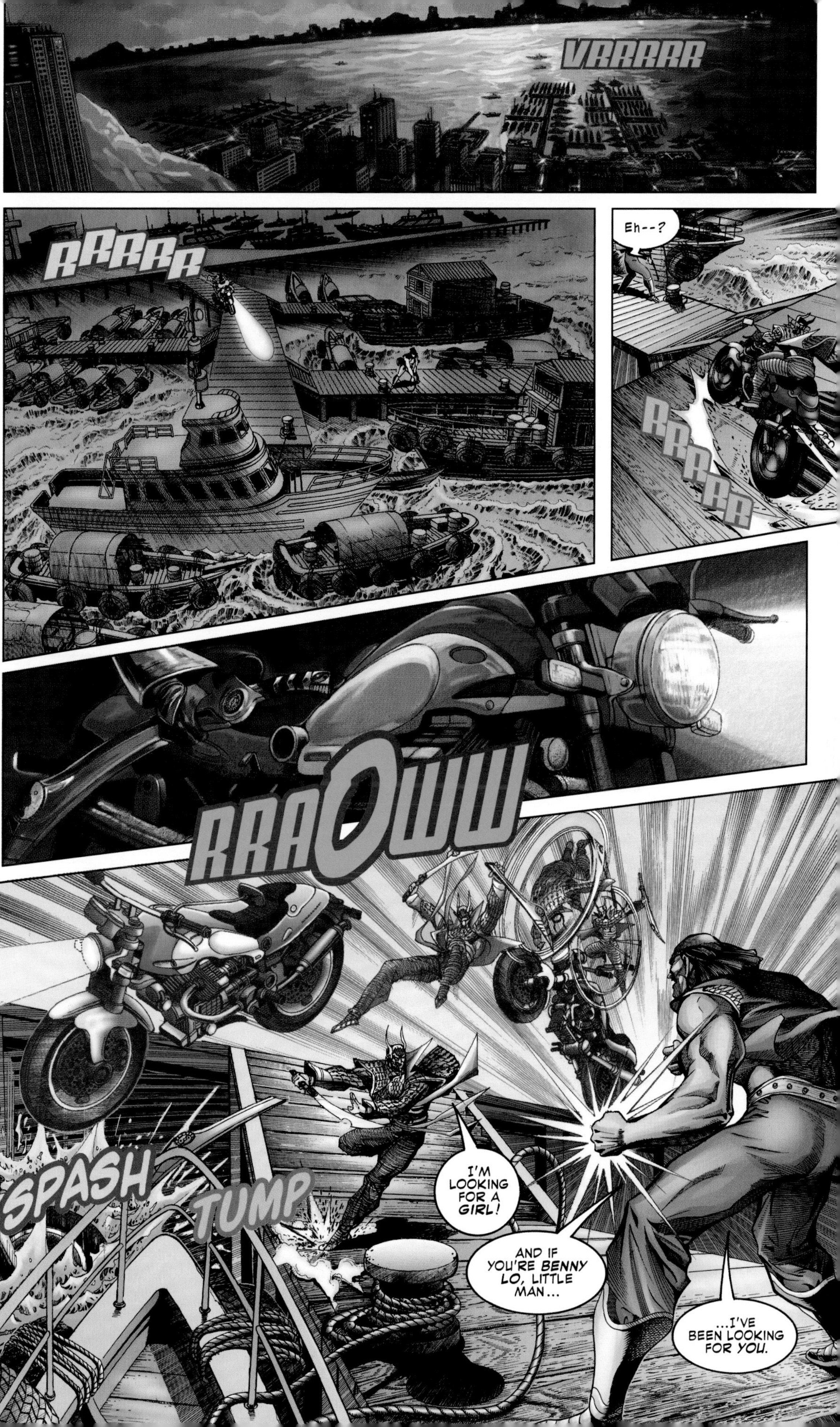
VRRRRR
RRRRR
Eh--?
RRRRR
RRAOWW
SPASH
TUMP
I'M LOOKING FOR A GIRL!
AND IF YOU'RE BENNY LO, LITTLE MAN...
...I'VE BEEN LOOKING FOR YOU.

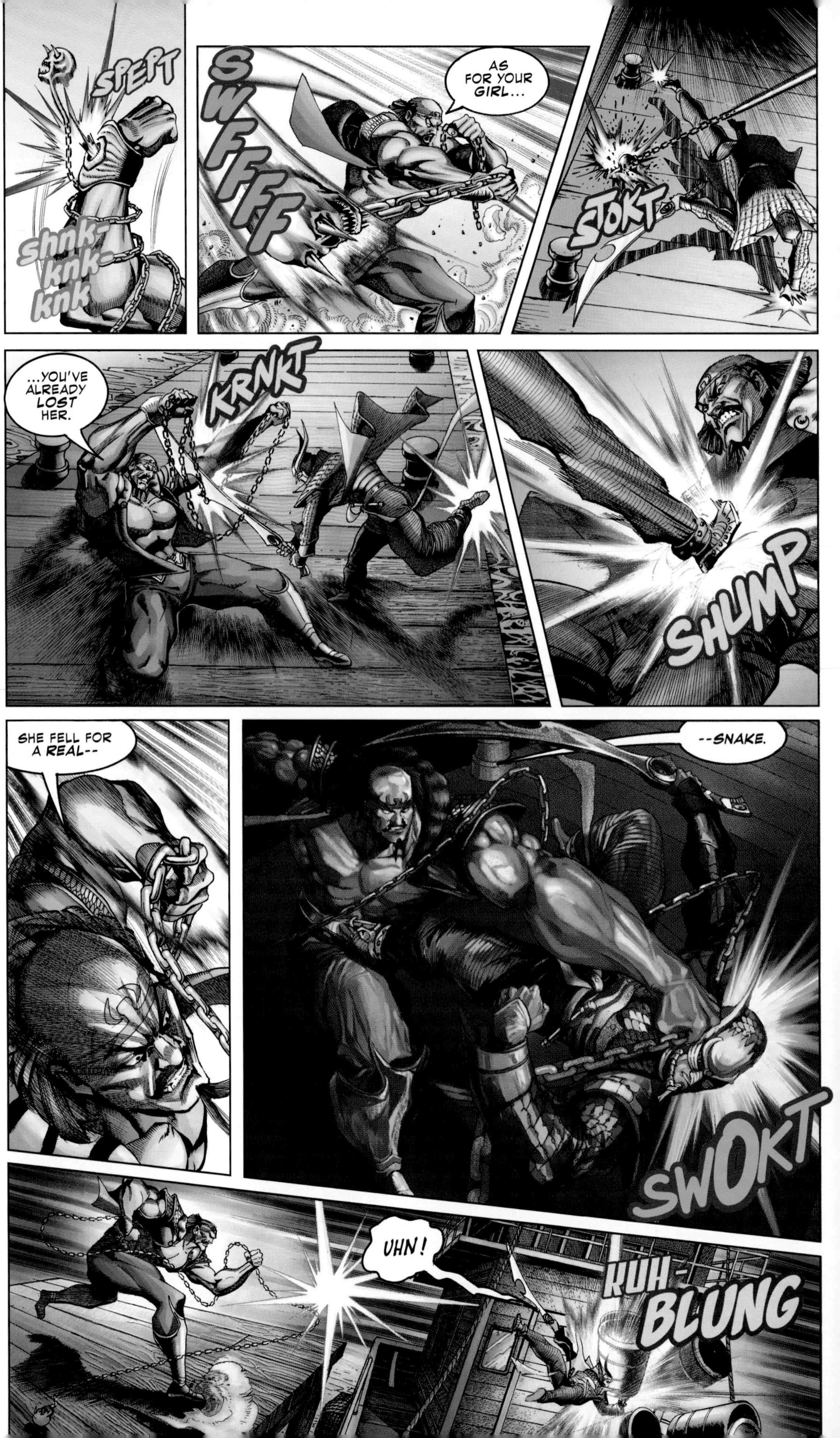
SPEPT
shnk-
knk-
knk
SWFFFF
AS FOR YOUR GIRL...
STOKT
...YOU'VE ALREADY LOST HER.
KRNKT
SHUMP
SHE FELL FOR A REAL--
--SNAKE.
SWOKT
UHN!
KUH-
BLUNG

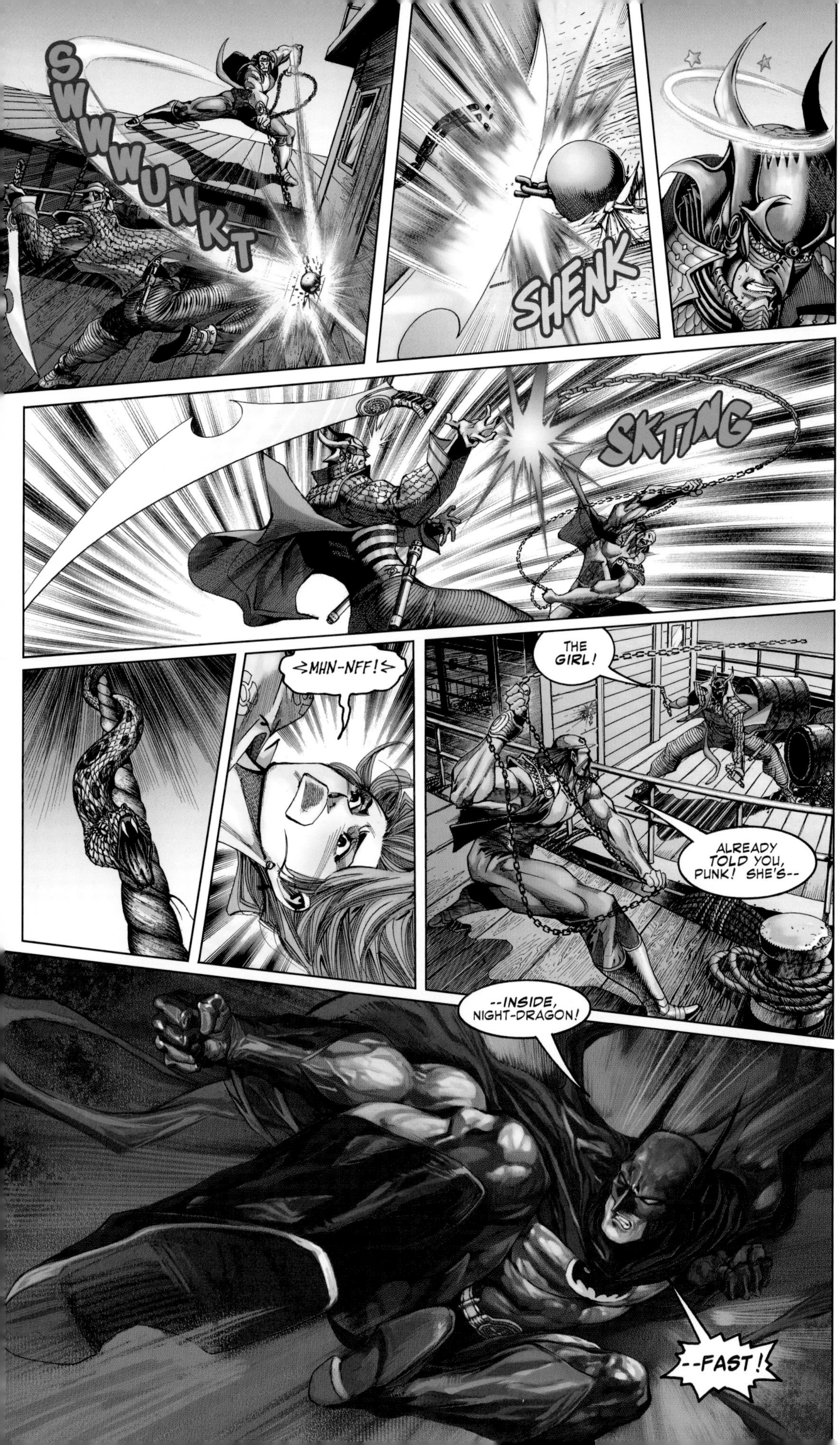
SWWWUNKT
SHENK
SKTING
≷MHN-NFF!≶
THE GIRL!
ALREADY TOLD YOU, PUNK! SHE'S--
--INSIDE, NIGHT-DRAGON!
--FAST!

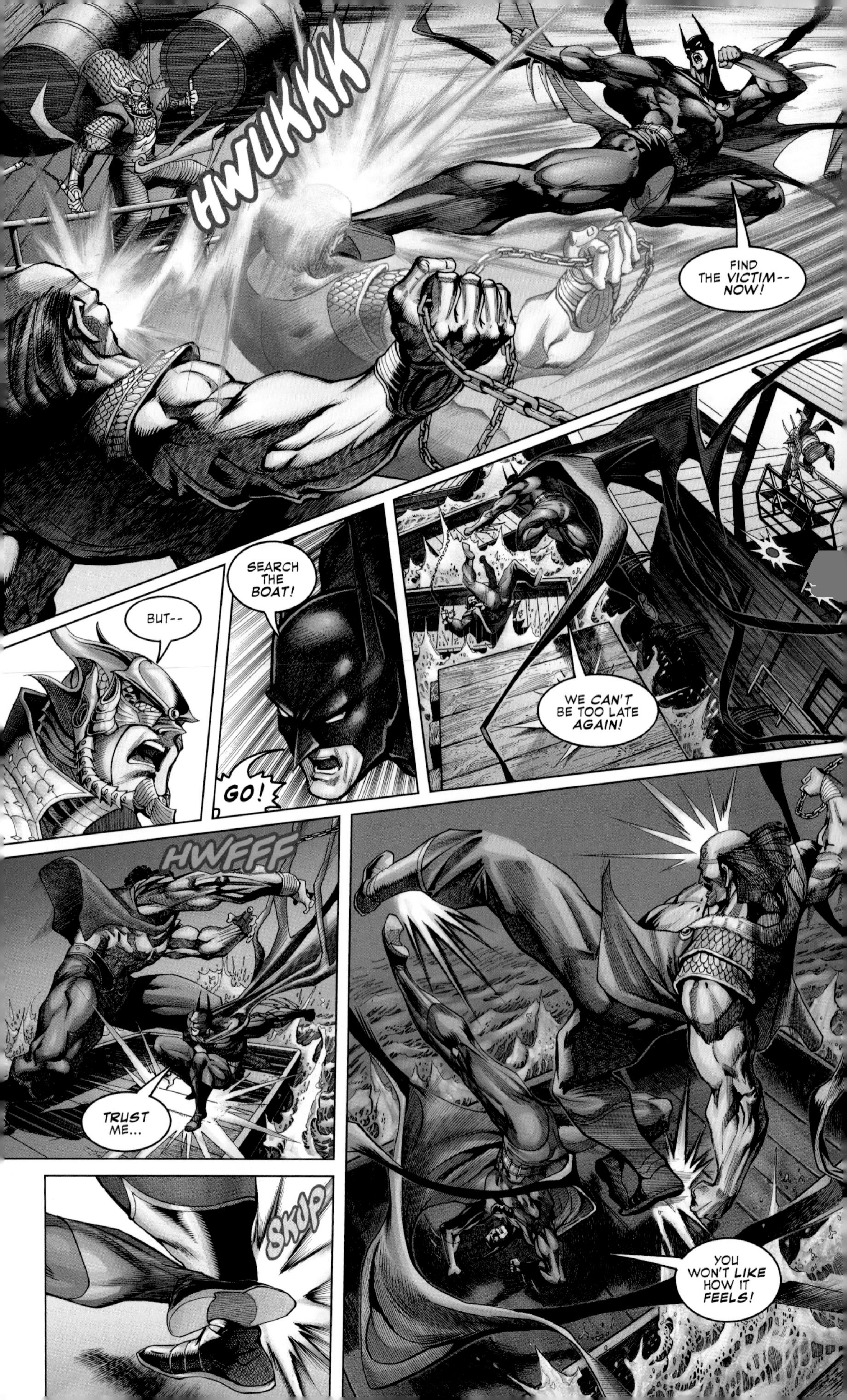
HWUKKK
FIND THE VICTIM-- NOW!
BUT--
SEARCH THE BOAT!
GO!
WE CAN'T BE TOO LATE AGAIN!
HWFFF
TRUST ME...
SKUP
YOU WON'T LIKE HOW IT FEELS!

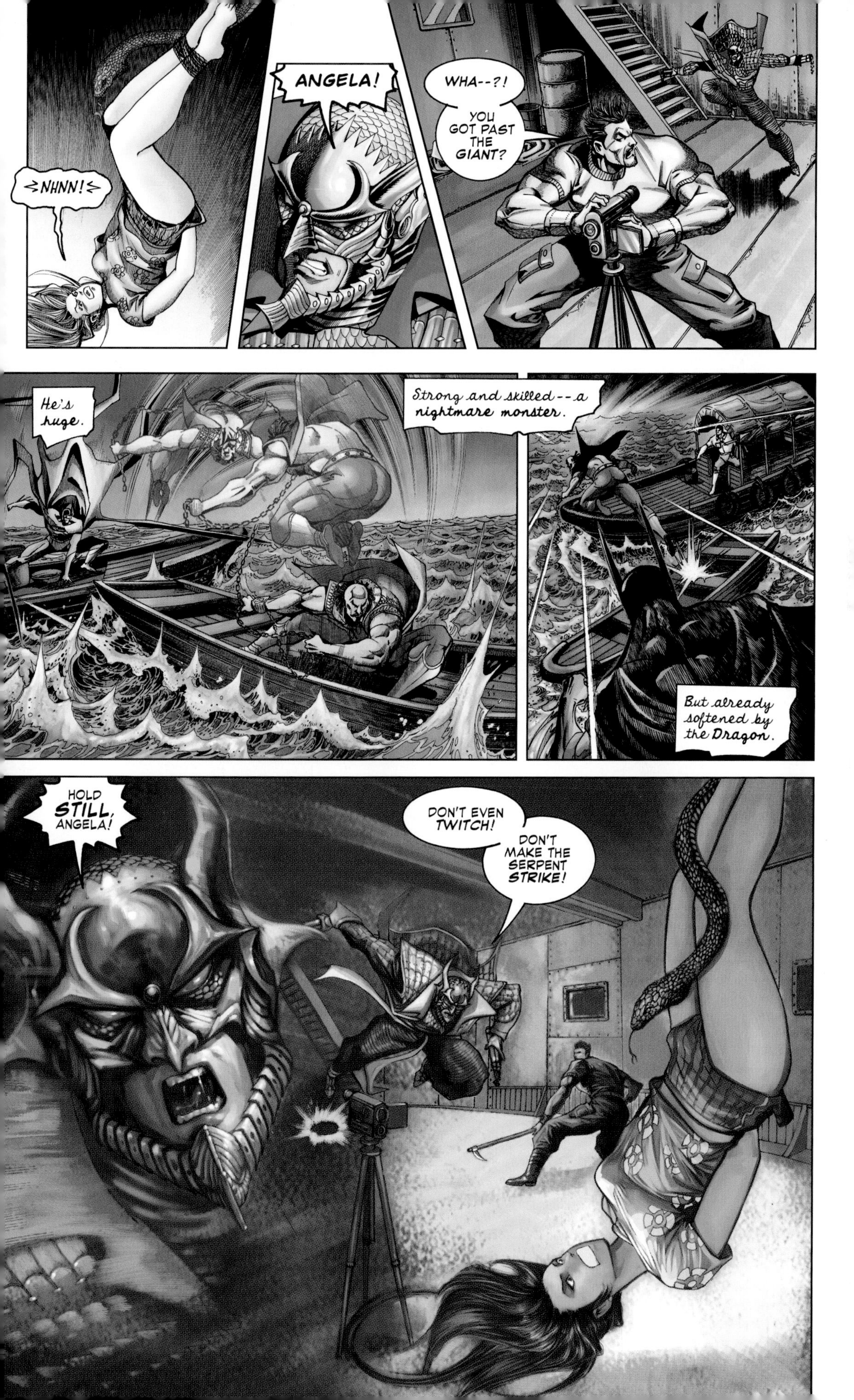

NHNN!
ANGELA!
WHA--?!
YOU GOT PAST THE GIANT?
He's huge.
Strong and skilled--a nightmare monster.
But already softened by the Dragon.
HOLD STILL, ANGELA!
DON'T EVEN TWITCH!
DON'T MAKE THE SERPENT STRIKE!

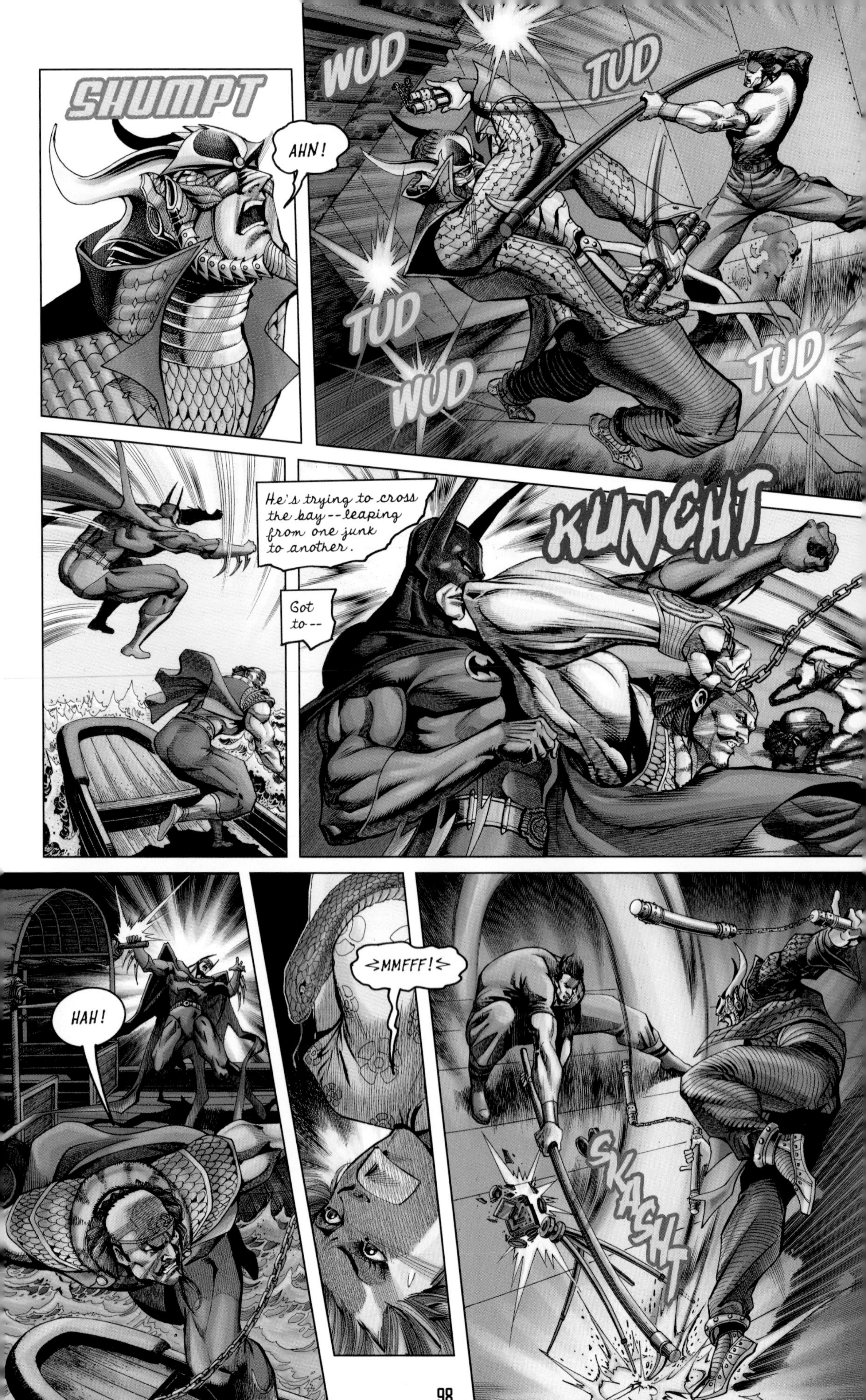
SHUMPT
AHN!
WUD
TUD
TUD
WUD
TUD
He's trying to cross the bay--leaping from one junk to another.
Got to--
KUNCHT
HAH!
<MMFFF!>
SKACHT

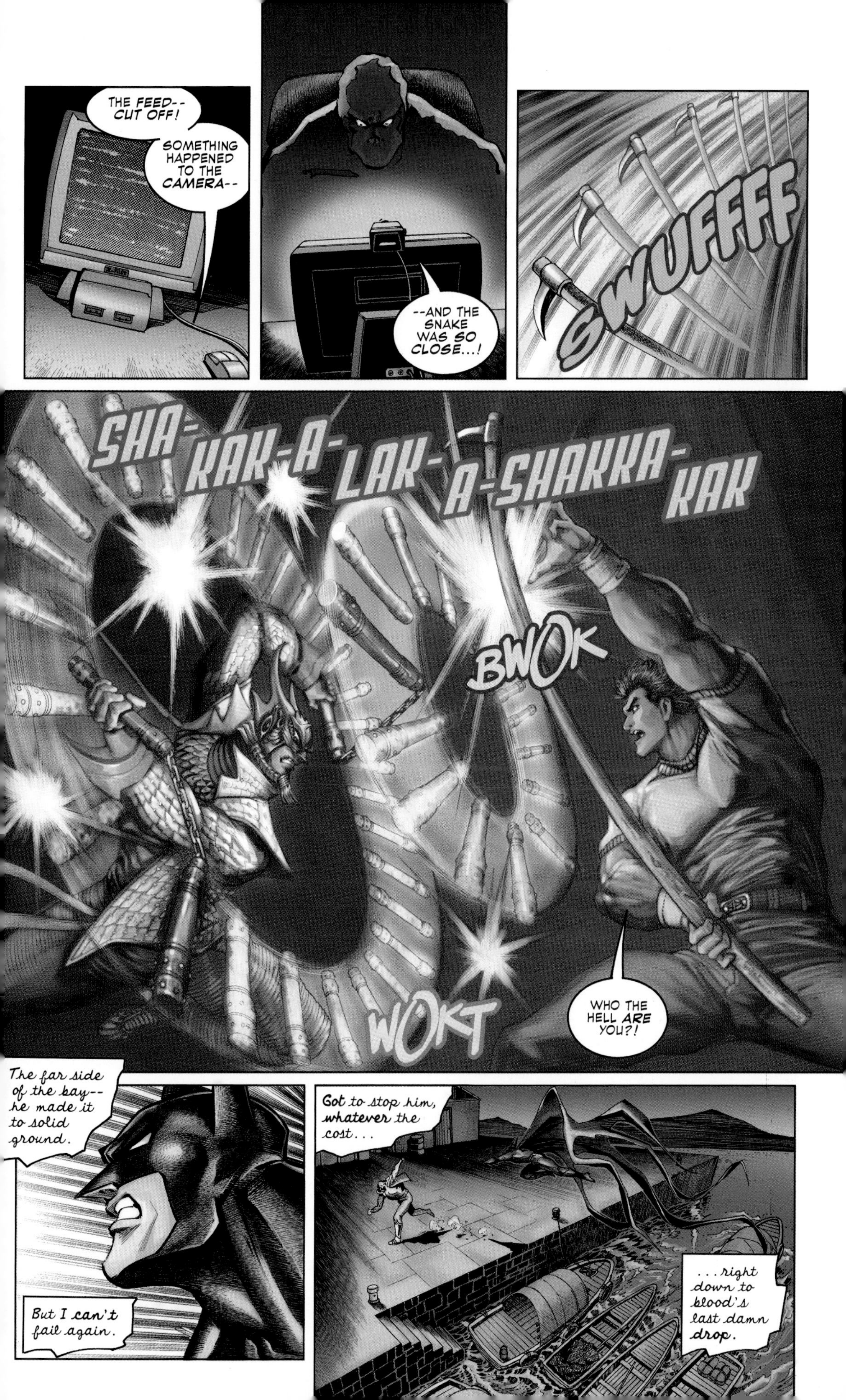
THE FEED--
CUT OFF!
SOMETHING HAPPENED TO THE CAMERA--
--AND THE SNAKE WAS SO CLOSE...!
SWUFFFF
SHA-KAK-A-LAK-A-SHAKKA-KAK
BWOK
WOKT
WHO THE HELL ARE YOU?!
The far side of the bay--he made it to solid ground.
But I can't fail again.
Got to stop him, whatever the cost...
...right down to blood's last damn drop.

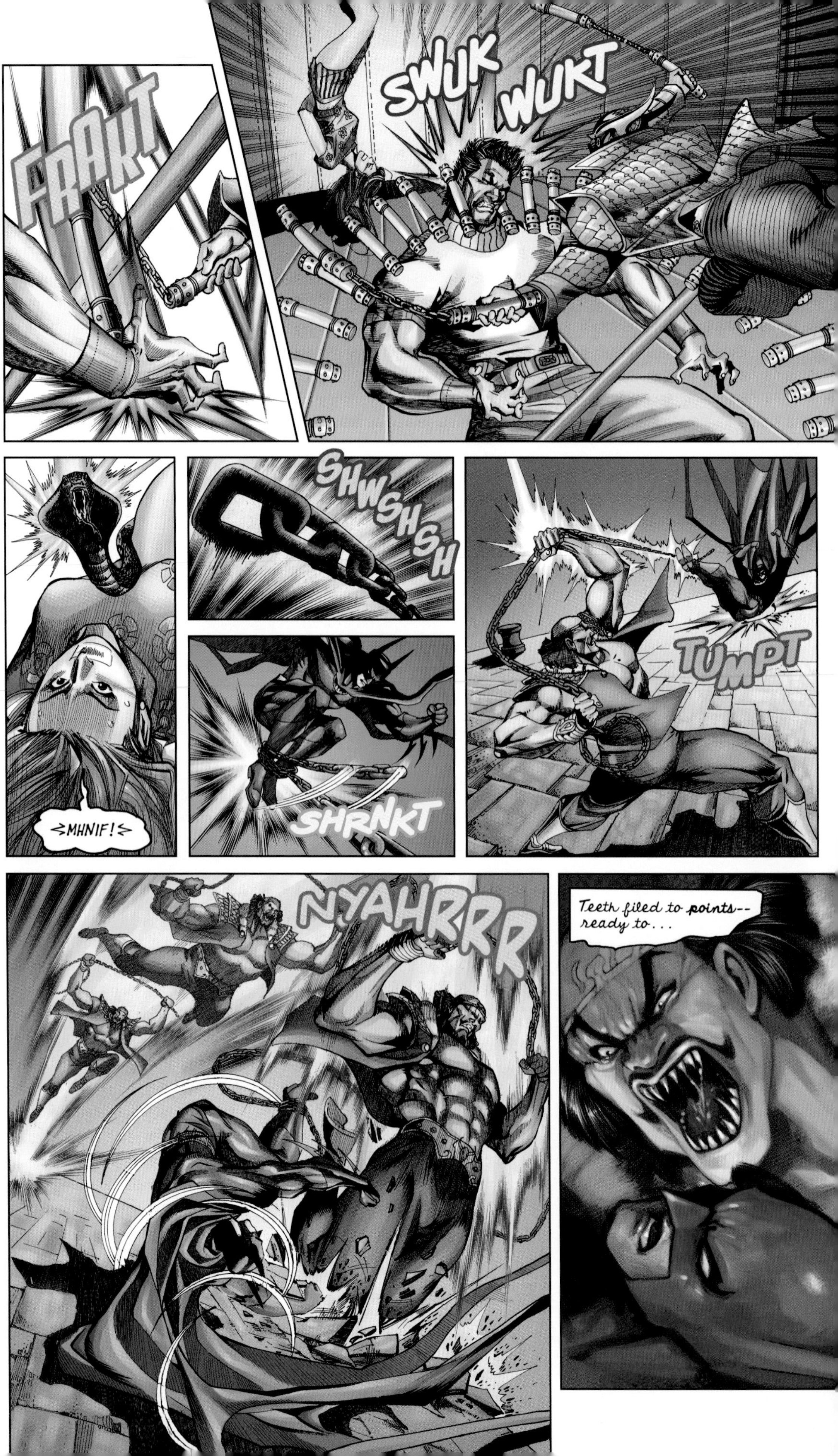

FRAKT
SWUK WUKT
SHWSHSH
SHRNKT
≤MHNIF!≥
TUMPT
NYAHRRR
Teeth filed to points--
ready to...

...bite.

KART

THE COBRA...

ABOUT TO STRIKE!

KRUNCHT

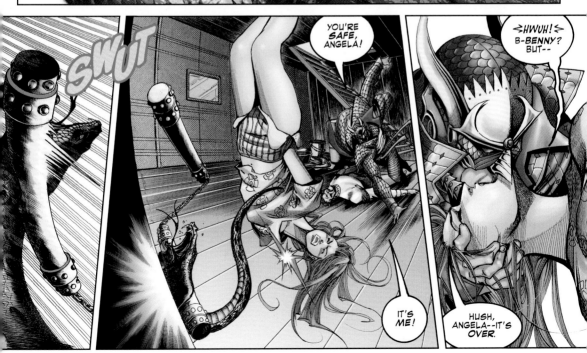

SWUT

YOU'RE SAFE, ANGELA!

IT'S ME!

≷HWUH!≷ B-BENNY? BUT--

HUSH, ANGELA--IT'S OVER.

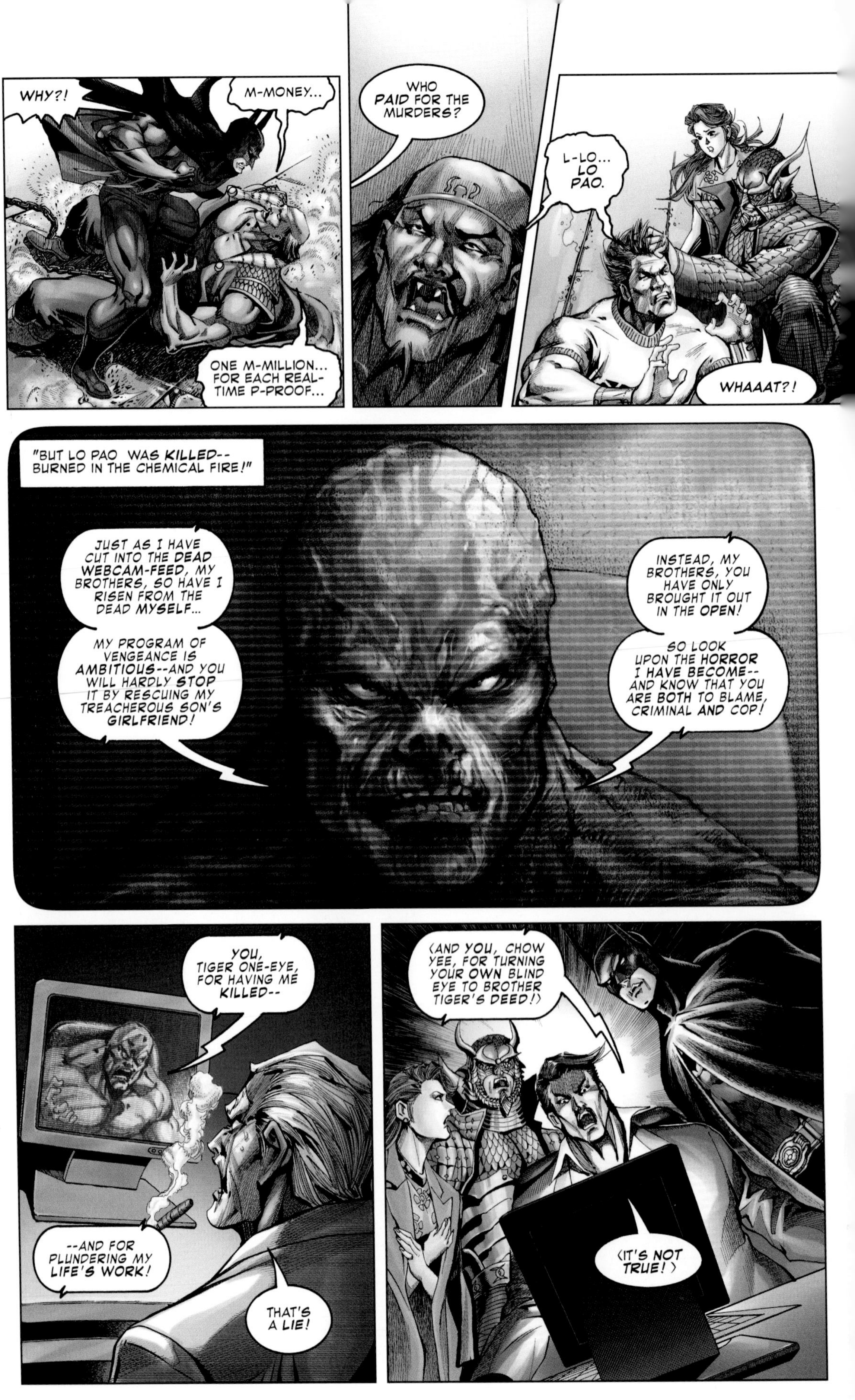
WHY?!
M-MONEY...
ONE M-MILLION... FOR EACH REAL-TIME P-PROOF...
WHO PAID FOR THE MURDERS?
L-LO... LO PAO.
WHAAAT?!
"BUT LO PAO WAS KILLED-- BURNED IN THE CHEMICAL FIRE!"
JUST AS I HAVE CUT INTO THE DEAD WEBCAM-FEED, MY BROTHERS, SO HAVE I RISEN FROM THE DEAD MYSELF...
MY PROGRAM OF VENGEANCE IS AMBITIOUS--AND YOU WILL HARDLY STOP IT BY RESCUING MY TREACHEROUS SON'S GIRLFRIEND!
INSTEAD, MY BROTHERS, YOU HAVE ONLY BROUGHT IT OUT IN THE OPEN!
SO LOOK UPON THE HORROR I HAVE BECOME-- AND KNOW THAT YOU ARE BOTH TO BLAME, CRIMINAL AND COP!
YOU, TIGER ONE-EYE, FOR HAVING ME KILLED--
--AND FOR PLUNDERING MY LIFE'S WORK!
THAT'S A LIE!
(AND YOU, CHOW YEE, FOR TURNING YOUR OWN BLIND EYE TO BROTHER TIGER'S DEED!)
(IT'S NOT TRUE!)

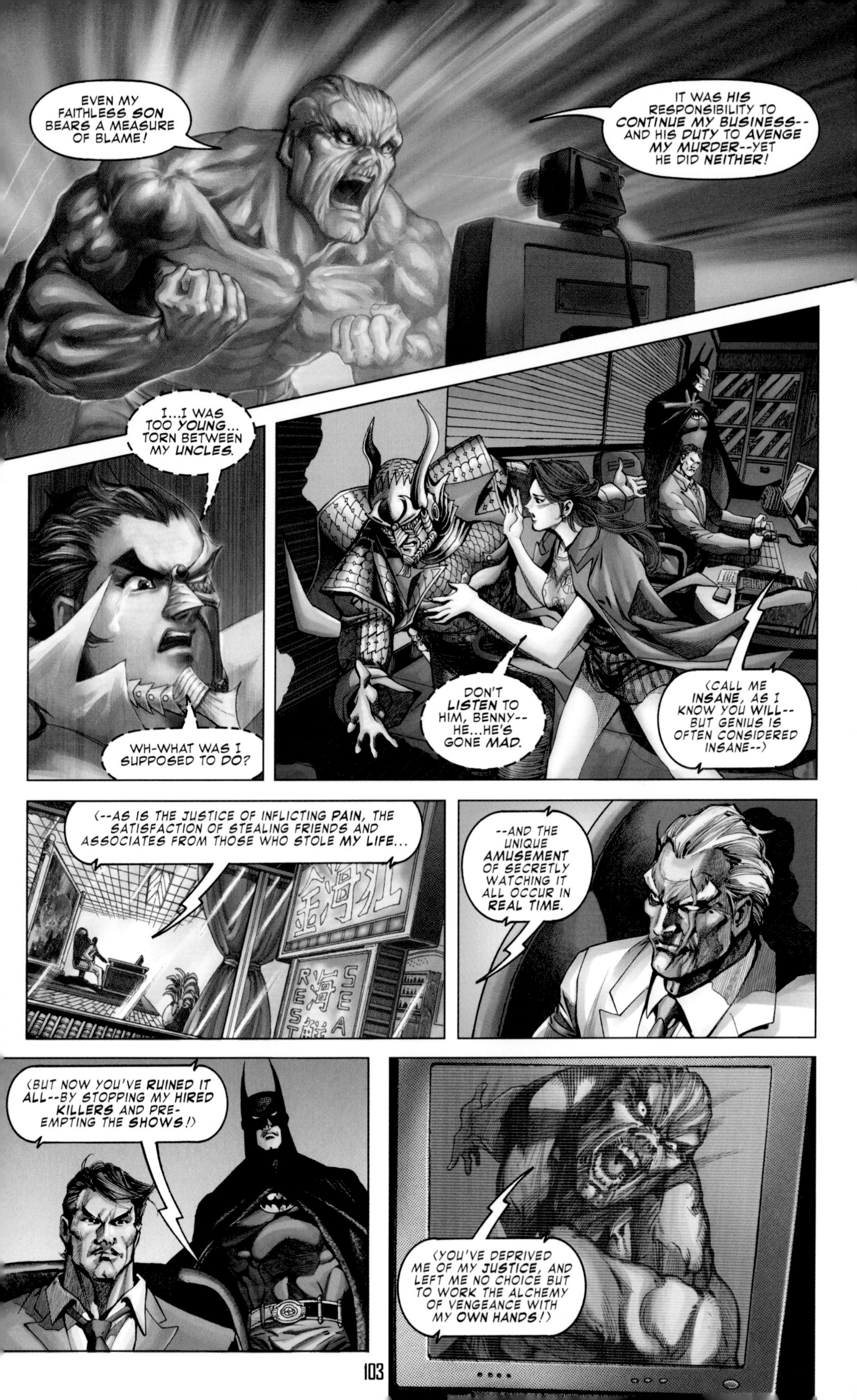

EVEN MY FAITHLESS SON BEARS A MEASURE OF BLAME!
IT WAS HIS RESPONSIBILITY TO CONTINUE MY BUSINESS--AND HIS DUTY TO AVENGE MY MURDER--YET HE DID NEITHER!
I...I WAS TOO YOUNG... TORN BETWEEN MY UNCLES.
WH-WHAT WAS I SUPPOSED TO DO?
DON'T LISTEN TO HIM, BENNY--HE...HE'S GONE MAD.
(CALL ME INSANE, AS I KNOW YOU WILL--BUT GENIUS IS OFTEN CONSIDERED INSANE--)
(--AS IS THE JUSTICE OF INFLICTING PAIN, THE SATISFACTION OF STEALING FRIENDS AND ASSOCIATES FROM THOSE WHO STOLE MY LIFE...
--AND THE UNIQUE AMUSEMENT OF SECRETLY WATCHING IT ALL OCCUR IN REAL TIME.
(BUT NOW YOU'VE RUINED IT ALL--BY STOPPING MY HIRED KILLERS AND PRE-EMPTING THE SHOWS!)
(YOU'VE DEPRIVED ME OF MY JUSTICE, AND LEFT ME NO CHOICE BUT TO WORK THE ALCHEMY OF VENGEANCE WITH MY OWN HANDS!)

⟨...BUT YOUR VERY WORLDS.⟩

⟨AND NOW, BROTHERS, I WILL DESTROY NOT JUST YOU AND YOURS...⟩

⟨YOU'VE FORCED ME BACK FROM THE DEAD-- AND OUT OF HIDING!⟩

CLEARLY A THREAT, CHIEF YEE, BUT WHAT KIND?

QUITE POSSIBLY... SUICIDAL TERRORISM.

I'LL PREPARE AN ENGLISH TRANSCRIPT.

BUT...WHAT REALLY HAPPENED TO LO PAO?

IF IT WASN'T TIGER, THEN WHO "KILLED" HIM?

⟨I DID.⟩

⟨YOU--!⟩

IT--IT CAN'T BE!

M-MOTHER?!

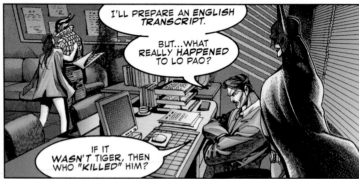

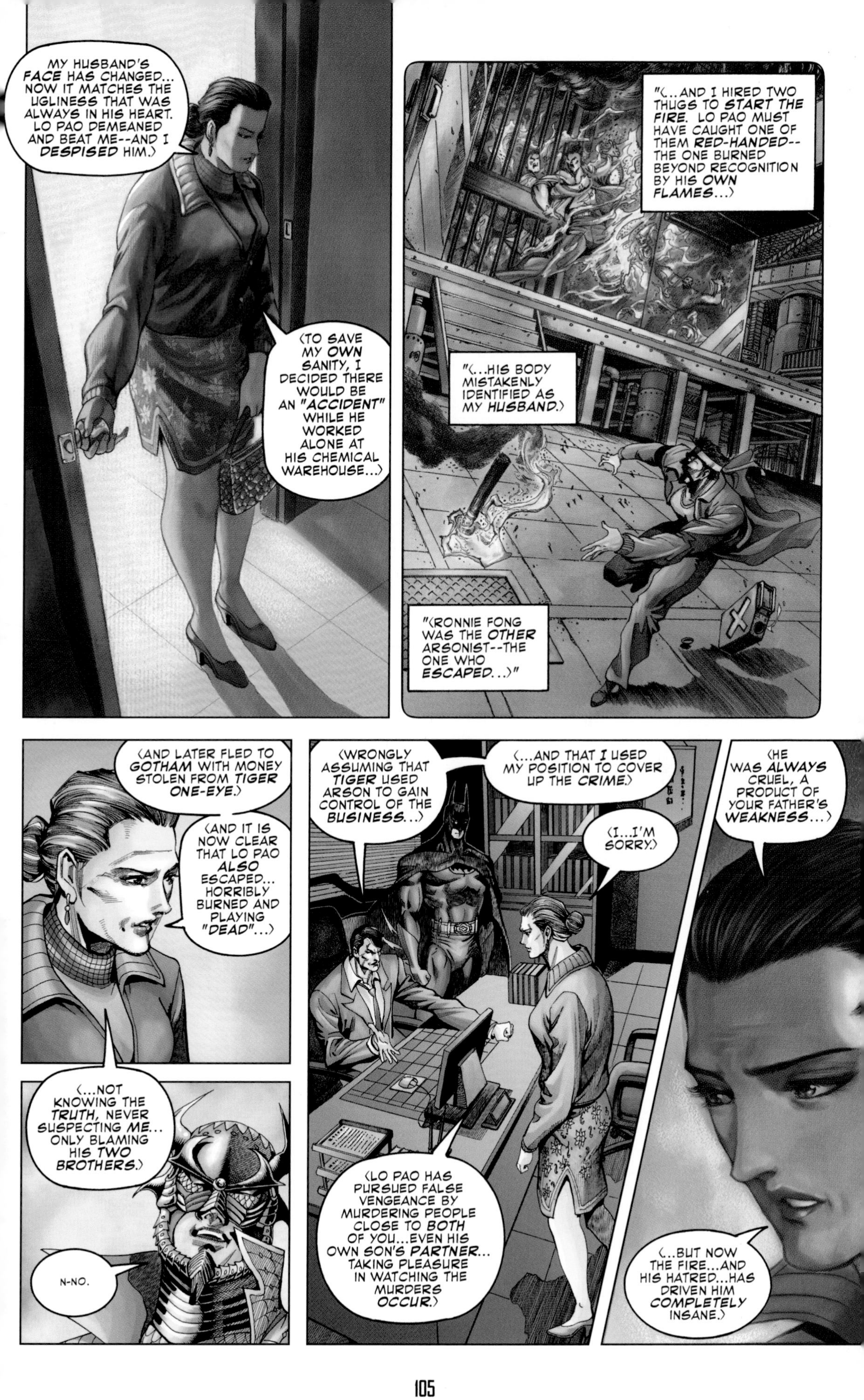

MY HUSBAND'S FACE HAS CHANGED... NOW IT MATCHES THE UGLINESS THAT WAS ALWAYS IN HIS HEART. LO PAO DEMEANED AND BEAT ME--AND I DESPISED HIM.〉
〈TO SAVE MY OWN SANITY, I DECIDED THERE WOULD BE AN "ACCIDENT" WHILE HE WORKED ALONE AT HIS CHEMICAL WAREHOUSE...〉
"〈...AND I HIRED TWO THUGS TO START THE FIRE. LO PAO MUST HAVE CAUGHT ONE OF THEM RED-HANDED-- THE ONE BURNED BEYOND RECOGNITION BY HIS OWN FLAMES...〉
"〈...HIS BODY MISTAKENLY IDENTIFIED AS MY HUSBAND.〉
"〈RONNIE FONG WAS THE OTHER ARSONIST--THE ONE WHO ESCAPED...〉"
〈AND LATER FLED TO GOTHAM WITH MONEY STOLEN FROM TIGER ONE-EYE.〉
〈AND IT IS NOW CLEAR THAT LO PAO ALSO ESCAPED... HORRIBLY BURNED AND PLAYING "DEAD"...〉
〈...NOT KNOWING THE TRUTH, NEVER SUSPECTING ME... ONLY BLAMING HIS TWO BROTHERS.〉
N-NO.
〈WRONGLY ASSUMING THAT TIGER USED ARSON TO GAIN CONTROL OF THE BUSINESS...〉
〈...AND THAT I USED MY POSITION TO COVER UP THE CRIME.〉
〈I...I'M SORRY.〉
〈LO PAO HAS PURSUED FALSE VENGEANCE BY MURDERING PEOPLE CLOSE TO BOTH OF YOU...EVEN HIS OWN SON'S PARTNER... TAKING PLEASURE IN WATCHING THE MURDERS OCCUR.〉
〈HE WAS ALWAYS CRUEL, A PRODUCT OF YOUR FATHER'S WEAKNESS...〉
〈...BUT NOW THE FIRE...AND HIS HATRED...HAS DRIVEN HIM COMPLETELY INSANE.〉

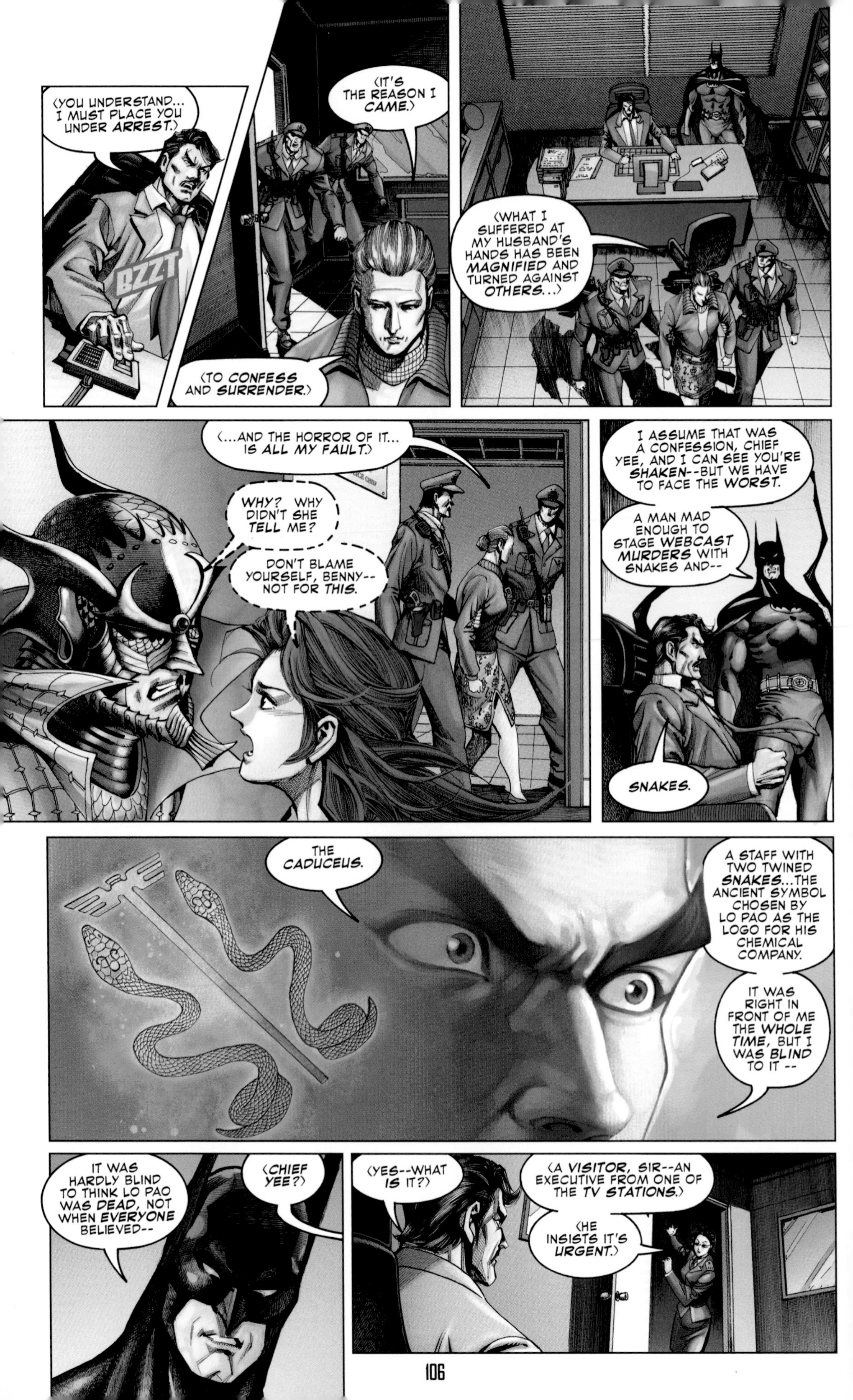

⟨YOU UNDERSTAND... I MUST PLACE YOU UNDER ARREST.⟩
BZZT
⟨IT'S THE REASON I CAME.⟩
⟨TO CONFESS AND SURRENDER.⟩
⟨WHAT I SUFFERED AT MY HUSBAND'S HANDS HAS BEEN MAGNIFIED AND TURNED AGAINST OTHERS...⟩
⟨...AND THE HORROR OF IT... IS ALL MY FAULT.⟩
WHY? WHY DIDN'T SHE TELL ME?
DON'T BLAME YOURSELF, BENNY-- NOT FOR THIS.
I ASSUME THAT WAS A CONFESSION, CHIEF YEE, AND I CAN SEE YOU'RE SHAKEN--BUT WE HAVE TO FACE THE WORST.
A MAN MAD ENOUGH TO STAGE WEBCAST MURDERS WITH SNAKES AND--
SNAKES.
THE CADUCEUS.
A STAFF WITH TWO TWINED SNAKES...THE ANCIENT SYMBOL CHOSEN BY LO PAO AS THE LOGO FOR HIS CHEMICAL COMPANY.
IT WAS RIGHT IN FRONT OF ME THE WHOLE TIME, BUT I WAS BLIND TO IT --
IT WAS HARDLY BLIND TO THINK LO PAO WAS DEAD, NOT WHEN EVERYONE BELIEVED--
⟨CHIEF YEE?⟩
⟨YES--WHAT IS IT?⟩
⟨A VISITOR, SIR--AN EXECUTIVE FROM ONE OF THE TV STATIONS.⟩
⟨HE INSISTS IT'S URGENT.⟩

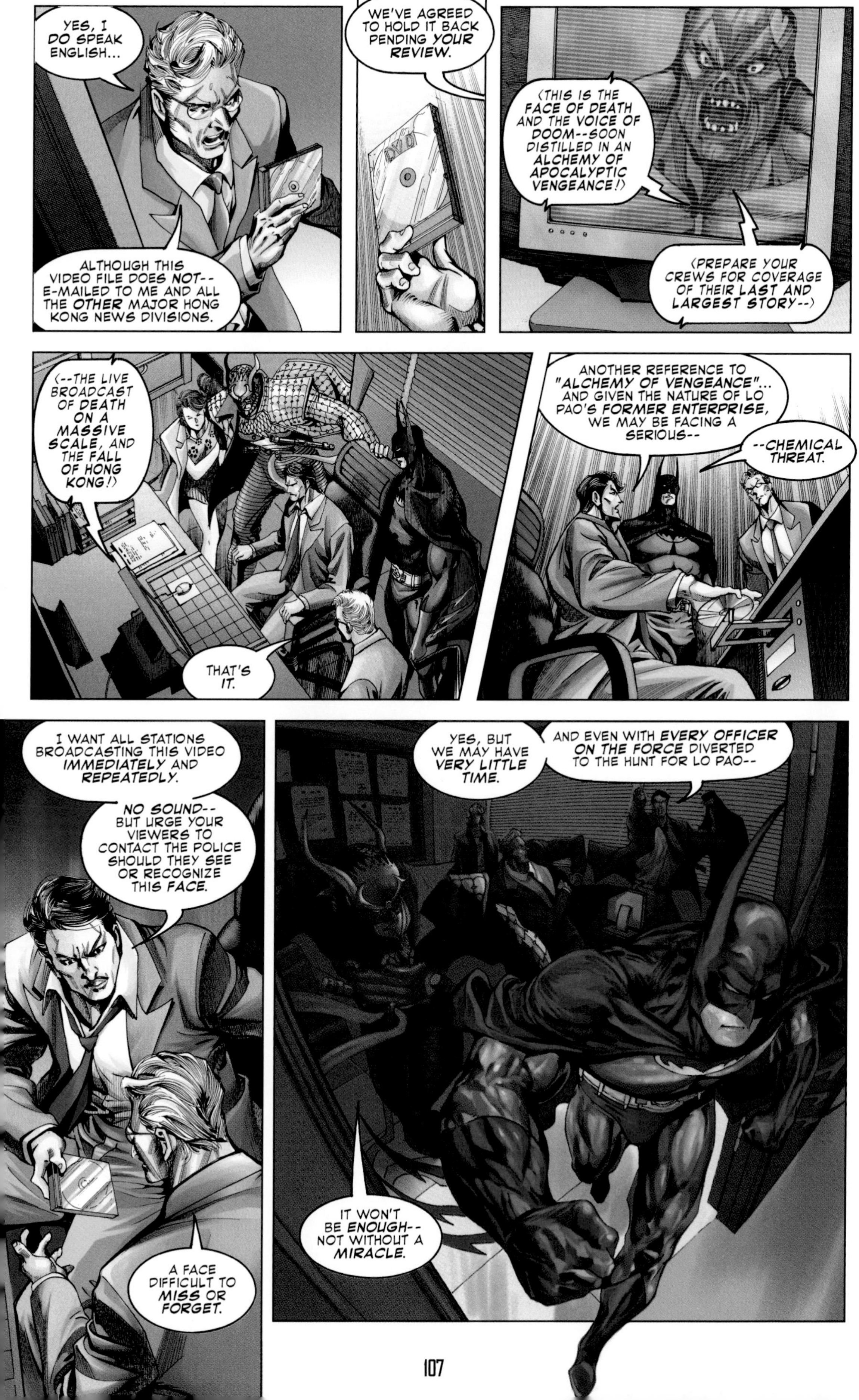
YES, I DO SPEAK ENGLISH...
ALTHOUGH THIS VIDEO FILE DOES NOT-- E-MAILED TO ME AND ALL THE OTHER MAJOR HONG KONG NEWS DIVISIONS.
WE'VE AGREED TO HOLD IT BACK PENDING YOUR REVIEW.
DVD
(THIS IS THE FACE OF DEATH AND THE VOICE OF DOOM--SOON DISTILLED IN AN ALCHEMY OF APOCALYPTIC VENGEANCE!)
(PREPARE YOUR CREWS FOR COVERAGE OF THEIR LAST AND LARGEST STORY--)
(--THE LIVE BROADCAST OF DEATH ON A MASSIVE SCALE, AND THE FALL OF HONG KONG!)
THAT'S IT.
ANOTHER REFERENCE TO "ALCHEMY OF VENGEANCE"... AND GIVEN THE NATURE OF LO PAO'S FORMER ENTERPRISE, WE MAY BE FACING A SERIOUS--
--CHEMICAL THREAT.
I WANT ALL STATIONS BROADCASTING THIS VIDEO IMMEDIATELY AND REPEATEDLY.
NO SOUND-- BUT URGE YOUR VIEWERS TO CONTACT THE POLICE SHOULD THEY SEE OR RECOGNIZE THIS FACE.
A FACE DIFFICULT TO MISS OR FORGET.
YES, BUT WE MAY HAVE VERY LITTLE TIME.
AND EVEN WITH EVERY OFFICER ON THE FORCE DIVERTED TO THE HUNT FOR LO PAO--
IT WON'T BE ENOUGH-- NOT WITHOUT A MIRACLE.

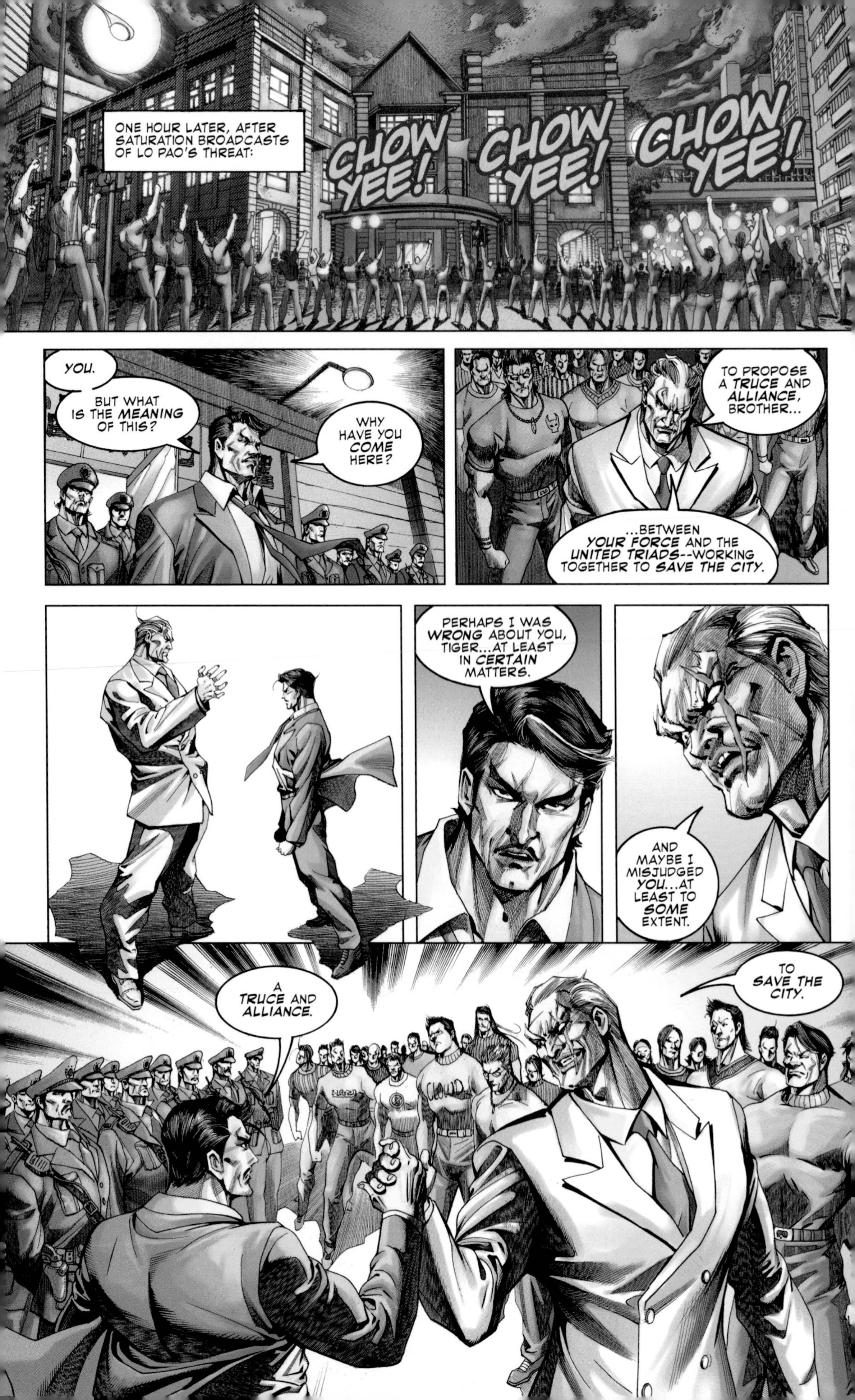
ONE HOUR LATER, AFTER SATURATION BROADCASTS OF LO PAO'S THREAT:
CHOW YEE! CHOW YEE! CHOW YEE!
YOU.
BUT WHAT IS THE MEANING OF THIS?
WHY HAVE YOU COME HERE?
TO PROPOSE A TRUCE AND ALLIANCE, BROTHER...
...BETWEEN YOUR FORCE AND THE UNITED TRIADS--WORKING TOGETHER TO SAVE THE CITY.
PERHAPS I WAS WRONG ABOUT YOU, TIGER...AT LEAST IN CERTAIN MATTERS.
AND MAYBE I MISJUDGED YOU...AT LEAST TO SOME EXTENT.
A TRUCE AND ALLIANCE.
TO SAVE THE CITY.

A BACK-STREET RENTED FLAT:

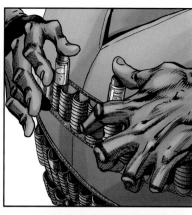

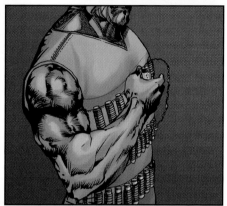

YOUR FANGS, MY FRIENDS, ARE NOW *TOO SHORT.*

BUT DON'T WORRY...

YOU WON'T HAVE *TIME* TO STARVE.

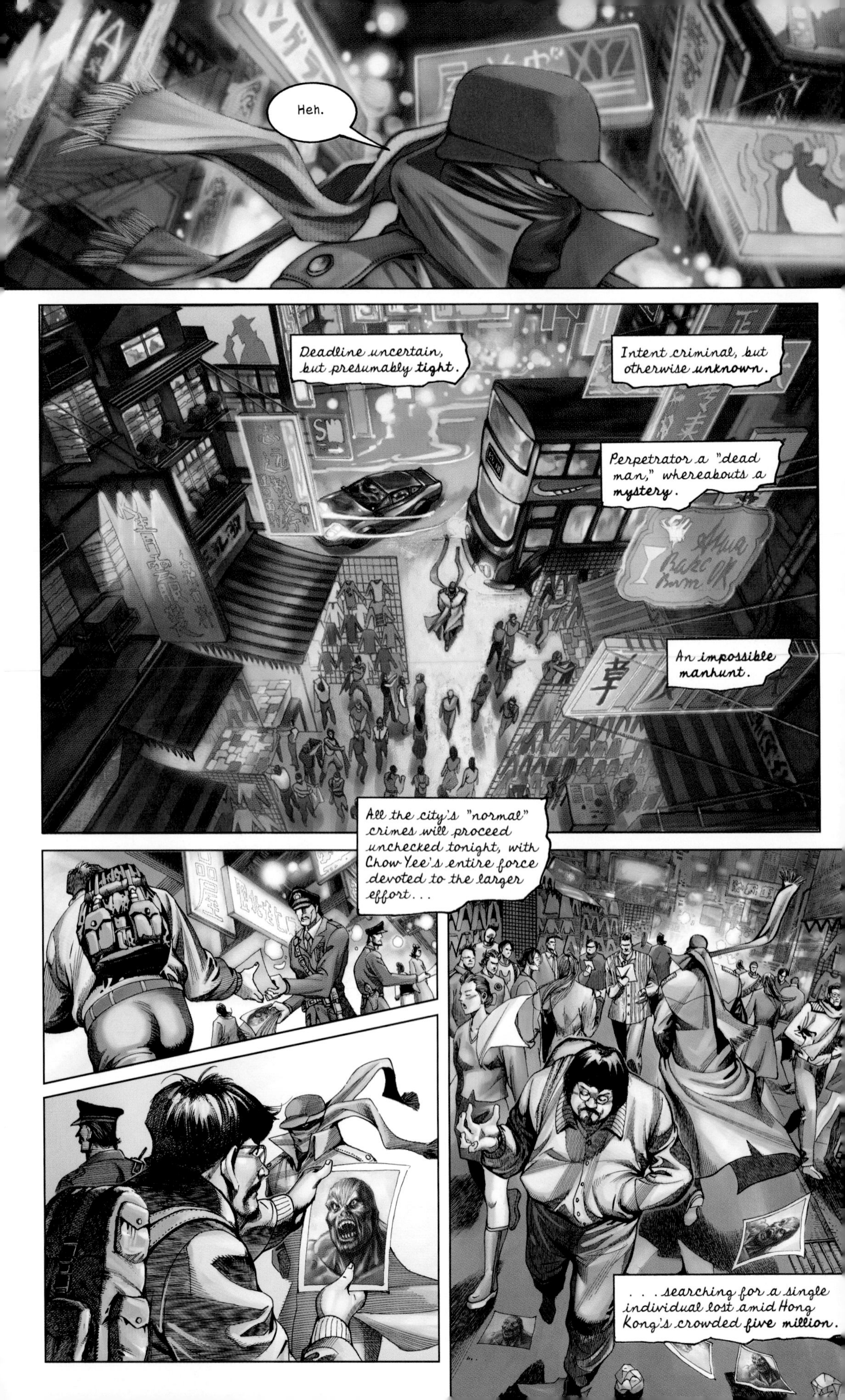

Heh.
Deadline uncertain, but presumably tight.
Intent criminal, but otherwise unknown.
Perpetrator a "dead man," whereabouts a mystery.
An impossible manhunt.
All the city's "normal" crimes will proceed unchecked tonight, with Chow Yee's entire force devoted to the larger effort...
...searching for a single individual lost amid Hong Kong's crowded five million.

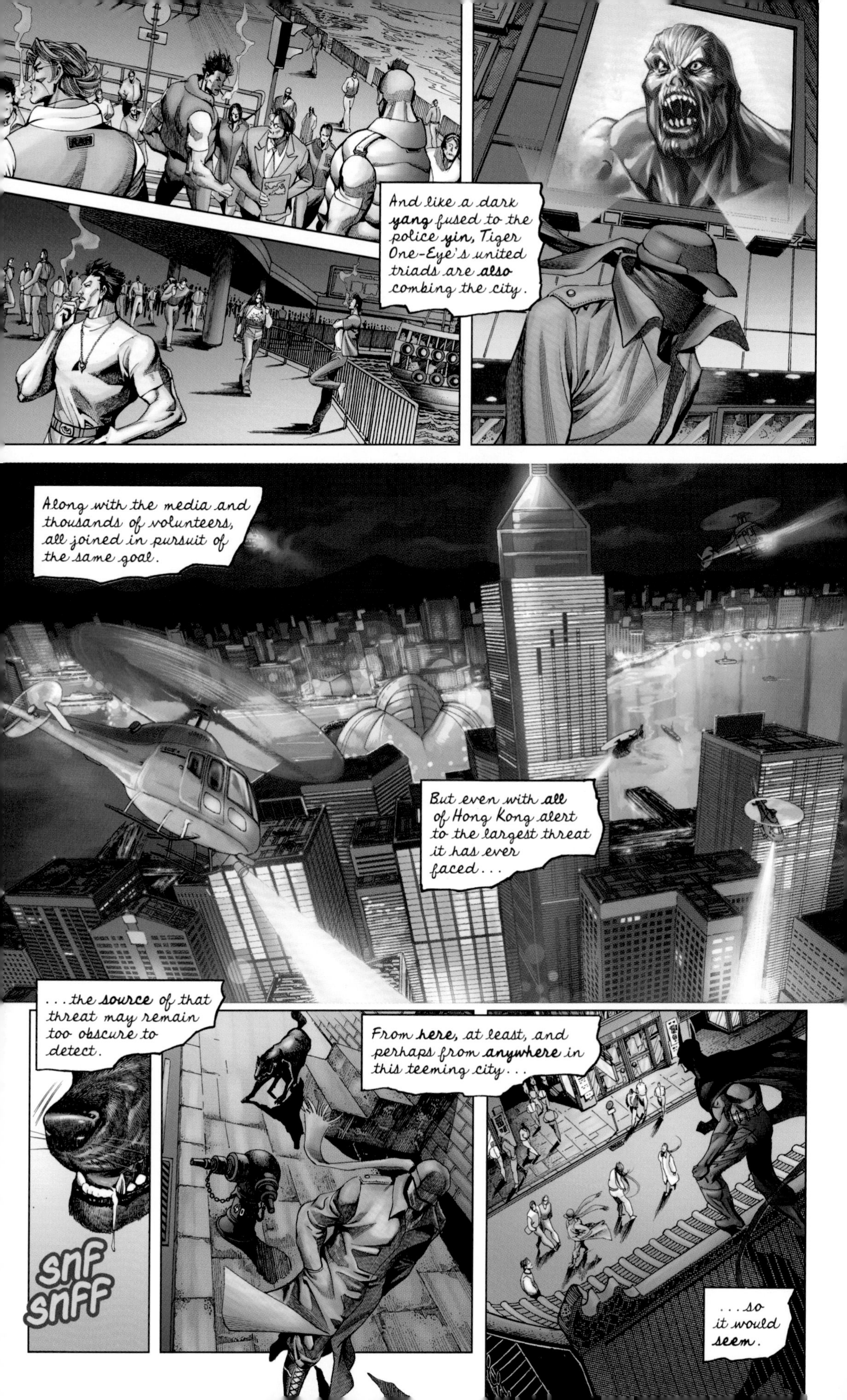
And like a dark **yang** fused to the police **yin**, Tiger One-Eye's united triads are **also** combing the city.
Along with the media and thousands of volunteers, all joined in pursuit of the same goal.
But even with **all** of Hong Kong alert to the largest threat it has ever faced...
...the **source** of that threat may remain too obscure to detect.
snf snff
From **here**, at least, and perhaps from **anywhere** in this teeming city...
...so it would **seem**.

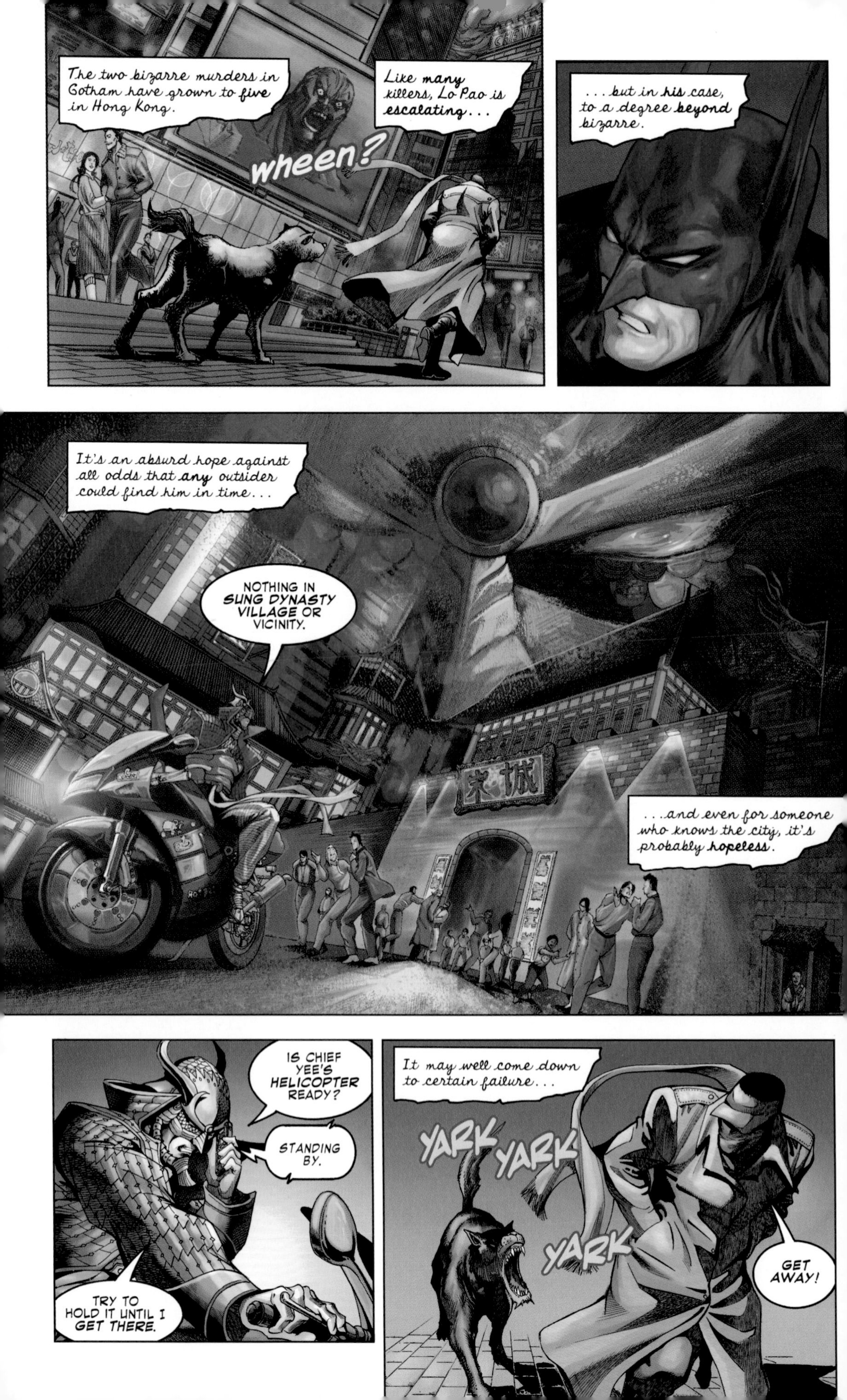
The two bizarre murders in Gotham have grown to five in Hong Kong.
Like many killers, Lo Pao is escalating...
wheen?
...but in his case, to a degree beyond bizarre.
It's an absurd hope against all odds that any outsider could find him in time...
NOTHING IN SUNG DYNASTY VILLAGE OR VICINITY.
...and even for someone who knows the city, it's probably hopeless.
IS CHIEF YEE'S HELICOPTER READY?
STANDING BY.
TRY TO HOLD IT UNTIL I GET THERE.
It may well come down to certain failure...
YARK YARK
YARK
GET AWAY!

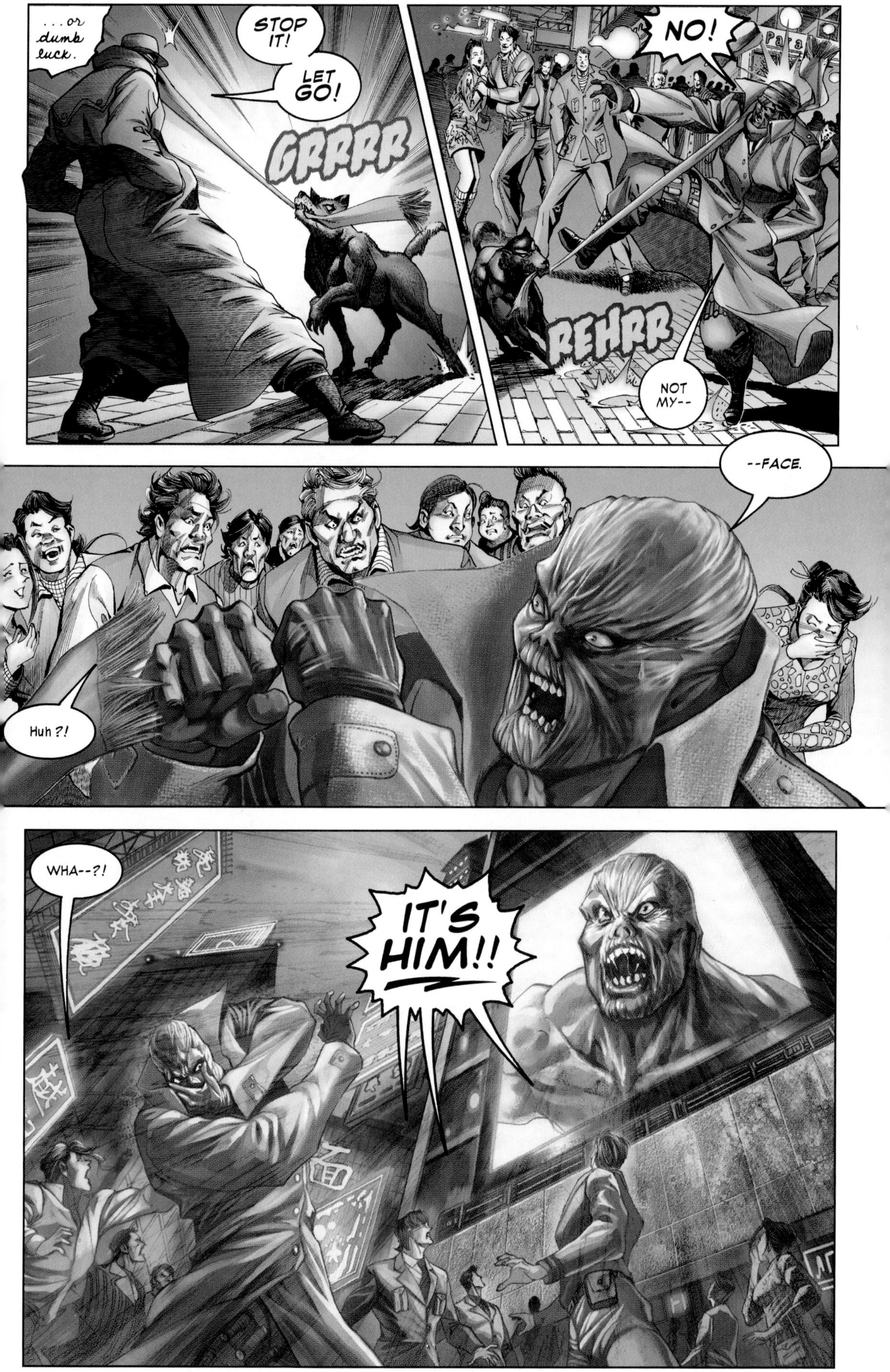

...or dumb luck.
STOP IT!
LET GO!
GRRRR
NO!
REHRR
NOT MY--
--FACE.
Huh?!
WHA--?!
IT'S HIM!!

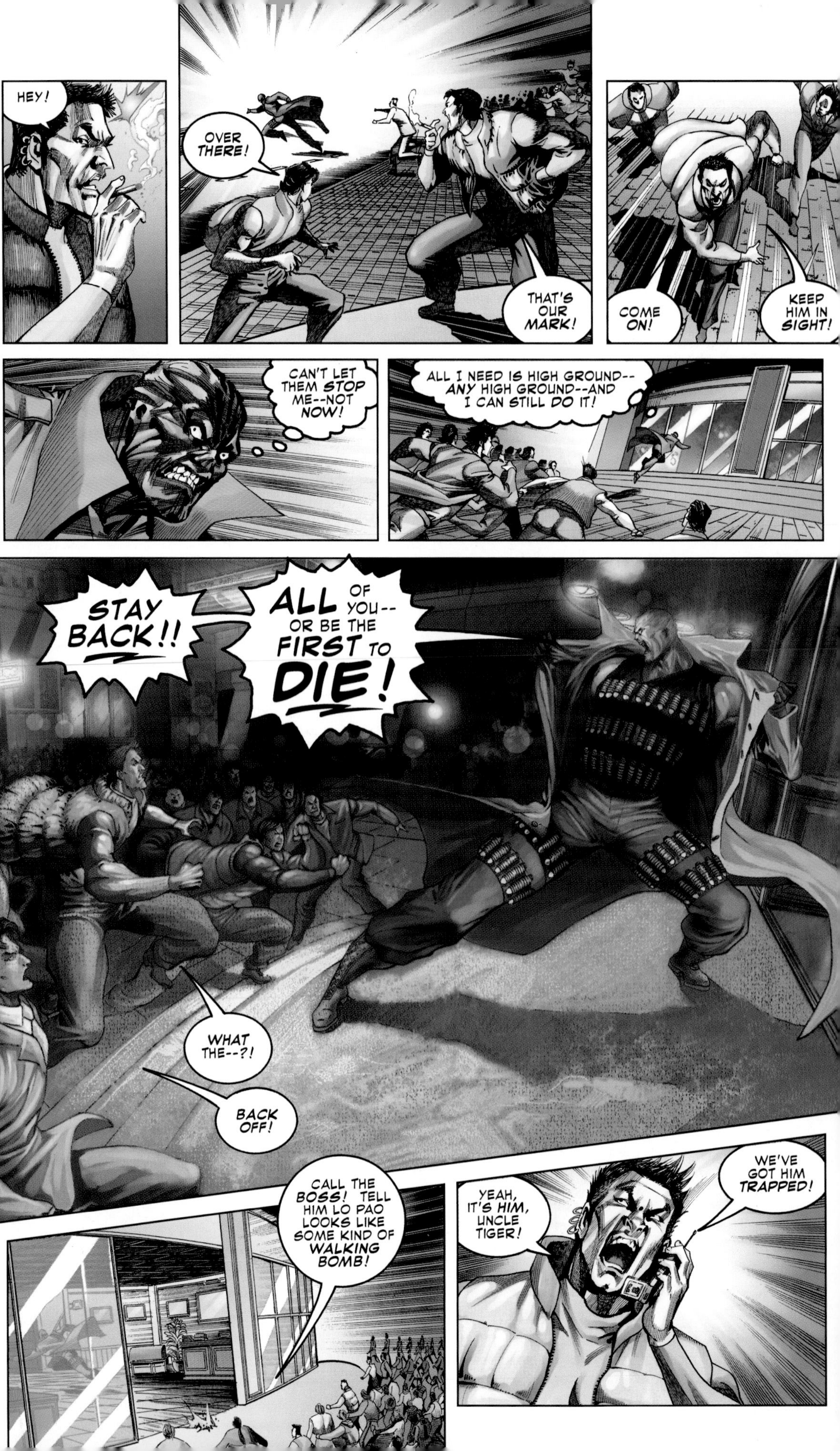
HEY!
OVER THERE!
THAT'S OUR MARK!
COME ON!
KEEP HIM IN SIGHT!
CAN'T LET THEM STOP ME--NOT NOW!
ALL I NEED IS HIGH GROUND--ANY HIGH GROUND--AND I CAN STILL DO IT!
STAY BACK!!
ALL OF YOU--OR BE THE FIRST TO DIE!
WHAT THE--?!
BACK OFF!
CALL THE BOSS! TELL HIM LO PAO LOOKS LIKE SOME KIND OF WALKING BOMB!
YEAH, IT'S HIM, UNCLE TIGER!
WE'VE GOT HIM TRAPPED!

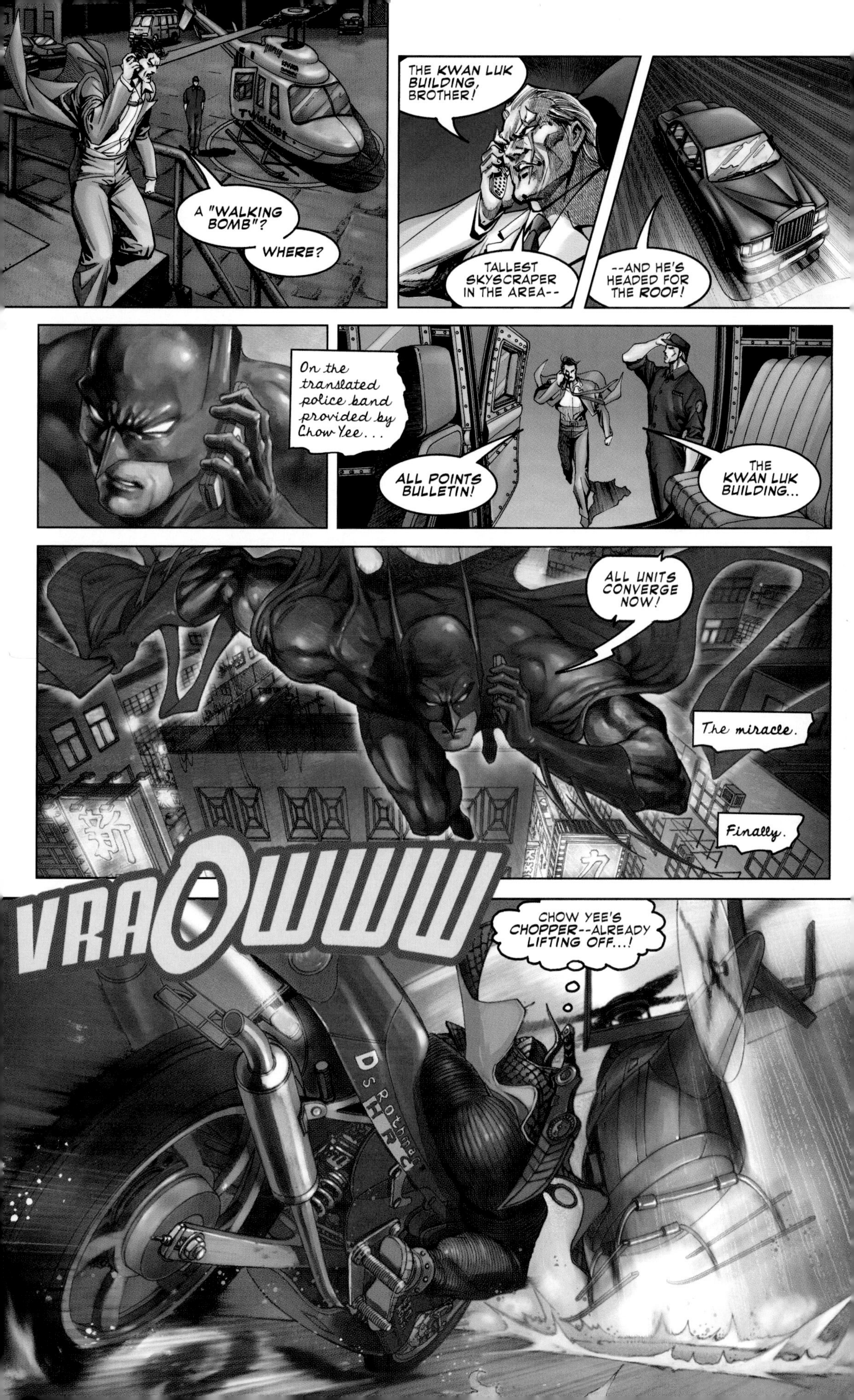
A "WALKING BOMB"?
WHERE?
THE KWAN LUK BUILDING, BROTHER!
TALLEST SKYSCRAPER IN THE AREA--
--AND HE'S HEADED FOR THE ROOF!
On the translated police band provided by Chow Yee...
ALL POINTS BULLETIN!
THE KWAN LUK BUILDING...
ALL UNITS CONVERGE NOW!
The miracle.
Finally.
VRAOWWW
CHOW YEE'S CHOPPER--ALREADY LIFTING OFF...!

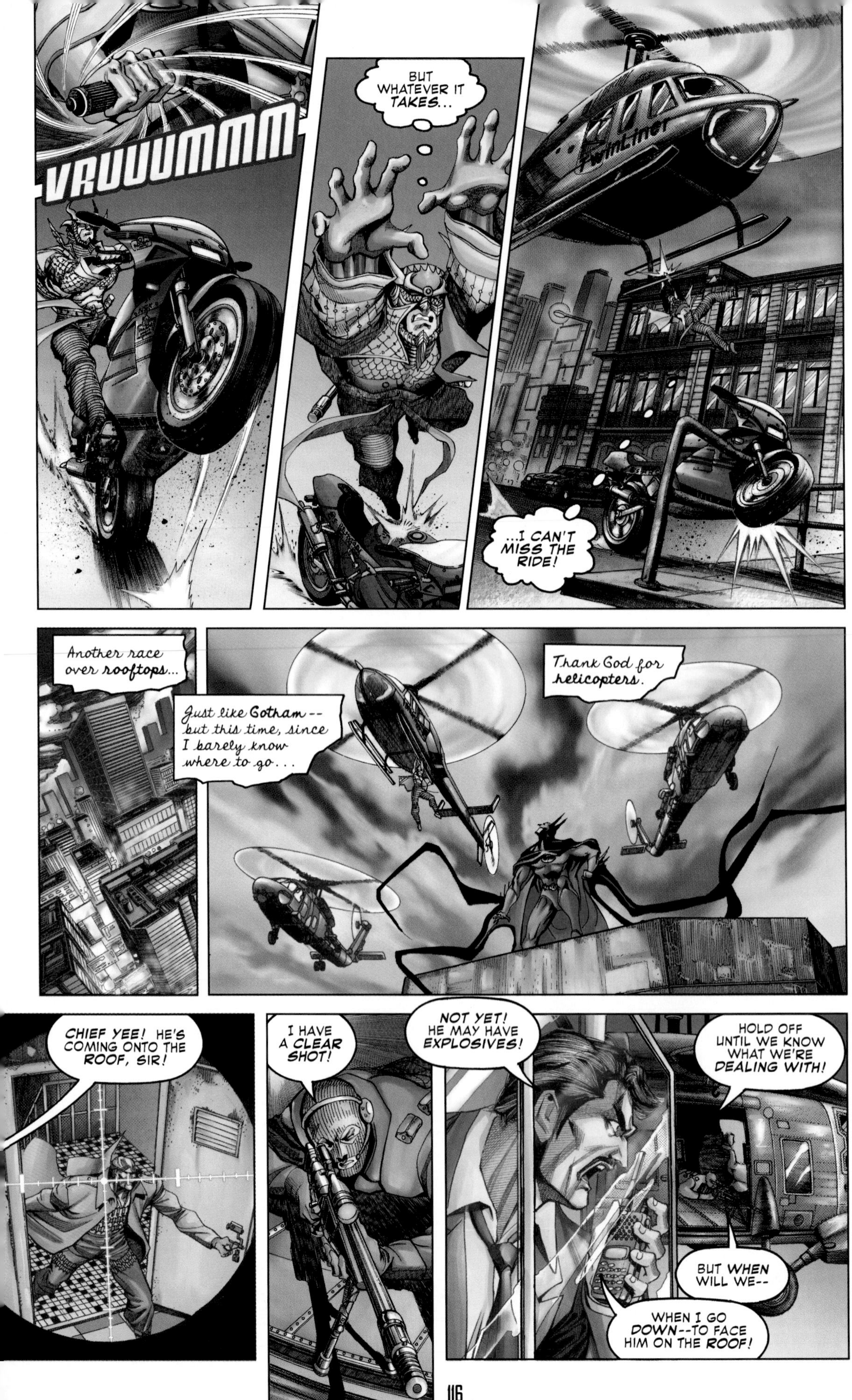
VRUUUMMM
BUT WHATEVER IT TAKES...
...I CAN'T MISS THE RIDE!
TwinLiner
Another race over rooftops...
Just like Gotham -- but this time, since I barely know where to go...
Thank God for helicopters.
CHIEF YEE! HE'S COMING ONTO THE ROOF, SIR!
I HAVE A CLEAR SHOT!
NOT YET! HE MAY HAVE EXPLOSIVES!
HOLD OFF UNTIL WE KNOW WHAT WE'RE DEALING WITH!
BUT WHEN WILL WE--
WHEN I GO DOWN--TO FACE HIM ON THE ROOF!

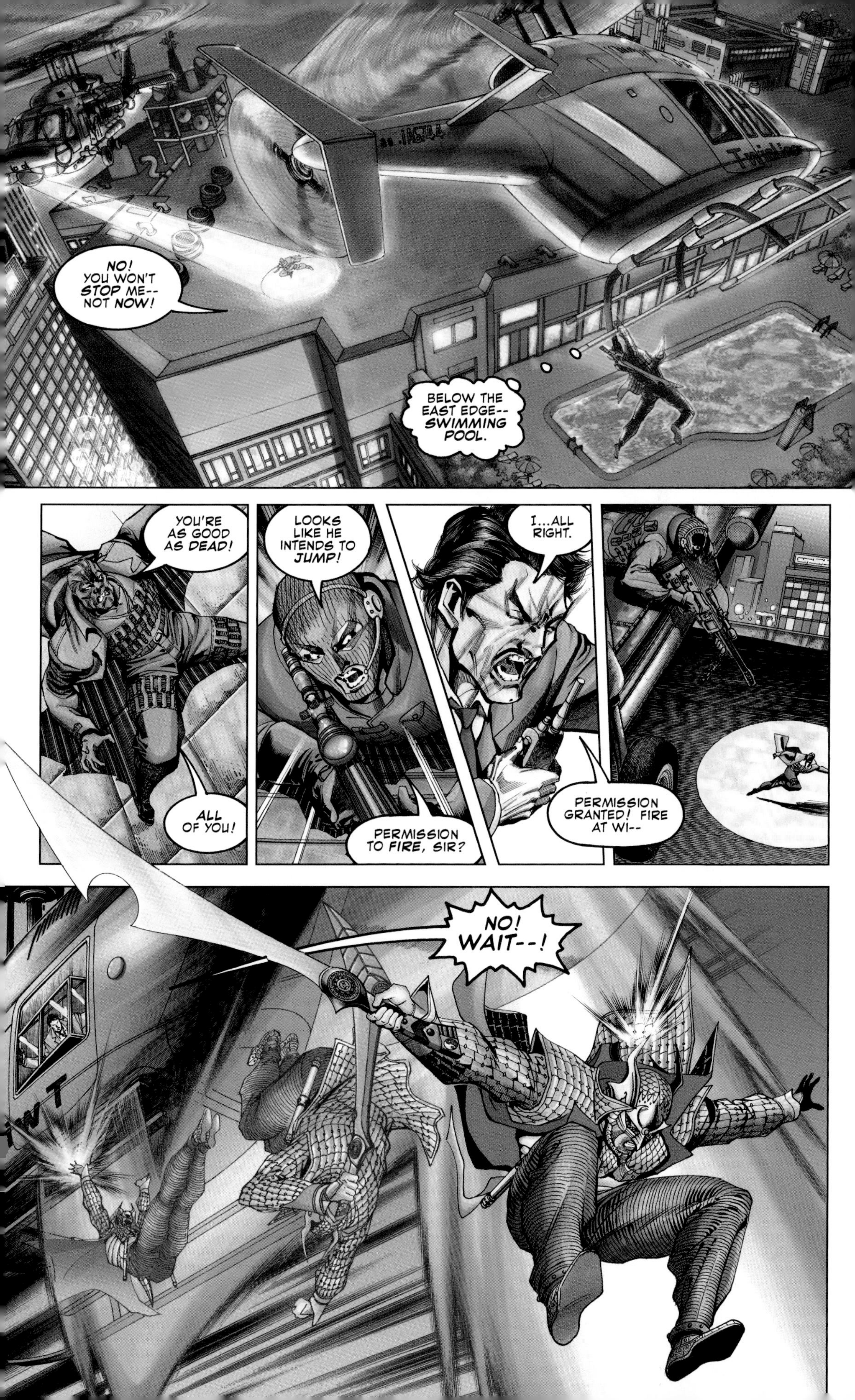
NO! YOU WON'T STOP ME-- NOT NOW!
BELOW THE EAST EDGE-- SWIMMING POOL.
YOU'RE AS GOOD AS DEAD!
ALL OF YOU!
LOOKS LIKE HE INTENDS TO JUMP!
PERMISSION TO FIRE, SIR?
I...ALL RIGHT.
PERMISSION GRANTED! FIRE AT WI--
NO! WAIT--!

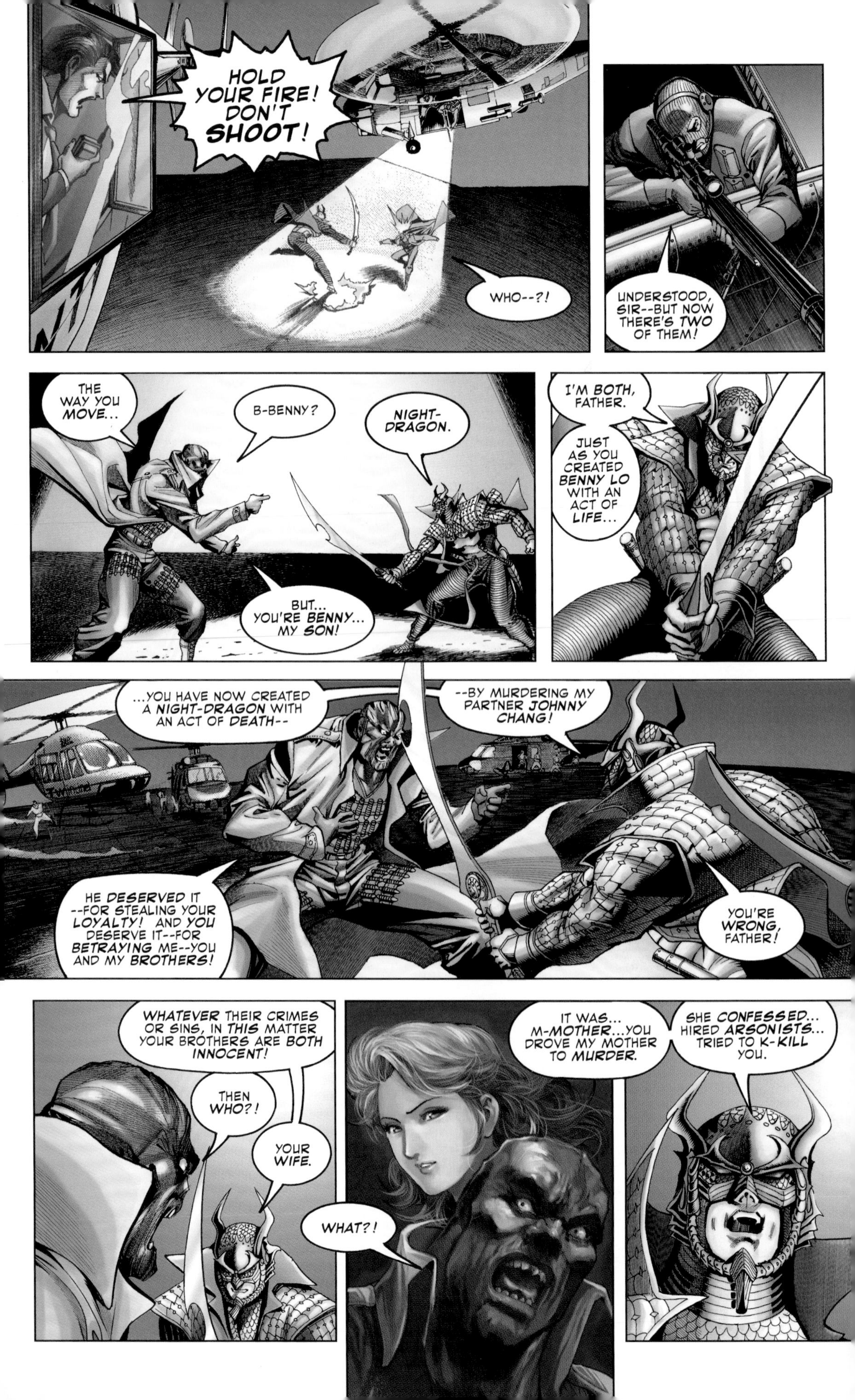
HOLD YOUR FIRE! DON'T SHOOT!
WHO--?!
UNDERSTOOD, SIR--BUT NOW THERE'S TWO OF THEM!
THE WAY YOU MOVE...
B-BENNY?
NIGHT-DRAGON.
BUT... YOU'RE BENNY... MY SON!
I'M BOTH, FATHER.
JUST AS YOU CREATED BENNY LO WITH AN ACT OF LIFE...
...YOU HAVE NOW CREATED A NIGHT-DRAGON WITH AN ACT OF DEATH--
--BY MURDERING MY PARTNER JOHNNY CHANG!
HE DESERVED IT --FOR STEALING YOUR LOYALTY! AND YOU DESERVE IT--FOR BETRAYING ME--YOU AND MY BROTHERS!
YOU'RE WRONG, FATHER!
WHATEVER THEIR CRIMES OR SINS, IN THIS MATTER YOUR BROTHERS ARE BOTH INNOCENT!
THEN WHO?!
YOUR WIFE.
WHAT?!
IT WAS... M-MOTHER...YOU DROVE MY MOTHER TO MURDER.
SHE CONFESSED... HIRED ARSONISTS... TRIED TO K-KILL YOU.

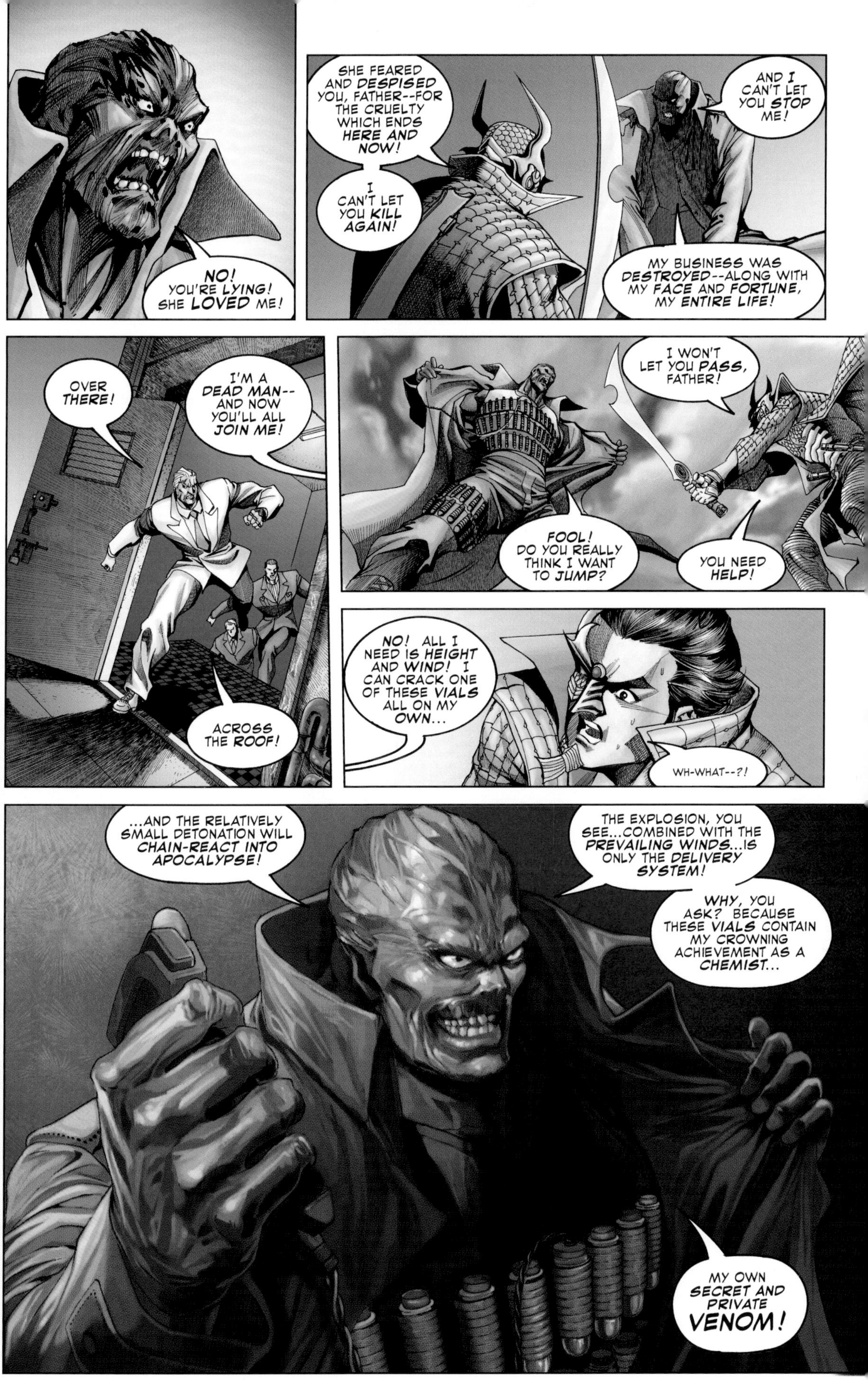
NO! YOU'RE LYING! SHE LOVED ME!
SHE FEARED AND DESPISED YOU, FATHER--FOR THE CRUELTY WHICH ENDS HERE AND NOW!
I CAN'T LET YOU KILL AGAIN!
AND I CAN'T LET YOU STOP ME!
MY BUSINESS WAS DESTROYED--ALONG WITH MY FACE AND FORTUNE, MY ENTIRE LIFE!
OVER THERE!
I'M A DEAD MAN-- AND NOW YOU'LL ALL JOIN ME!
ACROSS THE ROOF!
I WON'T LET YOU PASS, FATHER!
FOOL! DO YOU REALLY THINK I WANT TO JUMP?
YOU NEED HELP!
NO! ALL I NEED IS HEIGHT AND WIND! I CAN CRACK ONE OF THESE VIALS ALL ON MY OWN...
WH-WHAT--?!
...AND THE RELATIVELY SMALL DETONATION WILL CHAIN-REACT INTO APOCALYPSE!
THE EXPLOSION, YOU SEE...COMBINED WITH THE PREVAILING WINDS...IS ONLY THE DELIVERY SYSTEM!
WHY, YOU ASK? BECAUSE THESE VIALS CONTAIN MY CROWNING ACHIEVEMENT AS A CHEMIST...
MY OWN SECRET AND PRIVATE VENOM!

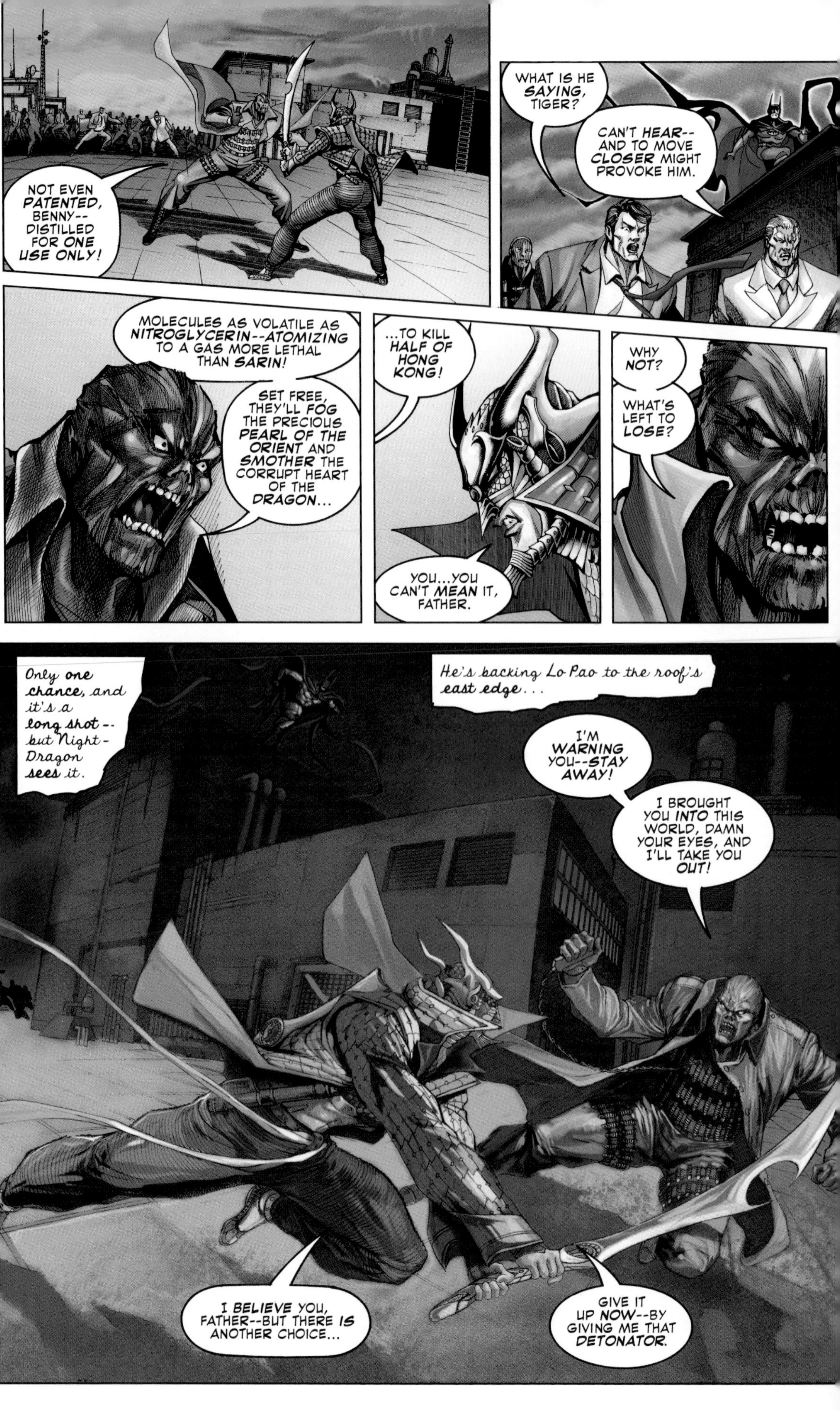
NOT EVEN PATENTED, BENNY--DISTILLED FOR ONE USE ONLY!
WHAT IS HE SAYING, TIGER?
CAN'T HEAR--AND TO MOVE CLOSER MIGHT PROVOKE HIM.
MOLECULES AS VOLATILE AS NITROGLYCERIN--ATOMIZING TO A GAS MORE LETHAL THAN SARIN!
SET FREE, THEY'LL FOG THE PRECIOUS PEARL OF THE ORIENT AND SMOTHER THE CORRUPT HEART OF THE DRAGON...
...TO KILL HALF OF HONG KONG!
YOU...YOU CAN'T MEAN IT, FATHER.
WHY NOT?
WHAT'S LEFT TO LOSE?
Only one chance, and it's a long shot--but Night-Dragon sees it.
He's backing Lo Pao to the roof's east edge...
I'M WARNING YOU--STAY AWAY!
I BROUGHT YOU INTO THIS WORLD, DAMN YOUR EYES, AND I'LL TAKE YOU OUT!
I BELIEVE YOU, FATHER--BUT THERE IS ANOTHER CHOICE...
GIVE IT UP NOW--BY GIVING ME THAT DETONATOR.

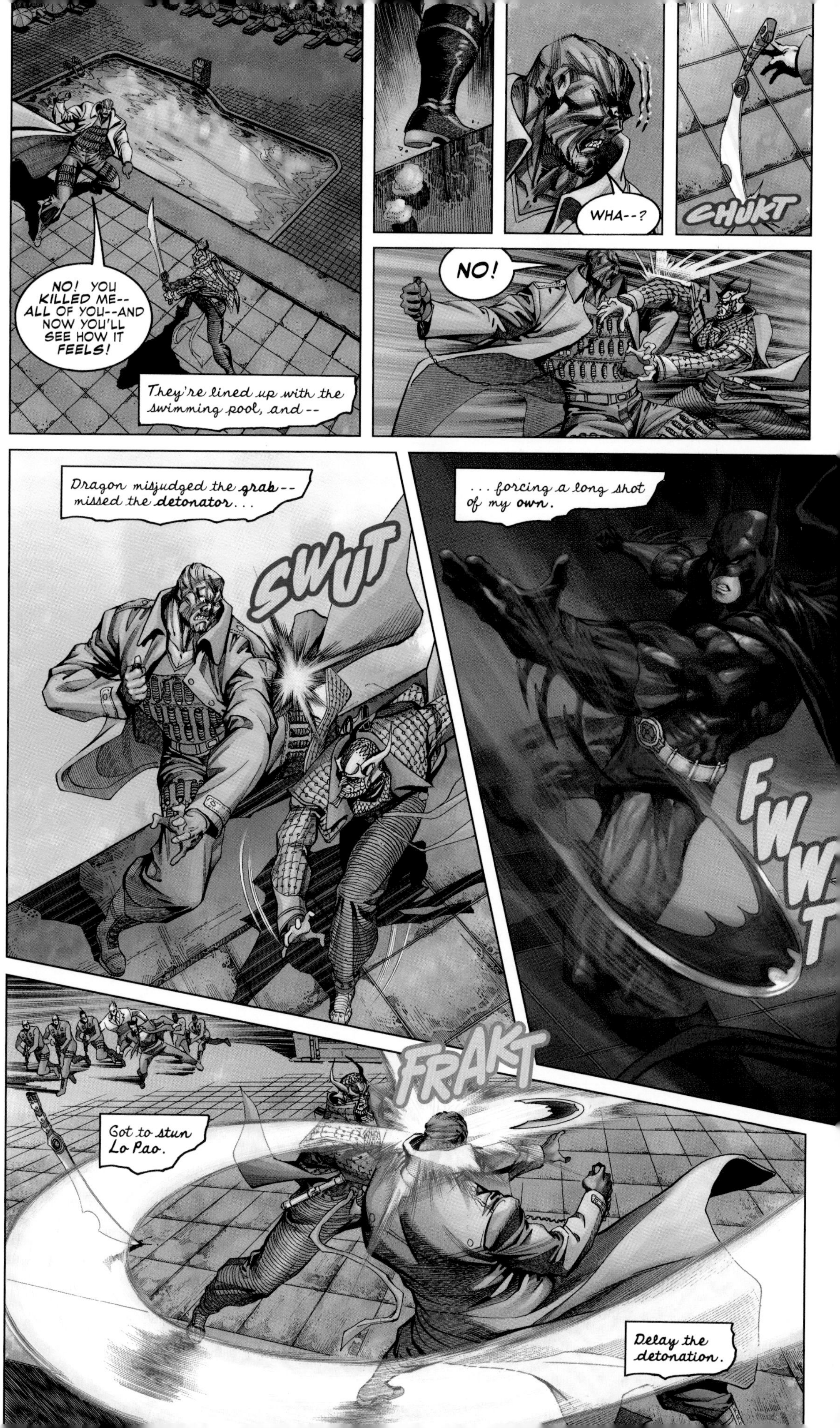
NO! YOU KILLED ME-- ALL OF YOU--AND NOW YOU'LL SEE HOW IT FEELS!
They're lined up with the swimming pool, and --
WHA--?
CHUKT
NO!
Dragon misjudged the grab-- missed the detonator...
SWUT
...forcing a long shot of my own.
FWWWT
FRAKT
Got to stun Lo Pao.
Delay the detonation.

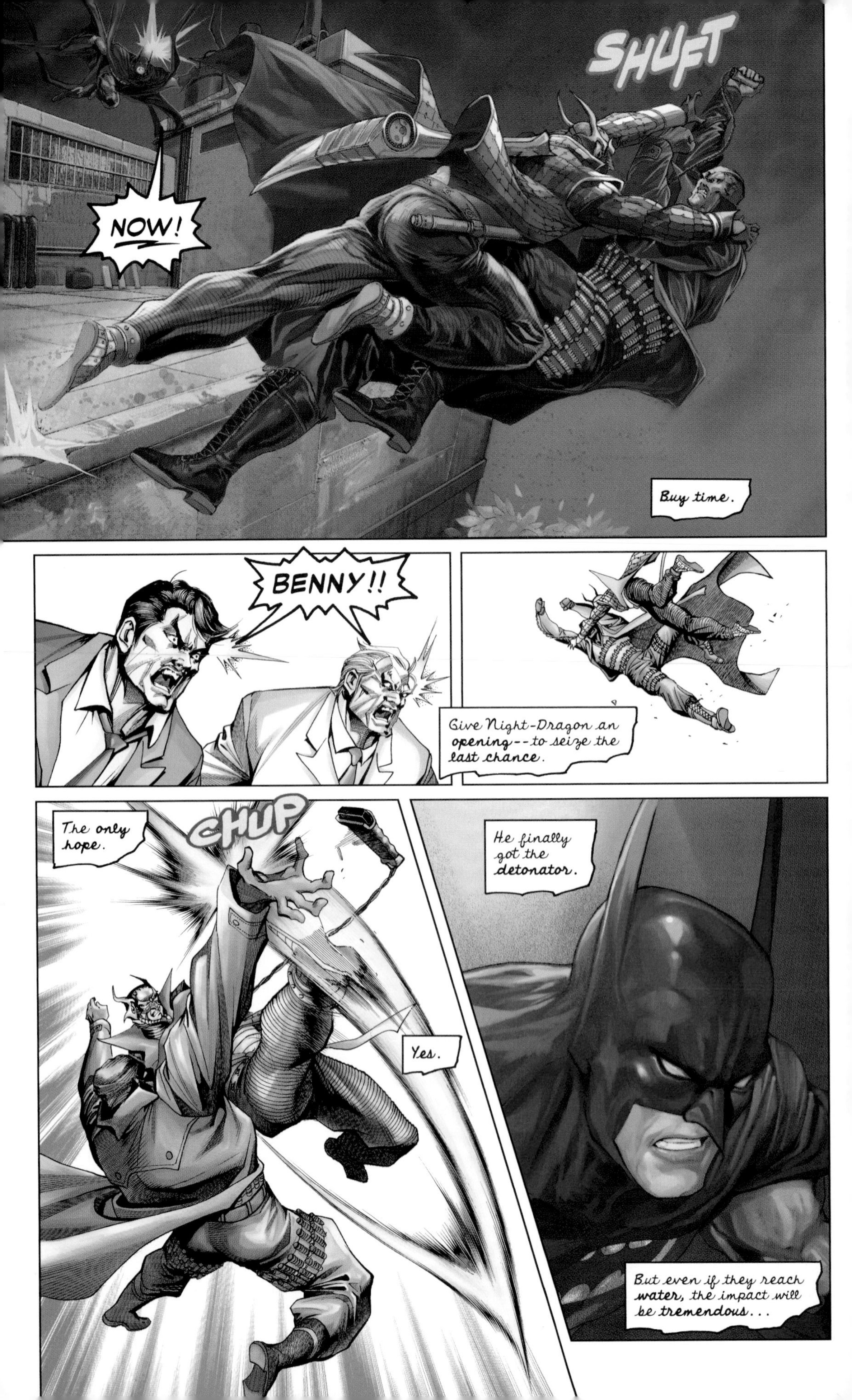
SHUFT
NOW!
Buy time.
BENNY!!
Give Night-Dragon an opening--to seize the last chance.
The only hope.
CHUP
Yes.
He finally got the detonator.
But even if they reach water, the impact will be tremendous...

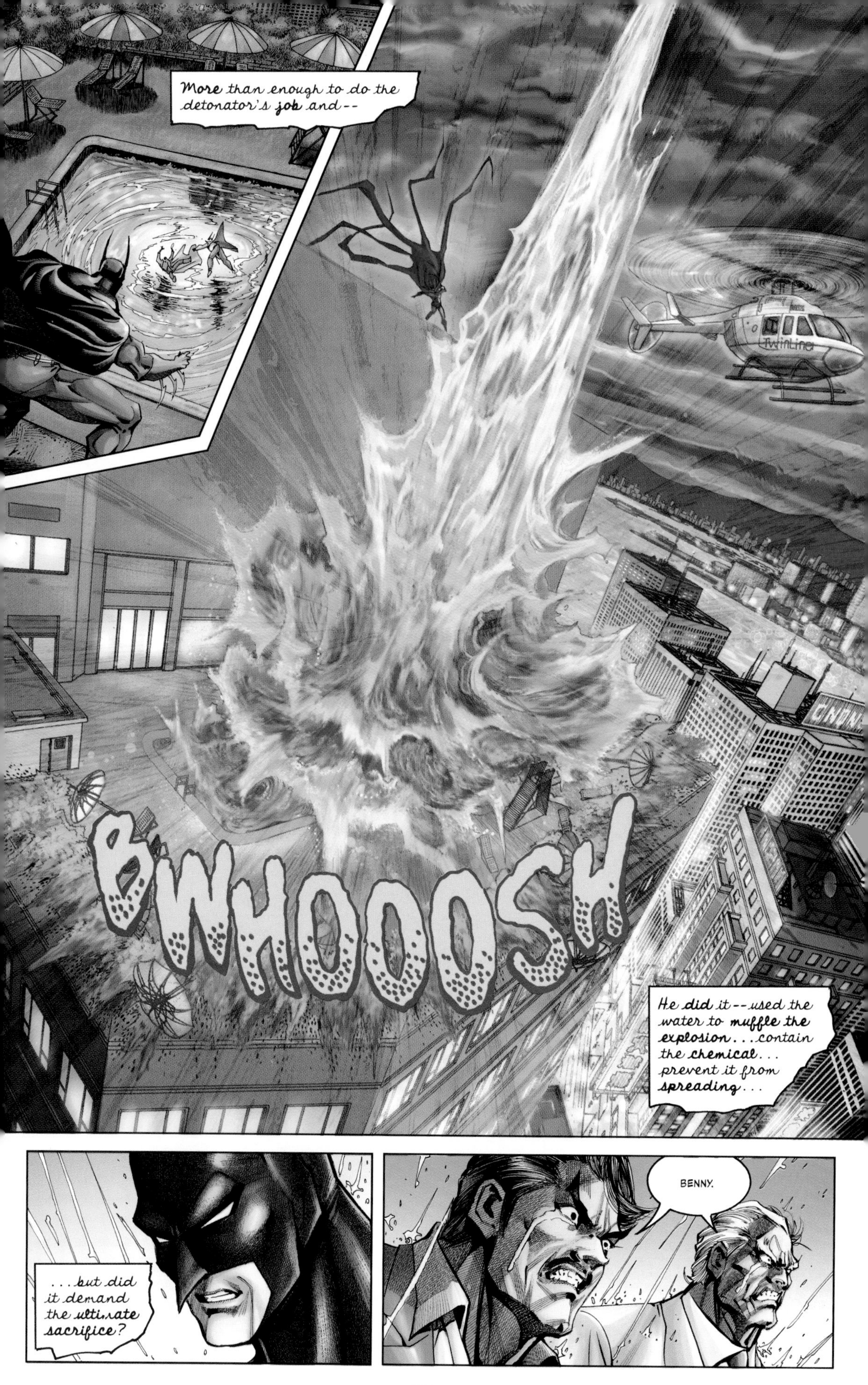
More than enough to do the detonator's job and--
BWHOOOSH
He did it--used the water to muffle the explosion...contain the chemical... prevent it from spreading...
...but did it demand the ultimate sacrifice?
BENNY.

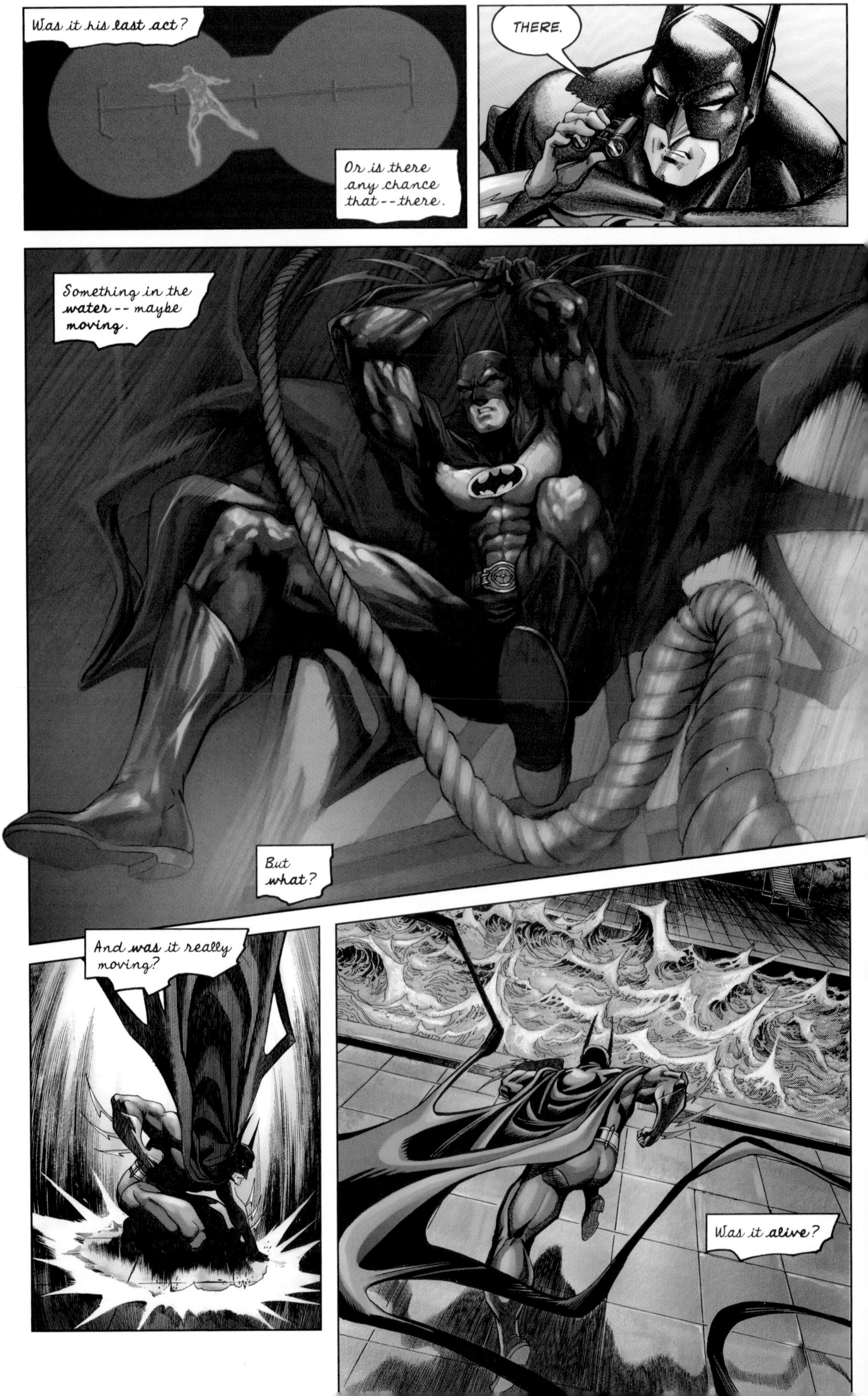
Was it his last act?
Or is there any chance that--there.
THERE.
Something in the water--maybe moving.
But what?
And was it really moving?
Was it alive?

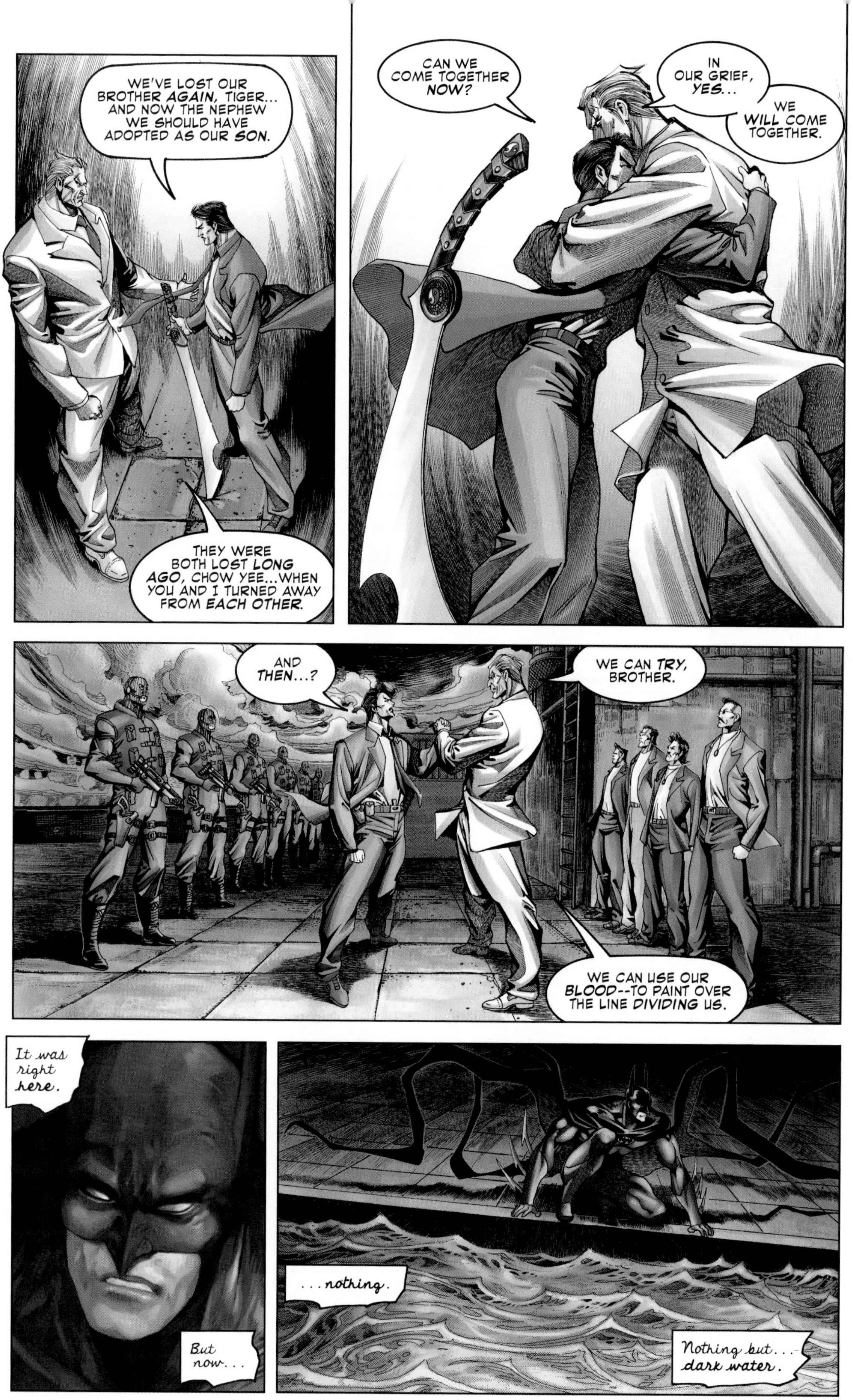
WE'VE LOST OUR BROTHER AGAIN, TIGER... AND NOW THE NEPHEW WE SHOULD HAVE ADOPTED AS OUR SON.
THEY WERE BOTH LOST LONG AGO, CHOW YEE...WHEN YOU AND I TURNED AWAY FROM EACH OTHER.
CAN WE COME TOGETHER NOW?
IN OUR GRIEF, YES...
WE WILL COME TOGETHER.
AND THEN...?
WE CAN TRY, BROTHER.
WE CAN USE OUR BLOOD--TO PAINT OVER THE LINE DIVIDING US.
It was right here.
But now...
...nothing.
Nothing but... dark water.

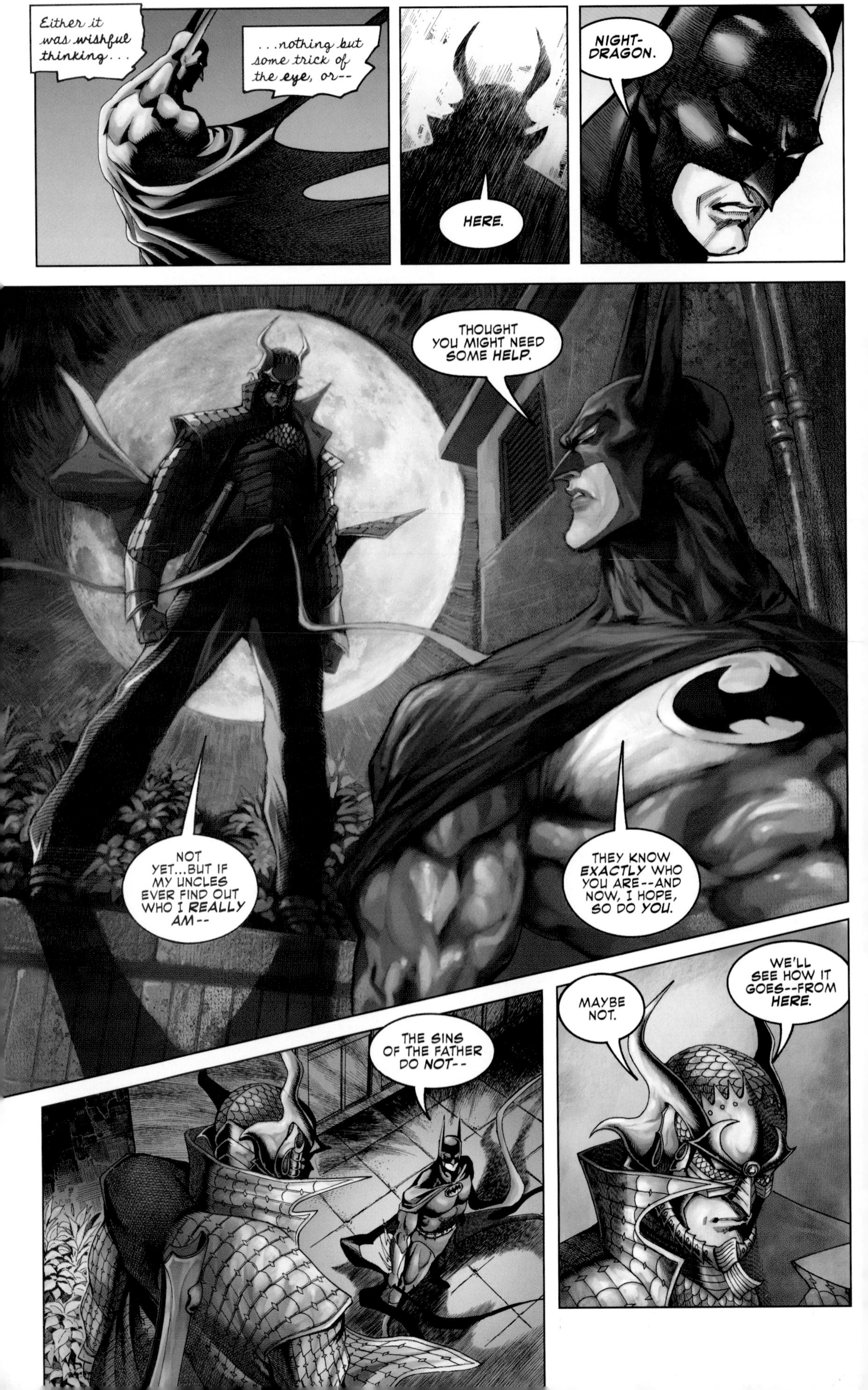
Either it was wishful thinking...
...nothing but some trick of the eye, or--
HERE.
NIGHT-DRAGON.
THOUGHT YOU MIGHT NEED SOME HELP.
NOT YET...BUT IF MY UNCLES EVER FIND OUT WHO I REALLY AM--
THEY KNOW EXACTLY WHO YOU ARE--AND NOW, I HOPE, SO DO YOU.
THE SINS OF THE FATHER DO NOT--
MAYBE NOT.
WE'LL SEE HOW IT GOES--FROM HERE.

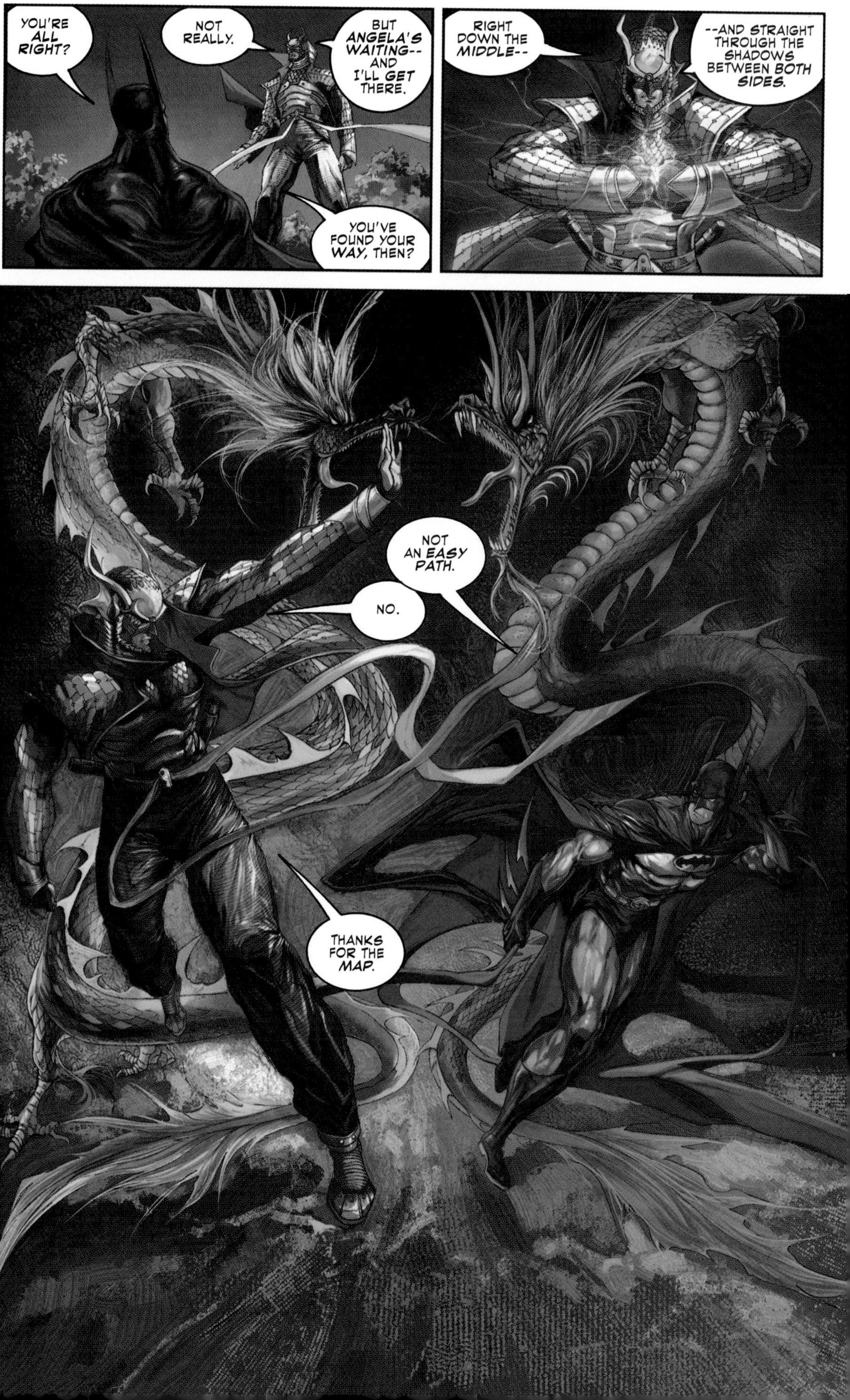
YOU'RE ALL RIGHT?
NOT REALLY.
BUT ANGELA'S WAITING-- AND I'LL GET THERE.
YOU'VE FOUND YOUR WAY, THEN?
RIGHT DOWN THE MIDDLE--
--AND STRAIGHT THROUGH THE SHADOWS BETWEEN BOTH SIDES.
NOT AN EASY PATH.
NO.
THANKS FOR THE MAP.

batman

THE QUEST FOR JUSTICE CONTINUES IN THESE BOOKS FROM DC

FOR READERS OF ALL AGES

THE BATMAN ADVENTURES
K. Puckett/T. Templeton/
R. Burchett/various

BATMAN BEYOND
Hilary Bader/Rick Burchett/
various

BATMAN: THE DARK KNIGHT ADVENTURES
Kelley Puckett/Mike Parobeck/
Rick Burchett

BATMAN: WAR ON CRIME
Paul Dini/Alex Ross

GRAPHIC NOVELS

BATMAN: ARKHAM ASYLUM
Suggested for mature readers
Grant Morrison/Dave McKean

BATMAN: BLOODSTORM
Doug Moench/Kelley Jones/
John Beatty

BATMAN: THE CHALICE
Chuck Dixon/John Van Fleet

BATMAN: CRIMSON MIST
Doug Moench/Kelley Jones/
John Beatty

BATMAN/DRACULA: RED RAIN
Doug Moench/Kelley Jones/
Malcolm Jones III

BATMAN: FORTUNATE SON
Gerard Jones/Gene Ha

BATMAN: HARVEST BREED
George Pratt

BATMAN: THE KILLING JOKE
Suggested for mature readers
Alan Moore/Brian Bolland/
John Higgins

BATMAN: NIGHT CRIES
Archie Goodwin/Scott Hampton

BATMAN: NINE LIVES
Dean Motter/Michael Lark

BATMAN: SON OF THE DEMON
Mike Barr/Jerry Bingham

CATWOMAN:
SELINA'S BIG SCORE
Darwyn Cooke

COLLECTIONS

BATMAN:
A DEATH IN THE FAMILY
Jim Starlin/Jim Aparo/
Mike DeCarlo

BATMAN:
A LONELY PLACE OF DYING
Marv Wolfman/George Pérez/
various

BATMAN BLACK AND WHITE
Vols. 1 & 2
Various writers and artists

BATMAN: BRUCE WAYNE — MURDERER?
Various writers and artists

BATMAN: BRUCE WAYNE — FUGITIVE Vol. 1
Various writers and artists

BATMAN: BRUCE WAYNE — FUGITIVE Vol. 2
Various writers and artists

BATMAN: CATACLYSM
Various writers and artists

BATMAN: CHILD OF DREAMS
Kia Asamiya

BATMAN:
DANGEROUS DAMES & DEMONS
Dini/Timm/various

BATMAN:
THE DARK KNIGHT RETURNS
Frank Miller/Klaus Janson/Lynn
Varley

BATMAN: THE DARK KNIGHT
STRIKES AGAIN
Frank Miller/Lynn Varley

BATMAN:
DARK KNIGHT DYNASTY
M. Barr/S. Hampton/G. Frank/
S. McDaniel/various

BATMAN: DARK VICTORY
Jeph Loeb/Tim Sale

BATMAN: EVOLUTION
Rucka/Martinbrough/Mitchell/
various

BATMAN: GOTHIC
Grant Morrison/Klaus Janson

BATMAN: HAUNTED KNIGHT
Jeph Loeb/Tim Sale

BATMAN/HUNTRESS:
CRY FOR BLOOD
Rucka/Burchett/T. Beatty

BATMAN IN THE FIFTIES
BATMAN IN THE SIXTIES
BATMAN IN THE SEVENTIES
Various writers and artists

THE KNIGHTFALL Trilogy
BATMAN: KNIGHTFALL
Part 1: Broken Bat
BATMAN: KNIGHTFALL
Part 2: Who Rules the Night
BATMAN: KNIGHTFALL
Part 3: KnightsEnd
Various writers and artists

BATMAN:
THE LONG HALLOWEEN
Jeph Loeb/Tim Sale

BATMAN: NO MAN'S LAND
Vols. 1 - 5
Various writers and artists

BATMAN: OFFICER DOWN
Various writers and artists

BATMAN: PRODIGAL
Various writers and artists

BATMAN:
STRANGE APPARITIONS
S. Englehart/M. Rogers/
T. Austin/various

BATMAN: SWORD OF AZRAEL
Dennis O'Neil/Joe Quesada/
Kevin Nowlan

BATMAN:
TALES OF THE DEMON
Dennis O'Neil/Neal Adams/
various

BATMAN: VENOM
Dennis O'Neil/Trevor Von Eeden/
various

BATMAN VS. PREDATOR:
THE COLLECTED EDITION
Dave Gibbons/Andy Kubert/Adam
Kubert

BATMAN: YEAR ONE
Frank Miller/David Mazzucchelli

BATMAN: YEAR TWO —
FEAR THE REAPER
Barr/Davis/McFarlane/various

BATGIRL: A KNIGHT ALONE
Puckett/D. Scott/Turnbull/
Campanella/various

BATGIRL: SILENT RUNNING
Puckett/Peterson/D. Scott/
Campanella

BIRDS OF PREY
Various writers and artists

BIRDS OF PREY:
OLD FRIENDS, NEW ENEMIES
Dixon/Land/Geraci/various

CATWOMAN: THE DARK END
OF THE STREET
Brubaker/Cooke/Allred

THE GREATEST BATMAN
STORIES EVER TOLD Vol. 1
Various writers and artists

THE GREATEST JOKER
STORIES EVER TOLD
Various writers and artists

NIGHTWING: A KNIGHT
IN BLÜDHAVEN
Dixon/McDaniel/Story

NIGHTWING: ROUGH JUSTICE
Dixon/McDaniel/Story

NIGHTWING:
LOVE AND BULLETS
Dixon/McDaniel/Story

NIGHTWING:
A DARKER SHADE OF JUSTICE
Dixon/McDaniel/Story

NIGHTWING:
THE HUNT FOR ORACLE
Dixon/Land/Guice/Zircher/various

ROBIN: FLYING SOLO
Dixon/Grummett/P. Jimenez/various

ROBIN: YEAR ONE
Dixon/S. Beatty/Pulido/
Martin/Campanella

ARCHIVE EDITIONS

BATMAN ARCHIVES Vol. 1
(DETECTIVE COMICS 27-50)

BATMAN ARCHIVES Vol. 2
(DETECTIVE COMICS 51-70)

BATMAN ARCHIVES Vol. 3
(DETECTIVE COMICS 71-86)

BATMAN ARCHIVES Vol. 4
(DETECTIVE COMICS 87-102)

BATMAN ARCHIVES Vol. 5
(DETECTIVE COMICS 103-119)

All by B. Kane/B. Finger/
D. Sprang/various

BATMAN: THE DARK KNIGHT
ARCHIVES Vol. 1
(BATMAN 1-4)

BATMAN: THE DARK KNIGHT
ARCHIVES Vol. 2
(BATMAN 5-8)

BATMAN: THE DARK KNIGHT
ARCHIVES Vol. 3
(BATMAN 9-12)

All by Bob Kane/Bill Finger/various

BATMAN: THE DYNAMIC DUO
ARCHIVES Vol. 1
(BATMAN 164-167,
DETECTIVE COMICS 327-333)
B. Kane/Giella/Finger/Broome/
Fox/various

WORLD'S FINEST COMICS
ARCHIVES Vol. 1
(SUPERMAN 76,
WORLD'S FINEST 71-85)
B. Finger/E. Hamilton/C. Swan/
Sprang/various

To find more collected editions and monthly comic books from DC Comics, call 1-888-COMIC BOOK for the nearest comics shop or go to your local book store.

Visit us at www.dccomics.com

BM0012